Learning Leadership in a Changing World

Learning Leadership in a Changing World

Virtue and Effective Leadership in the 21st Century

Mark W. McCloskey

palgrave
macmillan

Softcover reprint of the hardcover 1st edition 2014 978-1-137-47632-6

First published in 2014 by
PALGRAVE MACMILLAN®
in the United States—a division of St. Martin's Press LLC,
175 Fifth Avenue, New York, NY 10010.

Where this book is distributed in the UK, Europe and the rest of the world,
this is by Palgrave Macmillan, a division of Macmillan Publishers Limited,
registered in England, company number 785998, of Houndmills,
Basingstoke, Hampshire RG21 6XS.

Palgrave Macmillan is the global academic imprint of the above companies
and has companies and representatives throughout the world.

Palgrave® and Macmillan® are registered trademarks in the United States,
the United Kingdom, Europe and other countries.

ISBN 978-1-349-50195-3   ISBN 978-1-137-47637-1 (eBook)
DOI 10.1057/9781137476371

Library of Congress Cataloging-in-Publication Data

McCloskey, Mark W.
    Learning leadership in a changing world : virtue and effective
    leadership in the 21st century / Mark W. McCloskey.
       pages cm
    Includes bibliographical references and index.

    1. Leadership. I. Title.

HD57.7.M39527 2014
303.3'4—dc23   2014023295

A catalogue record of the book is available from the British Library.

Design by Newgen Knowledge Works (P) Ltd., Chennai, India.

First edition: December 2014

10 9 8 7 6 5 4 3 2 1

Transferred to Digital Printing in 2015

For Dawnelle, Kirsten, David, and Abby

Contents

Figures

Acknowledgments

I would like to offer special thanks to the Palgrave Macmillan team; to Casie Vogel for her encouragement and advice in the early stages of this project, to Bradley Showalter for his advice and support, to Bhavana Nair for her work in guiding the production process, and to Smitha Mathews for her exceptional work in the editing process.

SECTION I

The Twenty-First-Century Leadership Context

This section explores the new leadership landscape of the twenty-first century—a terrain full of disruptive threats, discontinuous change, and stomach-turning twists and turns.

CHAPTER 1

Two Leadership Myths

The Roaring 1990s

It was the decade of Steve Jobs and Bill Gates, Oprah and Tiger, Jack Welch and General Schwarzkopf. It was a time of unparalleled economic growth. The Dow began the decade at 2,810.15. It broke through the 10,000 mark on March 29, 1999, and ended the decade at 11, 497.12. The Nasdaq Composite broke through the 3,000 mark on November 3, 1999, and ended the decade at 4,069.31. Unemployment reached a 30-year low. The Soviet Union went out of business, and the prospect of a New World Order was tantalizingly within reach. The World Wide Web was born. The Human Genome Project and e-commerce were launched. Flat panel TVs, DVRs, and MP3 players entered our homes, over half of which owned a computer.

We entered the new millennium on a roll. The surging stock market typified a decade of expanding economic expectations. Companies grew in market capitalization at record rates. Investors anticipated record profits as a new breed of company—the dot-com—saw meteoric rises in stock prices. Fueled by low interest rates in 1998–1999, making start-up capital easy to come by, the dot-com trend looked promising. By 2000, these companies were collectively valued at $1.3 trillion, or approximately 8 percent of the US stock market.

The turn of the century featured a new breed of leader—risk-takers and charismatic mavericks, high-tech entrepreneurs and creative visionaries, problem-solvers and crisis-eaters, grand strategists and masters of mergers and acquisitions. Enron reported over 100 billion in revenues in 2000. *Fortune* magazine ranked it as one of the "100 Best Companies to Work For" in 2000, and named it "American's Most Innovative Company" for six consecutive years from 1996 to 2001. *Worth* magazine put CEO Jeff Skilling on the cover of its April 23, 2001, issue featuring "The 50 Best CEOs." We began the twenty-first century with an unqualified belief that things were trending positive and would continue to do so, as these purveyors of progress stood poised to take us to even greater economic heights.

The Myth of the Exceptional Leader

Kaiser et al. (2008) point out that the leadership literature over the last three decades has paid more attention to exceptional leaders—the creative visionaries and hypercompetent problem-solvers who build their careers and typically rise to high levels of organizational leadership—than leaders who build strong teams and enduring organizations, and often operate "under the radar." These "exceptional leaders" possess two sets of qualities that set them apart from the rest of us—personality power in the form of charisma, and high levels of technical–managerial competence. These are the "x-factors," the "right stuff" of a good leader. We believe this with such force and sincerity that a cultural mythology has grown up around leaders who manifest these qualities.

A myth is a narrative or story with explanatory power—whether factual or fictional. It offers insight into the way things are and how the world works. Myths are typically grounded in the exploits of heroic individuals, who serve as archetypes—a model for the rest of us mortals. Myths shape our worldview, ideals, and expectations, and exercise powerful conceptual, emotional, and moral sway over popular thought. The myths of charisma and technical–managerial competence continue to shape our collective images and expectations around what "good leaders" look like and what they should do for us.

These myths serve a larger, "Old Normal" leadership narrative that is the familiar story of manifest destiny wrapped in leadership language. The narrative tells us that progress is inevitable, assured by exceptional leaders. The Old Normal narrative assumes that we live in a rational and substantially predictable world. Although change is, indeed, a constant, it is relatively well behaved and can be effectively managed. Occurrences such as 9/11 or the economic collapse of 2008 are aberrations—"extreme" or "outlier" events. On normal days, we operate in a predictable cause-and-effect world that maintains its equilibrium even in the face of powerfully destabilizing forces. Large deviations from the norm are rare and inconsequential. When extreme events do occur, they quickly pass. Crises get resolved, wars get won, and recessions give way to relatively quick and robust recoveries due to the leadership of individuals with the right stuff.

This is Isaac Newton's world. Since an apple hit him on the head in 1665 (as the popular story by Voltaire goes), physicists, astronomers, mathematicians, and engineers have been making predictions based on physical laws that govern the macrophysical world. They have done an exceptional job in those arenas amenable to linear cause-and-effect sequences and mathematical precision. For instance, when it comes to the gravitational pull of planets, the thrust of a jet engine, or the load-bearing capacity of a bridge, we know with certainty—often to the decimal point—what will happen, how, when, and why. Our predictive capacities in these contexts are so well developed that we have, mistakenly, come to believe that most everything operates in a precise, linear, cause-and-effect manner.

The Old Normal narrative extends the idea of a predictable world to leadership practice. Good leaders shape the world in accord with their will, based on the assumption of "unrestricted malleability"—that the future is "makeable" and can be shaped in accordance with the persuasive influence or planning intellect of an elite few (Rittel & Webber, p. 158). Good leaders know where they are going and how to get there. They forge out ahead of followers, showing the way forward on a journey to progressively higher ground, the organization's version of the next level of effectiveness, and on the way to the summit, the organization's idea of peak performance. The journey may be difficult at times; it is always uphill. However, problems dissolve and obstacles give way to the extraordinary personal assets of the elite few who know most, perform best, and decide all.

Along the way, good leaders adhere to the two unbreakable Old Normal commandments: "Thou shalt be resolutely optimistic—always," and "Thou shalt produce results—today." Accordingly, good leaders are uplifting and ever productive. They keep everyone reasonably happy and optimistic about the organization's progress. They slay the dragon of uncertainty by anticipating events and protecting the organization from negative outcomes. When problems do arise, they fix them immediately. Moreover, perhaps most important, they deliver the comforting message that things are good and getting better, that progress is inevitable, and tomorrow will find us at least one step closer to the summit.

The Myth of Charisma

The myth of the charismatic leader (sometimes called the heroic or inspirational leader) is seductively simple. It is premised on the elitist notion that leadership is the province of an exceptional few who are advantaged from birth with the right stuff—the DNA of good leadership. We call this complex of uncommon gifting *charisma*. Charisma refers to a special quality deeply embedded in the personality of the leader that captures the popular imagination and inspires allegiance and devotion. These "anointed ones" have a hereditary advantage over the rest of us in that they possess an array of gifts that mark them as exceptional human beings and even better leaders.

Charisma comes from the Greek *charis* meaning "grace, beauty, or kindness." The word carries the idea of a favored person who possesses a magnetic appeal, allure, or social presence—someone with an unusually strong and attractive personality and unique ability to influence others. German sociologist Max Weber (1947) believed charisma was a quality of personality associated with "extraordinariness." Charismatic leaders rely on personality power to accomplish extraordinary things, typically, at extraordinary times in history. The idea of heroic leadership is often associated with charismatic appeal, especially when the leader performs unusually powerful feats during a time of crisis.

The charismatic leader possesses that unmistakable, certain something; a winsome, dramatic, dynamic personality. They offer a highly personalized, exceptionally attractive, even exciting, version of leadership. They have a way with words and a winning way with people. An engaging personality—not experience, technical competence, or moral character—is the source of the charismatic's leadership capital.

The Power of the Myth

Anyone who has studied leadership—or worked with a charismatic leader for a sustained period—knows this myth is decidedly false. Many good leaders lack charisma, and many charismatic leaders do not perform well over time. However, the myth has remarkable staying power. It is firmly ingrained in the popular consciousness, and continues to powerfully shape our expectations around what good leaders look like and what they should do for us.

The Charisma–Leadership Connection

Charismatic leaders possess extraordinarily attractive and powerful personalities. They are charming and creative, exceptionally insightful and inspirational (Conger & Kanungo, 1987; Shamir et al., 1993). Conger and Kanungo (1994) note, "Charismatic leaders differ from other leaders by their ability to formulate and articulate an inspirational vision and by behaviors and actions that foster an impression that they and the mission are extraordinary" (p. 442). Weber (1947) used the idea of charisma as an umbrella concept for the forces of change and innovation in a society, contrasting it with the "unadaptive and bureaucratic" forces that support the status quo.

Crisis is fertile ground for the rise of a charismatic leader. A crisis is a "low probability, high impact event that threatens the viability of the organization and is characterized by ambiguity of cause, effect, and means of resolution, as well as by a belief that decisions must be made swiftly" (Pearson & Clair, 1998, p. 59). Crisis calls for quick, decisive action, and the charismatic leader delivers. Energized by difficulty, charismatic leaders are nothing if not supremely confident. When pressing problems mount, as disaster looms and anxiety spreads, the charismatic leader is at his or her best.

Crisis and charisma go hand in glove. Khurana (2002) noted that corporate boards are prone to turn to charismatic outsiders promising change unencumbered by the people or culture that may have got the company in trouble in the first place. Shamir and Howell (1999) note that followers in crisis "will readily, even eagerly, accept the influence of a leader who seems to have high self-confidence and a vision that provides both meaning to the current situation and promise of salvation from the currently acute distress" (p. 260). In trying circumstances, the exceptional qualities of the leader may be highlighted, or even exaggerated, in order to alleviate anxiety—the worse it gets, the better a charismatic leader looks.

Historian Sydney Hook (1943) points out that the hope for resolution of a crisis is bound up in the hope for the appearance of a strong leader to cope with the crisis—the more urgent the crisis, the more intense the longing for such a leader. Weber (1947) believed that charismatic authority arose under conditions of distress, whether physical, religious, economic, or political. In these situations, leaders and followers form a "charismatic bond" in which followers readily submit to the leader. The leader, now perceived as possessing extraordinary capabilities relevant to the distressing circumstances, becomes the object of enthusiastic devotion. The principle: the greater the uncertainty, the more insecure are the followers, and, thus, the greater the appeal of the charismatic leader.

Cracks in the Myth

It is unlikely we will experience a crisis shortage in the next decade, and, therefore, we will continue to place a premium on charismatic leaders. When the next crisis erupts, we will scan the horizon for an extraordinary person to deliver us from peril and take us to the Promise Land. There will be no shortage of charismatic leaders ready and eager to respond. Although this may be reassuring, our unqualified belief in this myth merits two words of warning.

First, charisma is ineffective in the day-to-day grind. Although charismatic leaders are unmatched at starting things, they are notorious for not finishing them. Dramatically venturesome and interested primarily in grand endeavors, charismatic leaders are profoundly uninterested in mundane details and do not relish the homework and hard work required to move their change agenda forward 1 day at a time. In political language, campaigning and promise making is the province of the charismatic leader; governing and promise keeping is not (Bligh & Kohles, 2009; Lubit, 2001). In business language, charismatic leaders are often long on ideas, but short on implementation—great at inspiring, but poor at executing.

Second, charisma eventually fades and inevitably disappoints. Charismatic influence, apart from other essential personal qualities— moral character being foremost—is not sustainable. Two dynamics come into play. Charismatic leadership capital is a fluid and fleeting commodity, unstable and exceedingly fragile, dependent on a rare confluence of events. Like a crisis, it may come and go as quickly as events play out and circumstances change. If the crisis ends, if the leader fails to deliver results, or if a more attractive leader shows up, the leader's charismatic influence will diminish. Or ironically, if the leader solves the problem or resolves the crisis, they may be victims of their own success as the anxiety of followers is lessened, thus reducing the need for a charismatic leader such as they—Churchill was thrown out of office in the first election after World War II. Either way, the effectiveness of a charismatic leader may be surprisingly short lived, especially in comparison to the initial level of enthusiasm displayed by followers.

To compound these cracks in the myth, charisma is alarmingly disarming, and potentially destructive. Charismatic appeal has long been known to be a seductive and often destructive force in organizational life. The virtuosity of a winsome personality, combined with high ideals and lofty promises, captivate and thrill us, and bring instant relief to our anxiety about the future. Herein resides the irony and danger of our unabashed love affair with charismatic leaders: they are at their best just when we need them most. Crisis breeds the conditions for charismatic leaders to match their extreme self-confidence—grandiosity in some cases—with the organization's sense of dependence and helplessness (Kets de Vries, 1980).

Isaacson (2011) notes that Steve Jobs turned charm into a "cunning force, to cajole and intimidate and distort reality with the power of his personality" (p. 42). Jobs's "friends" and employees were treated to regular, high doses of his dark side—insincere flattery, dissembling, piercing insults, and even outright cruelty. Isaacson reflected on the mixed legacy of Jobs's leadership over the decades:

> He was not a model boss or human being, tidily packaged for emulation. Driven by demons, he could drive those around him to fury and despair. But his personality and passions and products were all interrelated, just as Apple's hardware and software tended to be, as if part of an integrated system. His tale is thus both instructive and cautionary, filled with lessons about innovation, character, leadership, and values. (p. xxi)

The lesson: beware of the ominous fit between the desire for a strong and attractive leader, and the charismatic individual who is all-too-ready to take over the reins of power. Although a highly inspirational personality may give a leader an edge, it comes in the form of the proverbial double-edged sword. A charismatic leader is highly susceptible to destructive narcissism and, with it, the tendency to overestimate his or her capabilities, underestimate the difficulty of change, and operate in a world of invalidated hunches and wishes, rather than the facts—a toxic, at times, lethal combination in organizational life (Kets de Vries, 1980; Lubit, 2001).

Summary

Charismatic leaders are a force to be reckoned with. It is impossible to ignore them. They have that certain something we call command presence or star quality. They are insightful and assertive, independent and influential, innovators and risk-takers—the would-be world-changers among us. They inspire us with a grand vision for a better future. They galvanize support for their change agenda. However, there are cracks in the myth. Charisma is not effective in the day-to-day grind of leadership. Charisma is fleeting. Finally, because it is alarmingly disarming, we ignore these downsides at our peril.

The Myth of Technical–Managerial Competence

The myth of technical–managerial competence affirms that good leaders possess the "right stuff" in the form of innate drive and intelligence—or shrewdness, in some cases—mixed with the requisite competencies—knowledge, skill, and ability—that fuel performance in a given leadership context. Competent leaders are energetic, analytically powerful, and unusually productive. They are typically good planners, organizers, and decision-makers. They take charge, set clear direction, identify strategic priorities, overwhelm inertia, drive out inefficiencies, and fix hard-to-fix problems. A virtuoso performance, not a magnetic personality, is the source of their leadership capital. Although the competent leader may not initially inspire people like the charismatic leader, they quickly gain the confidence of others by getting results.

The Power of the Myth

There is something deeply engrained in our collective psyche that yearns for a determined, smart, and competent leader to take charge and lead us to the summit. We want a firm hand at the wheel, someone who operates in the currency of results. When performance lags, we turn to turnaround artists and scan the horizon for the next all-star performer. We seek out individuals with the drive, intelligence, and competence mix to overcome obstacles, solve difficult problems, and deliver results. When we find them, we put them in charge and keep them there—as long as they win. And they do—for a time. They dazzle us with their energy and know-how. We stand amazed that they are exhilarated, not diminished, by the sheer volume of work and the daunting challenges set before them.

The myth of technical–managerial competence is firmly established in many, perhaps most, organizations. It finds expression in the ubiquitous competency list—the wish list most organizations have for prospective leaders. These lists have been around since the early 1970s and, by the 1990s, they had achieved great popularity in business organizations and, yes, even the federal government (Spencer & Spencer, 1993). However inadvertently, these lists support and extend the myth of technical–managerial competence in two ways.

First, these lists suggest that good leaders embody an almost superhuman range of knowledge, skill, and ability. Competence lists typically include everything from moral and relational traits like integrity and compassion to personality-dependent qualities like drive, command, and initiative, to competitive differentiators such as strategic thinking and learning agility, to more prosaic "workshop skills" like delegation, effective listening, and process management (Goleman 1995; Boyatzis, et al., 2000; Lombardo & Eichinger, 2009). Although noting the full range of what it takes to lead effectively is certainly helpful, too often, these lists perpetuate the belief that a good leader is not merely multicompetent or even hypercompetent, but rather, Omnicompetent—a self-contained critical mass of drive, intelligence, and expertise.

Second, these lists support a core affirmation of the myth of technical–managerial competence—the belief that technical–managerial expertise is the fundamental driver of effective leadership: that a good leader is someone who has mastered a wide range of knowledge and skill. Here is how it plays out.

Competency lists implicitly define "competence" in the broadest terms as any attitude, trait, or behavior related to effective performance. The authors of these lists typically make a distinction between technical competence and foundational moral, emotional, and relational competence. Boyatzis (1982) distinguishes between skill, motive, and trait competencies, noting that each type of competence is acquired differently, with trait competencies (integrity, courage, compassion) grounded in deeper, stable personality characteristics that are difficult to change in the short term through training interventions. The Lominger list ranks 67 competencies from "easiest" to "hardest" to master. For instance, "functional and technical skills" and "planning" are among the easiest, whereas "managerial courage" and "understanding others" are among the hardest (Lombardo & Eichinger, 2009).

However, this broad definition blurs the distinction between technical competencies like planning, budgeting, and customer focus—skills that can be learned by most anyone in a training workshop—and foundational moral, emotional, and relational competencies like compassion, integrity, earning trust, and understanding others—decidedly not skills of the workshop variety. The result, often unintended, is that moral, emotional, and relational competencies are placed in a technical frame, with the implication that all competencies are of equal importance and acquired in a similar manner—in a workshop setting in a relatively short time frame. A case in point is the bourgeoning emotional intelligence industry. In spite of warnings that emotional intelligence (EQ) is a higher order configuration of attitudes and behaviors requiring strenuous effort, significant time, and consistent feedback to develop (Goleman, 1995; 1998), a growing number of seminars, workshops, and books frame emotional intelligence as a technical skill that can be learned quickly by most anyone in a workshop setting (Lynn, 2007).

Cracks in the Myth

As with charisma, cracks appear in the myth of technical–managerial competence. The most important flaw is the equation of moral, emotion, and relational competence with technical competence. The drive, intelligence, and know-how of the competent leader convince us—at times, these assets seduce us—into thinking the individual is exactly what the organization needs. When the pressure to win reaches a critical level—when performance lags—organizations are desperate to find an Omni-competent leader, rendering them vulnerable to ignoring his or her lack of moral, emotional, or relational capacity.

Organizations that confuse technical–managerial competence with moral, emotional, and relational competencies are vulnerable to catastrophic leadership failure. A case in point is that of Dennis Kozlowski, the former CEO of the global manufacturing giant, Tyco. For most of Kozlowski's 27 years at Tyco, he was an enterprising and shrewd leader, growing the company at an exceptional rate and creating enormous shareholder value. Kozlowski employed a rare combination of logic and intuition to drive business results. Renowned for his ability to cut deals and acquire companies, Wall Street hailed him as a business genius. In 2001, he appeared on the cover of *Business Week* under the headline "The Most Aggressive CEO." The numbers did not lie. In the first decade of his leadership, Tyco increased 70-fold in market-capitalization. From 1997 to 2001, Tyco's revenues rose a remarkable 48.7 percent a year. Tyco's stock price soared, and everyone was happy. His board rewarded him with hefty raises, and authorized him to share in an unrestricted stock-ownership plan.

Perhaps blinded by his dazzling success, Kozlowski developed a severe case of moral myopia, habitually blurring the line between the good of the company and private gain. His wretched excesses are well known— the $6,000 shower curtain in his Gilded-era Manhattan apartment, the $15,000 doggie umbrella stand, and the two million dollar birthday party for his wife on the island of Sardinia disguised as a shareholder meeting to get corporate funding—Tyco paid for half the bill.

His personal excesses diminished his formidable business judgment. After a two-decade long string of sound deals, he closed out his leadership tenure at Tyco with a tangled mess of acquisitions and strategic errors that cost shareholders over 90 billion dollars. In 2005, Kozlowski was found guilty on 22 of 23 counts of grand larceny and conspiracy, falsifying business records, and violating business law. In an ironic twist, the scope of the disaster and degree of harm perpetrated on Tyco and its shareholders was in direct proportion to his unparalleled technical–managerial competence. It is impossible to conceive of the Tyco debacle as separate from the exceptional drive, calculating shrewdness, and consummate managerial skill that earned Kozlowski the CEO job.

It is unlikely we will experience a shortage of underperforming organizations in the next decade. Therefore, we will continue to place a premium on leaders with drive, intelligence, and an impressive repertoire of technical competence. When performance lags, when the next obstacle blocks the way, we will scan the horizon for an energetic, smart, results-driven leader with the technical know-how to turn things around and take us to the summit. There will be no shortage of driven, intelligent, and technically competent leaders ready and eager to respond. Although this may be reassuring, our unqualified belief in this myth merits extreme caution.

Summary

The Old Normal narrative is the familiar story of organizational manifest destiny wrapped in leadership language—progress is inevitable, assured by one or a few special leaders armed with charisma or technical–managerial competence—or both. The staying power of these myths is no mystery. If a leader inspires us, if they quell our nerves and relieve our anxiety, if they convince us that they will get results, we count ourselves fortunate to have them in charge.

CHAPTER 2

The Mess: Say Hello to the New Normal

Introduction

In the second decade of the twenty-first century, the Old Normal narrative and its supporting myths have fallen on hard times. A new version of "normal"—a New Normal—is fast arriving, and it shows no signs of slowing down. The idea of a "New Normal" describes a series of social, economic, and cultural sea changes, a confluence of extreme events, the cumulative effect of which is to create a fundamentally new leadership landscape full of disruptive threats, discontinuous change, and stomach-turning twists and turns. Although disruptive change has been with us for millennia, it has reached unprecedented levels in the twenty-first century, increasing dramatically in scope and intensity, rendering organizations vulnerable to forces outside their control.

Old Normal myths and New Normal realities are on a collision course, and leaders find themselves at the intersection. Ellen Kullman, CEO of DuPont, observed:

> These days, there are things that just come shooting across the bow—economic volatility and the impact of natural events, like the Japanese earthquake and tsunami—at much greater frequency than we've ever seen. You have to be able to react very quickly. And the world is so connected that the feedback loops are more intense. Our supply chains are global. Our financial markets are global. So uncertainty in on part of the world infiltrates all parts of the world. And then you have the global megatrends. You've got population growth an the world passing seven billion people last year, and the stresses that causes, whether its feeding the world, creating enough energy, or protecting the environment. (Kirkland, 2012a)

The Old Normal is fast passing away, replaced by a convergence of social and economic forces reshaping the global operating environment. Obstacles refuse to bow to personality power. Events cannot be controlled. Problems increasingly defy technical solution. Although charisma and competence are still useful leadership assets, the New Normal generates an extraordinary mix of cognitive, moral, and emotional demands, exposing charisma and technical–managerial competence as woefully inadequate drivers of leadership performance.

The New Normal Unleashed

The term "New Normal" was coined by investment industry visionary Roger McNamee (2004) to describe the new state of affairs in the twenty-first century. What was once the exception is now a new version of "normal."

Old Change–New Change

Change is a constant, and disruptive change has asserted itself throughout history. As Halstead (2003) observed:

> American history reveals that periods of fundamental reform are typically triggered by one or more of the following: a major war; a large-scale shift from one industrial era to another; extreme levels of economic inequality; a dramatic change in the composition of the political parties. On the rare occasions when these forces coincide, they fundamentally transform society. That is what happened when Reconstruction coincided with the dawn of the first industrial revolution; it is also what happened when the Roaring Twenties and the Great Depression coincided with the beginning of the second industrial revolution. All the requisite ingredients for change are now coming together again, at the onset of the post-industrial age. If patterns hold, our nation's next major reinvention cannot be far away. (p. 124)

The pattern is holding. The "New Normal" has been arriving in bits and pieces the last three decades at an increasing pace. Daniel Yankelovich (1981) explained the monumental shifts occurring in our societal landscape using the metaphor of plate tectonics. Giant plates undergird the Earth's surface to keep things stable. However, at times, they shift their position and grind against each other. These shifts may be slight, an inch or so, but the plates are so massive that even the slightest movement releases enormous energy along the fault line, causing shifts in the Earth's surface—earthquakes—and activating volcanoes. In light of these massive shifts, Drucker (1992) predicted we were headed into an "age of discontinuity."

Disruptive change has reached unprecedented levels in the twenty-first century, increasing dramatically in scope and intensity. The double blow of 9/11 and the burst of the dot-com bubble at the turn of the century put us on alert that the twenty-first century will feature regular doses of unruly and disruptive change—the constant threat of terrorism, economic roiling, geopolitical instability, failed leaders, and failed institutions. The economic meltdown of the fall of 2008 confirmed that "normal" is a thing of the past.

The giant plates of societal trends and technological change are shifting, releasing enormous energy along economic, cultural, and political fault lines, powerfully transforming the social landscape such that it is fast losing its familiarity. Like the shifting of tectonic plates, these social, political, and economic changes break the continuity of our experience in decisive and irreversible ways. Hagel et al. (2009) describe a "Big Shift" in the global business environment and competitive landscape, resulting in a dramatic increase in performance pressures on US companies, with competitive intensity doubling in the past 40 years. Henton et al. (2004) call this decade "an uncertain time of transition, similar to the 1760s, 1850s, 1900s, and 1950s, just before major change." Christensen (1997, 2013) warns of the rising trend of disruptive innovation that buffets modern organizations with gale-like forces (Murray, 2010).

These drivers of disruptive change have worked their way into all facets of life, making it increasingly difficult to remain untouched by the seismic activity. Those living closest to the social, economic, political, and cultural fault lines—leaders—are, typically, the first to experience these shifts.

Vuca-Me: A Framework for Understanding the New Normal

Since the early 1990s, the acronym VUCA has been employed to describe the increasing volatility, uncertainty, complexity, and ambiguity of the emerging New Normal world. This framework was first used at the US Army War College in Carlisle Pennsylvania to help officers get a handle on the dynamic cultural, technological, and geopolitical forces shaping the world—conceptual challenges that leaders in all walks of life must constructively engage if their organizations are to survive and thrive in the twenty-first century.

Volatility

The term volatile comes from the Latin *volare* meaning, "to fly," and refers to something that is quick to vaporize or disappear and, thus, difficult to capture or hold permanently. The New Normal landscape is marked by extreme volatility. Volatility speaks to the rapid, escalating, and discontinuous change driven by what statisticians call "extreme" or "outlier" events. Outlier events are sudden, random jumps or large deviations from the norm. These events do not appear on the horizon and politely announce themselves days or weeks in advance, giving us time to prepare. Like heart attacks or earthquakes, they happen suddenly, without warning or antecedent—that is the nature of volatility. When these events unfold, they require our undivided attention.

Hertz CEO Mark Frissora, notes:

> In 34 years, I've never seen a more volatile business environment than the one we are operating in today. Technology and media have completely changed the concept of competitive advantage...Now, whatever you do and say is almost instantly transferrable to your competitors...What used to be a two-year competitive advantage is two minutes today. This is all due to the exponentially increased use of the Internet, social media and other technology-based advances. (Frissora and Kirkland, 2013)

In the last decade, outlier events have occurred with greater frequency. Although large deviations from the norm are still rare—that is what makes them outliers—days like 9/11, economic downturns like the fall of 2008, and earthquakes and tsunamis like the ones that struck Indonesia and Japan are game changers. The Richter level is high, transforming the social, political, and economic landscape—and, in the case of the Japanese earthquake, even the physical landscape. The fact that these events are rare is little consolation. They cannot be dismissed as mere outliers and, thus, as being unimportant. The implication? Predictable trend lines, whether for unemployment, economic growth, or stock market performance are harder and harder to find. Leaders must face the hard fact that the rare extreme—the unusual—is fast becoming the normal. Instability is the order of the day.

Uncertainty

The word conjures up images of something variable, in flux, irregular, and indefinite. The New Normal world is dimly light. Surprises lurk in the shadows. The impact of change and the problems associated with it are so confusing, vague, and imprecise as to make solutions nothing more than educated guesswork. Little is clear. Final proof is rare. Nothing is conclusive. Doubt and skepticism abound. Closure is suspended. Outcomes hang in the balance. Prediction is a fool's game, as the future is less and less an extrapolation of the past. Leaders are often caught off guard, and find themselves perpetually off balance and wavering in a chronic state of anxious indecision.

Uncertainty is more than a lack of certainty—what might be called "mild uncertainty." Mandelbrot and Taleb (2006) note that the present economic and political environment offers up a "wild uncertainty" or "wild randomness." Wild randomness is "an environment in which a single observation or a particular number can impact the total in a disproportionate way" (p. 2). The so-called Law of Large Numbers implies that the midpoint of a random sample is likely to be close to the mean of the entire population, provided the population is sufficiently large. The typical Bell curve assumes that large, outlier events are, indeed, possible (they are found in the "thin tail" of the graph), but statistically uncommon. Daily life is made up of small deviations from the normal that are, typically, inconsequential. However, rare deviations can have a lasting impact. For instance, on the New York Stock Exchange, only ten trading days represent 63 percent of the returns of the past 50 years or so.

Nature, typically, works with a mild randomness, as in an exceptionally high or low temperature, a thunderstorm producing hail, or dry spells. Wild randomness breaks through in the form of more severe activity like droughts, hurricanes, tornadoes earthquakes, and tsunamis. Similarly, wild uncertainty has manifested itself in extreme events that have shaped the cultural landscape in the last decade; terrorist attacks, extreme stock market swings, election surprises, the collapse of once proud and prosperous business organizations, and the impending collapse of entire national economies. The only certainty is that there will be more wild uncertainty.

Complexity

The word comes from the Latin *complecti*, with *com* meaning, "to encircle or embrace," and *plectere* meaning "to weave." When something is complex, it is interwoven and entangled, consisting of many interdependent and interconnected strands. Complexity is a hallmark of the New Normal, where events are driven by multiple, factors, none of which is determinative and all of which is interrelated.

The shifting New Normal landscape is the product of a dense, interwoven overlay of constantly interacting economic, social, political, and cultural factors, producing a dynamic situation impossible to understand, let alone predict and control. The number of factors and actors is overwhelming, as entire systems interact with one another to create a dizzying array of cause and effect sequences. This intricate mix of multiple, varied, and interconnected factors generates situations where almost nothing, perhaps nothing at all, is the result of just one thing, and almost everything, perhaps everything, is the result of many things, some small, some hidden, and all consequential.

The Butterfly Effect. MIT professor Edward Lorenz (1963) was the first to recognize what is now called "chaotic behavior" in the mathematical modeling of weather systems. In 1961, Lorenz was inputting numbers in a computer model to run a weather prediction. He inputted 0.506127 on the first day, but used a shortcut and rounded off to 0.506 the second day. He was shocked to find that this seemingly insignificant change in the initial conditions of his weather model resulted in a completely different weather scenario. This led Lorenz to hypothesize what is now called "the butterfly effect." The term came from a paper he presented in 1972 titled: "Predictability: Does the Flap of a Butterfly's Wings in Brazil Set Off a Tornado in Texas?" The idea is that the flaps of a butterfly's wings—a small, random input into initial atmospheric conditions—could lead to a chain of systemic events potentially impacting a significant weather event, like a tornado in Texas, thousands of miles away. If the butterfly had not flapped its wings, so goes the theory, the trajectory of the system might have been altered, thus leading to a vastly different outcome. Of course, the butterfly does not directly cause the tornado in a linear cause–effect model—a tornado needs far more energy to emerge than that provided by the flap of butterfly wings. However, it does "lead" to the tornado in that the flap of wings is a necessary prior condition in a highly interactive weather system. Without the wings flapping in Brazil, the tornado in Texas might not have developed.

The butterfly effect is symbolic of the radical interconnectedness and ultrasensitivity of systems. The assumption that small inputs yield small outputs—small changes in one part of the system yield only small changes in any other part, and these changes can be reliably predicted—is simply wrong. Our world is more chaotic, non-linear, and unpredictable than we can imagine. Small inputs in one part of the system may lead to unanticipated and consequential outputs in other parts of the system. This is especially true in unstable, interactive systems like the economy, making prediction notoriously difficult.

The butterfly effect applies to the internal life of organizations as well. Organizational life is shaped by an open and interactive system of "circular causality." The "players" in the system (positional leaders, employees, customers, and shareholders) are continuously acting, interacting, reacting, and adapting to each other. Individuals exchange information, make decisions, and adjust their next set of interactions based on the feedback. Information "jumps channels" and moves quickly through the organization. People interpret this information and interact in unscripted ways, escalating the rate of internal change. The outcomes of these multiple factors and actors are impossible to control, let alone predict.

Ambiguity

Our term comes from the French *ambigere* meaning "to wander about." Ambiguity is the condition of admitting two or more possible meanings or multiple, plausible interpretations of the same facts. In a New Normal landscape lacking clear-cut cause and effect sequences, there is, often, more than one reasonable way to make sense of a situation. The flow of events is puzzling. The facts, such as they are, may be vague and misleading, and their ramifications indefinite and difficult to interpret. Multiple perspectives breed confusion about the meaning of an event or decision. Alternative interpretations abound. Final clarity is exceedingly difficult. In our vagueness and confusion, we waver between conclusions. Leaders may have difficulty recognizing opportunities before they disappear, and threats before they become lethal. They may find it difficult to wisely choose priorities, and may easily lapse into a "busy but unproductive" pattern.

Beyond these conceptual challenges, the New Normal makes stringent moral and emotional demands.

Moral

Leadership is an inherently relational endeavor as well as an exercise in public stewardship. Personal interactions, setting priorities, and making critical leadership decisions are consequential moral actions. This is nothing new. However, the unpredictability, interconnectedness, and increasing transparency of the New Normal operating environment raises the moral stakes to an entirely new level.

Hamel (2012) notes, "The worst economic downturn since the 1930s wasn't a banking crisis, a credit crisis, or a mortgage crisis—it was a moral crisis, willful negligence in extremis" (p. 10). The economic crisis of 2008 was a perfect storm of vice. Arrogance, deceit, shortsightedness, ideological rigidity, cowardice, dereliction of duty, moral myopia, and Olympic levels of denial and blame deflection mixed in a toxic brio that made most of the world economically sick. We are still sorting through the wreckage to determine how these factors combined and interacted, and who was ultimately responsible (Morgenson & Rosner, 2011; Hamel, 2012).

The crisis has yielded one clear lesson: in this densely networked operating environment, it is increasingly difficult to make a decision devoid of moral consequence. In a globally interconnected economy and geopolitical system, the decisions of one or a few reverberate from one end of the world to the other at the speed of light. A morally careless or corrupt decision on Wall Street will impact a family on Main Street. Consequently, those entrusted with making decisions are held to a higher moral standard. Hamel (2012) states, "Because the decisions of global actors are uniquely consequential, their ethical standards must be uniquely exemplary" (p. 5). There is no such thing as a morally inconsequential decision.

Emotional

The New Normal operating environment generates considerable emotional stress and anxiety. In the aftermath of the recession of 2008–2009, social commentators and, most recently, Rachman (2011), labeled this decade the "age of anxiety." This is not a new phrase—it has been around for decades dating back to descriptions of post-World War I Europe. W. H. Auden made the term famous in the 1947 poem of that name.

The "age of anxiety" is a fitting description for the last decade. Entire economies in Western Europe are on the verge of collapse, unemployment in the United States and Western Europe still remains high, a massive federal deficit threatens the long-term welfare of the American experiment, and the spread of drug-resistant viruses threaten entire populations—all against the backdrop of civil unrest and the constant threat of terrorism. Five minutes watching a newscast can send us into an emotional tailspin.

The internal life of our organizations offers no respite from these external forces. In fact, organizations often reflect and, at times, magnify the turbulence of the New Normal, serving as incubators of anxiety, confusion, cynicism, conflict, and mistrust. In times of disruptive change, leaders and organization members must look beyond and beneath a purely rational and cognitive response to organizational problems, to understand the emotional dimension of organizational life—the hopes and fears, aspirations and interests of members. Feelings are facts, and emotions are powerful drivers of behavior and organizational performance.

Summary

The velocity of change is accelerating by the day. Tectonic plates shift beneath our feet and the landscape changes before our eyes—and keeps shifting. Like volcanic structures, new, unprecedented problems erupt without warning. Old Normal myths and New Normal realities are on a collision course.

CHAPTER 3

Myths Meet Mess: Old Normal Leaders in New Normal Times

Introduction

As the New Normal grows in scope and intensity, leaders increasingly face harsh realities and unprecedented demands. Although charisma and technical–managerial competence are useful, the New Normal operating environment features an extraordinary mix of cognitive, moral, and emotional demands, diminishing the value of these assets.

The New Normal Narrative: Leadership as a Wilderness Journey

During the Age of Discovery, maps were incomplete, with entire areas designated *Terra Incognita*—unknown land, a region yet to be explored and charted. Uncharted seas were labeled *mare incognitum*, Latin for "unknown sea." Ancient Roman and medieval cartographers marked uncharted areas with the Latin, *Hic sunt leones*—Here are lions. Some maps carried the warning "Here be dragons." Whatever the terminology, the warning was clear: potentially lethal dangers awaited those who dared to explore unknown terrain.

Newton's predictable world is fast disappearing. In its place, looms a twenty-first century version of Terra Incognita. Playing off Norman Mailer's observation that "civilized life is akin to a moral wilderness," the New Normal operating environment is a vast and unexplored social, economic, political, and cultural wilderness. Our term *wilderness* comes from the Old English word for a wild beast. In this sense, it is the wildness of a place that makes it a wilderness. A wilderness is an unexplored, uncharted environment beyond the control of humans and, thus, an inhospitable place, a landscape that has never been inhabited, influenced, or significantly modified by human activity—no roads, no infrastructure, no settlements. This does not mean the wilderness is a barren wasteland. On the contrary, it is a vast, complex, and richly diverse landscape.

The wilderness, as an uncharted and dangerous environment, is a fitting analogy for the unprecedented and unrelenting cognitive, moral, and emotional challenges of the New Normal. The work of leading is aptly compared to a wilderness journey—a collective process of exploration. Six distinctive features of a wilderness environment frame the challenge of leading in the New Normal.

First, a wilderness is an unexplored, uncharted, and unfamiliar place. There are no maps to point the way, no established, well-marked route forward. No ready reference points to direct the journey and mark progress. Leaders invite others on a journey to a place they themselves have never been, over terrain they have never traveled, and facing challenges and perils they have never encountered. In the New Normal, "good leaders" may not have the slightest idea of where to head next. Like everyone on the journey, leaders may find themselves confused, off balance, and ill-equipped for the unfamiliar terrain.

Second, a wilderness is a bewildering and, at times, wildly unpredictable place. There is no "normal" day. Rather, instability is the norm, with each day bringing novel circumstances, unprecedented challenges, and unpredictable "outlier" events—a twenty–first-century dragon of uncertainty prowling the landscape. Crises are a regular occurrence. No one knows what might be over the next hill or around the next river bend, including leaders. Like everyone else on the journey, leaders must learn how to deal with the anxiety of not knowing.

Third, a wilderness is, often, a dangerous place. The first glimpse of the wild terrain may be exciting, but the privilege of exploration comes at an exacting price. The wilderness is ruthlessly efficient. It does not accommodate our wishes or respect our feelings. It deals quickly and harshly with the casual and careless, the rigid and arrogant, those who show reckless indifference to the consequences of their decisions and actions, and those slow to adapt and learn. Like everyone else on the journey, leaders have to learn quickly and make wise adjustments to unprecedented events and novel circumstances.

Fourth, an extended wilderness journey is emotionally draining. The wilderness serves up a steady diet of stubborn obstacles and intractable problems. It is easy to get lost. Confusion reigns. Difficulty and disappointment abound. There is, often, no direct correlation between effort and progress. Leaders do not have the power to protect fellow travelers from negative circumstances or disappointing outcomes. Problems defy solution and may linger for extended periods. Some never get resolved. Even if solutions are found, tomorrow is certain to offer up a new set of problems and crises. Many succumb to fear and anxiety.

Fifth, the unpredictability and dangers inherent in a wilderness journey raise the moral stakes. The decisions and relationships of everyone on the journey, not just leaders, are consequential. How fellow travelers are treated is a matter of utmost importance. Vital and precious resources must be carefully protected and wisely spent—no one knows how long the journey may take. Everyone must be trusted to do the right thing for others.

Sixth, the wilderness offers up challenges beyond the capabilities of any one person. No leader is prepared for what lies ahead—dangers, some lethal; a staggering array of difficulties, some insurmountable; unprecedented challenges, and bewildering circumstances. No leader can meet these demands from their personal repertoire of assets, no matter how talented or experienced.

A Case Study in Wilderness Leadership: The Panama Canal

For four decades, two nations worked in a literal wilderness to construct the Panama Canal. Ferdinand de Lesseps, the nineteenth-century French diplomat, engineer, and builder of the Suez Canal, was the intellectual and financial force behind the first unsuccessful attempt to build the Canal. His attitudes, actions, and decisions as a leader are rich in lessons on how not to lead in the New Normal. The American government, under the leadership of President Teddy Roosevelt, led the second attempt, which is rich in lessons on how to survive and thrive in wilderness conditions.

Contemporaries describe de Lesseps as a man of mediocre talent, but extraordinary vision and determination. His capacity for hard work and perseverance would earn him worldwide fame, but his diminished capacity for "wilderness leadership" would bring him to public ruin.

De Lesseps stepped on the world stage in 1854 when Said Pasha, the Viceroy of Egypt, invited him to start preparations for what would become the world's most ambitious engineering project—the construction of the Suez Canal. De Lesseps took 5 years to put together the financing and organization for this monumental undertaking. His construction plan called for a 100-mile long canal extending from Port Said on the Mediterranean Sea to Port Suez on the Red Sea. If successful, the canal would shorten the trade route between Great Britain and India by more than 6,000 miles. In the blazing heat of the desert, the task that most thought impossible was completed in 10 years—a monument to de Lesseps's superb planning, organizing, raw determination, and engineering ability. The canal opened in 1869, and was an instant financial success. To this day, the Suez Canal is considered an engineering marvel.

In 1882, the government of Columbia (owner of Panama) asked de Lesseps to build the Panama Canal. The invitation was based largely on his prior success in building the Suez Canal. The Canal would be 50.72 miles long and, if successful, would shorten the 13,000-mile sea route from New York to San Francisco to a little more than 5,000 miles. De Lesseps accepted the challenge and set about arranging the financing and completing the engineering design of the canal. However, after 4 years of design work, planning, and initial construction, de Lesseps gave up on the project. "A sea level canal," de Lesseps stated, "would be impossible in the higher altitudes of Panama." Financially and creatively bankrupt (his Panama Canal Company went bankrupt in 1889), de Lesseps ended the project in utter failure. Over 76 million cubic yards of earth had been moved to no avail. Thousands of workers died of malaria and other diseases. The project—as well as de Lesseps's heavy machinery—sat idle in the Panamanian jungle for more than 20 years.

Two decades later, the United States, led by Roosevelt and motivated by strategic naval concerns at the end of the Spanish American War, gave the Panama Canal Project another look. American engineers evaluated the feasibility of the project and determined it could, indeed, be built. Work began in 1904. After a few missteps, the Americans made an unorthodox decision. An Army physician, Colonel William C. Gorgas, who had eliminated yellow fever in Havana after the Spanish American War, was put in charge of wiping out malaria and yellow fever in Panama.

Workers cleared brush and drained wilderness to rid the construction area of disease-carrying mosquitoes. By 1906, Gorgas had wiped out yellow fever and eliminated the rats that carried bubonic plague. Over $20 million, an astronomical sum in its day, was spent on the initial medical–sanitation phase of the project.

The Americans invented technology to suit the specific needs of building a canal in Panama. Engineers designed a lock canal system to prevent flooding and compensate for the significant variation in sea level encountered in the path of the canal—something de Lesseps was unable to do. (It is of note that the Suez Canal did not require locks to raise and lower the water level because there was no great variation in sea level in the land between the Red Sea and the Mediterranean.) Three sets of locks were built that would raise and lower ships from one water level to another. Electric locomotives, on tracks, called "mules" were designed to pull ships through the locks. Custom-designed steam shovels were built to scoop the loose volcanic dirt found in Panama. Two large lakes in the Canal's path were utilized to cut down on the labor and expense of digging.

It took 380 million dollars (an unheard of expense in its time) and 43,000 men 10 years to complete the work. The Panama Canal opened for business in 1913, and stands, today, as one of the engineering marvels of the twentieth century (see McCullough, 1979; Parker, 2009).

Wilderness Lessons for New Normal Leaders

The stark contrast in attitude and behaviors that drove failure and success in building of the Panama Canal provide insight in how to lead—and how not to lead—in a New Normal operating environment. De Lesseps's experience illustrates the fundamental mismatch between the perspective and skill-set of leaders immersed in Old Normal assumptions, and the demands of the New Normal operating environment.

We learn three "wilderness leadership lessons" from the failure of de Lesseps and the American success.

First, in the wilderness, past success may hinder future effectiveness. Past success carries the seeds of future failure in the form of a deadly leadership disease called "success blindness." Those infected employ the insight gleaned in a past situation as the exclusive interpretive reference point for addressing present challenges. This severely restricts a leader's perceptive capabilities, causing him or her to interpret a present challenge only in terms of the prior success. De Lesseps was a prisoner of precedent, binding him conceptually and emotionally to what worked in Egypt—fatal assumptions with respect to building a canal in Panama.

De Lesseps ignored an important fact: Panama is not Egypt. His mental map for how a canal ought to be built did not correspond to the novel realities of the Panamanian landscape. The Panamanian wilderness offered up an unprecedented set of challenges—a unique landscape with vastly different requirements for success. The Suez Canal was a historic success, but it was built at sea level and most of the digging was done through sandy, low-lying desert. In sharp contrast, the Panamanian terrain was a complex wilderness landscape—a rare combination of swamps and higher elevation, lakes, and dense jungle. Unlike the sand of Egypt, the Panamanian soil was composed of soft, volcanic material that was difficult to shovel. Perhaps, the greatest challenge to the project in its initial phase was not in the field of engineering, but in the new field of tropical medicine. Panama was a vast mosquito-breeding ground, and epidemics of malaria and yellow fever plagued de Lesseps's work force, causing thousands of deaths.

De Lesseps never came to terms with the realities of the leadership challenge set before him. He superimposed the Egyptian desert over the Panamanian jungle, the Suez Canal over the challenges of building a canal in Panama, with disastrous results. In this sense, he was a casualty of his own success.

Second, in the wilderness, sustained effectiveness requires humility, flexibility, and constant learning. The wilderness deals severely with those who cannot learn and adapt quickly to unprecedented circumstances and new realities. Boorstin (1985) reminds us, "The great obstacle to discovering the shape of the earth, the continents, and the ocean was not ignorance but the illusion of knowledge" (p. 86). De Lesseps operated under this illusion. Disciplined and logical—a prototypical engineer—he had supreme confidence that the same canal design, construction tools, and work process that brought him success in Egypt would bring success in Panama. If these failed, "technical genius" would meet any new set of challenges the Panamanian landscape put before them. However, humility, flexibility, and a love of learning were not in his repertoire. He had long since formed his opinion on the right way to build a canal and, predictably, he saw no need to develop new tools or make special accommodations to the new situation. Consequently, de Lesseps never appreciated how little he knew about building a canal in Panama and how ill-prepared he was to take on this challenge.

Third, in the wilderness, leaders who do not face reality and learn quickly are dangerous to themselves and those they lead. De Lesseps had a world-class capacity to suppress troubling information—his shovels were not working, hundreds were dying every week of malaria and yellow fever, money was running out, unscrupulous public officials were robbing the till, and investors were losing confidence by the day. However, he preferred presumptuous certainty to the stress of facing troubling information. He ignored the negative feedback, "doubled down," and worked harder. The pride of past success combined with an overestimation of his personal assets and underestimation of the Panamanian landscape proved a deadly mixture. Rampant disease and the Panamanian terrain ultimately prevailed, leaving de Lesseps to preside over an unmitigated disaster. Tens of thousands of workers perished, and the project almost bankrupted the French government.

Spared from success blindness, the Americans approached the project with a fresh, honest assessment of the Panamanian terrain. This gave them an important edge on de Lesseps—they did not share his fatal assumptions about success in canal building. Armed with creative insight and the willingness to learn as they went, they confronted the demands of the Panamanian terrain and its novel medical and engineering challenges. They abandoned the idea of a sea-level canal, and designed new tools, including a lock system to raise and lower ships over the uneven terrain and custom-designed steam shovels to scoop the loose volcanic dirt. Perhaps, most importantly, they made the highly unorthodox decision to invest millions of dollars in addressing medical and hygiene issues to insure safe working conditions.

Summary

Cognitively and emotionally unable—or unwilling—to adjust and learn, de Lesseps failed to adapt to the realities of Panama. He argued with reality, and lost. Although he did not realize it, he desperately needed a set of assets better suited for his new leadership challenge. Similarly, Old Normal leaders armed only with charisma and technical–managerial competence are unlikely to succeed in the New Normal. As Heifetz et al. (2009) note, "The skills that enabled most executives to reach their positions of command—analytical problem solving, crisp decision making, the articulation of clear direction—can get in the way of success" (p. 65). Fernandez-Araoz (2014) notes, "In the past few decades, organizations have emphasized 'competencies' in hiring and developing talent. Jobs have been decomposed into skills and filled by candidates who have them. But 21st century business is too volatile and complex—and the market for top talent too tight—for that model to work anymore" (p. 49).

A new set of emerging realities and unprecedented challenges threaten the viability of the Old Normal version of "good leadership." The mythology of the leader as Oz is over. Effective leadership in the New Normal requires a new set of assets better suited for a wilderness journey.

SECTION II

Next Practices and Ancient Assets

This section explores the leadership landscape of the twenty-first century. Seven leadership performance shifts are identified. A New Normal leadership "next practice," necessitated by each shift, is discussed. The ancient assets—virtues—associated with each next practice are identified and discussed.

CHAPTER 4

Next Practices: Part I

Introduction

The New Normal operating environment calls into question Old Normal orthodoxies around leadership performance. Effective twenty-first century leadership practice is not only changing, it is evolving into something fundamentally different.

Old Normal assets such as drive, intelligence, a winning personality, and technical–managerial skill—although still useful—are, nevertheless, increasingly inadequate in the face of the emerging New Normal landscape. Two foundational performance shifts are powerfully shaping the New Normal leadership operating environment and, with it, the requirements of "good leadership."

Performance Shift #1: From Formal Authority to Moral Authority

Effective leadership in the New Normal is less and less about the exercise of formal authority and more and more about the exercise of moral authority.

Clarifying Terms

Exploring this performance shift requires clarification around two terms: *power* and *authority*. Power is the ability to act, to affect an outcome, and, in the case of leadership, to influence the behavior of others in a given direction to bring about a desired result. Authority is the right to do so. Authority legitimates the expression of power, and designates the boundaries within which power is properly exercised.

Both Old Normal and New Normal narratives view leadership as the exercise of authority and power to get important things accomplished.

However, it is necessary to distinguish between two types of power—*position* power and *personal* power.

Position power is what we, typically, think of as formal authority. The individual's office, rank, or place on the organizational chart gives him or her the right to control the agenda and resources—money, personnel, and information—to make good things happen for the organization. Position power may carry great influence, as others comply due to either respect for those in authority, contractual obligation, or awareness of the negative ramifications of not complying—or, perhaps, a mix of the three.

In contrast, personal power—sometimes referred to as informal authority—is based on an individual's professional reputation and credibility, and, most importantly, the moral quality of his or her relationships. With respect to personal power, the individual's authority is based, not on rank or position, but, rather, is derived from followers who grant the individual the right to influence them based on whether he or she is perceived as trustworthy. Greenleaf (1977) observed:

> A fresh and critical look is being taken at the issues of power and authority and...A new moral principle is emerging which holds that the only authority deserving one's allegiance is that which is freely and knowingly granted by the led to the leader in response to, and in proportion to, the clearly evident servant stature of the leader. (pp. 3–4)

Fromm (1965) noted that power is expressed either as domination—as in the exercise of power over others, or what he calls "potency," or "generative power"—power used to make and do, create and serve (p. 160). Personal power is akin to Fromm's potency and generative power. If power is used to dominate, control, and pursue self-serving ends, followers withhold influence from the leader. When people use power to serve others, the moral authority to influence others is granted.

Who Can Lead?

The implications for who is capable of leading are profound. If leading is framed as the personal power to influence others based on one's moral authority and credibility, anyone, regardless of rank, is capable of functioning as a "leader." The inverse is also true. If an individual occupies a formal position, but lacks moral authority, his or her influence will suffer regardless of rank. There are leaders, and there are those that lead. Those that lead can show up anywhere on the organizational chart.

John Kotter (1990) makes a helpful distinction between a "LEADER," "Leader" and "leader." LEADERS are history-making individuals like F. D. Roosevelt or Churchill. Leaders are those holding positions of formal authority—CEO's VPs, division heads, team leaders, etc. Kotter's small "l" "leader" refers to organization members who, although lacking formal authority, still exercise considerable personal influence. For the purpose of clarity, in the remainder of the book, those with formal, positional authority are referred to as Leaders, and those without positional authority, but who have considerable influence due to their moral authority, are referred to as "member-leaders" or leaders with the "L" not capitalized.

Old Normal Expectations and New Normal Realities

The Old Normal narrative presumes that position power is fundamental to leadership effectiveness—only those with positional authority can, or should, lead. A few at the top of the organization possess the authority and power to command and control the people, processes, and resources to get important things accomplished. These few know most, perform best, and decide all.

Position power is still a valuable leadership asset in the New Normal; however, it is less and less the coin of the realm and is, in fact, rapidly depreciating in value. Carol Bartz, former CEO of Yahoo goes so far as to say, "The online era has made command-and-control management as dead as dial-up internet" (2009, p. 128). This may be an overstatement, but it highlights the diminishing value of formal authority, especially in contexts of rapid change where many member-leaders have access to important information typically reserved for only a few Leaders.

A Timeless Leadership Irony

The New Normal operating environment highlights a timeless leadership irony: positional power, typically, comes with powerful constraints. Four factors contribute to the limits of formal authority.

First, the reach and effectiveness of position power has always been over stated. Presidential advisor and historian Richard Neustadt's (1960) dictum with respect to the power of US Presidents applies to those holding positional power in the New Normal: Presidential power is, simply and only, the power to persuade. When Harry Truman contemplated the possibility that Eisenhower would succeed him as president, he predicted that the Five Star General would have difficulty adjusting to the difference between his exercise of formal authority as a military commander, and the reality that leading as president was dependent on the practice of moral persuasion and personal influence. "He'll sit here...and he'll say, 'Do this! Do that!' And nothing will happen. Poor Ike—it won't be a bit like the Army. He'll find it very frustrating" (Rodman, 2009, p. 5).

Truman spoke from personal experience. Reflecting on his limited power, he bemoaned, "I sit here all day trying to persuade people to do the things they ought to have sense enough to do without my persuading them...That's all the powers of the President amount to" (Rodman, 2009, p. 5). Former presidential advisor David Gergen (2001) strikes a similar note, observing that it is more realistic to conceptualize the effective Leader, even executives with vast formal authority like the President of the United States, as operating at the "center of a web" rather than the top of a pyramid (p. 349). Without personal power, one's position power, even at the highest levels, is insufficient to get important things accomplished.

Second, Collins (2005) notes that Leaders do not have the same concentration of pure executive power they once enjoyed. Naim (2013) argues that power is undergoing a historic and world-changing transformation, imposing constraints on those who possess formal authority. "In the twenty-first century, power is easier to get, harder to use—and easier to lose" (p. 2). In light of the leadership catastrophes of the last decade—Enron, 3Com, Global Crossing, and the like—regulators are watching Leaders more closely. Leaders face stricter rules on corporate governance and regulatory compliance, such as those mandated by the Sarbanes–Oxley Act of 2002, as well as pressures from investors, constituents, and organization members to exhibit greater transparency in handling corporate finances and sharing information.

Third, it is an iron law of organizational life that attempts to exert central control, often, stimulate powerful countertrends that severely limit the Leader's ability to impose a specific course of action on others. These come in various forms—disengagement, rival agendas, sabotage, and even outright rebellion. Moreover, in times of increasing complexity and uncertainty, a consensus decision on how to allocate scarce resources is, often, unattainable. Hard choices must be made. Leaders make promises and arouse expectations that they cannot fulfill, and often find themselves in the unenviable position of having to disappoint some in order to meet the expectations of others. Consequently, Leaders make an easy target for those disappointed in the direction or performance of the organization.

Fourth, it is increasingly ineffective and even dangerous to give a few Leaders unilateral authority to make critical decisions. Hamel (2007) notes, "Right now, your company has twenty-first century, internet-enabled business processes, mid-20th century management processes, all built atop 19th century management principles" (p. 255). One of the outdated management principles is the practice of entrusting most critical business decisions to a few Leaders even as it is becoming more apparent that no one person or central group is smart enough or fast enough to deal effectively with rapid changes in the operating environment.

The New Normal Next Practice: Moral Persuasion

As the New Normal wilderness replaces the familiar Old Normal landscape, Leaders find position power less and less the currency of the day, and the expression of personal power increasingly valuable. Personal power is primarily expressed in the practice of moral persuasion. Moral persuasion is the process of influencing others' attitudes or behaviors without resorting to the controls derived from position power—duress in the form of "pulling rank," threatening force, or prompting fear. The practice of moral persuasion calls on Leaders and member leaders to make the case that a particular course of action is consistent with what is "good," "right," and "important," and, thus, in the best interests of others.

Moral Persuasion in Action. Moral persuasion depends, to a degree, on technical competence—how to frame arguments or appeal to the interests of one's audience—but it is, fundamentally, an exercise in demonstrating trustworthiness, earning credibility, understanding others, and translating these into personal influence.

As the practice of moral persuasion typically begins and ends with the attitudes and behaviors of those with formal authority (although member-leaders must also participate), this section is focused on what Leaders must believe and do to extend this leadership practice throughout the organization. Here is how it works.

First, Leaders embrace the fundamental importance of personal credibility, which is earned trust in the eyes of others. The connections among trust, credibility, and persuasive power are obvious and ancient. More than two millennia ago, Aristotle made the case for the connection between a speaker's personal credibility and persuasive ability. Aristotle argued that an individual's projected character, which he calls *ethos*, is a crucial element in the art of persuasion.

> Persuasion is achieved by the speaker's personal character when the speech is so spoken as to make us think him credible. We believe good men more fully and more readily than others: this is true generally

whatever the question is, and absolutely true where exact certainty is impossible and opinions are divided...It is not true, as some writers assume in their treatises on rhetoric, that the personal goodness revealed by the speaker contributes nothing to his power of persuasion; on the contrary, his character may almost be called the most effective means of persuasion he possesses. (2006, p. 8)

His observations have powerful contemporary relevance. According to Rousseau et al. (1998), trust is "a psychological state comprising the intention to accept vulnerability based upon positive expectations of the intentions or behavior of another." Trust is at a premium in the New Normal, where, in Aristotle's words, "exact certainty is impossible." New Normal Leaders ask others to follow them on a journey through a wilderness along an unmarked route, often with little or no signs of progress. In this context, relationships based on shared values and mutual trust carry the greatest influence (Covey, 2006). As Aristotle reminds us, we do not tend to listen to people we do not trust or believe have our best interests at heart. We will not volunteer to follow them, especially into a situation filled with uncertainty and risks. Leaders cannot command that kind of trust; they must earn it.

Second, Leaders establish a trusting, personal connection with others. Aristotle called this *pathos*. "Our judgments when we are pleased and friendly are not the same as when we are pained and hostile. It is toward producing these effects, as we maintain, that present-day writers on rhetoric direct the whole of their efforts (Aristotle, 2006, p. 8). We trust people who, we have good reason to believe, listen to us, understand us, and connect in meaningful ways with our concerns.

The New Normal narrative affirms that, although formal authority is a valuable asset, Leaders have influence only to the degree that others actually follow. This is always the follower's choice, and the choice is based largely on his or her sense of relational connection with those doing the leading. This highlights the fundamental importance of putting followers in the frame of mind to say "yes" to the challenges and opportunities set before them. This "yes" is more likely when those leading resonate with the concerns of others and communicate genuine interest in their welfare.

Third, Leaders make an effective case for their agenda. They reason logically and marshal evidence for their point of view. Aristotle called this *logos*, which is the rational content of an argument. Here, expertise comes into play (Aristotle devotes the third book of *Rhetoric* to the technical aspects of argumentation). However, technical–managerial competencies like clear communication and the use of persuasive rhetoric must be backed up by moral, emotional, and relational competencies that enable those leading to establish a genuine connection with others (*pathos*) and honor their best interests (*ethos*).

Summary

According to the Old Normal narrative, power, information, and value flow down, through the organization's hierarchy. Leaders speak, and followers listen. Leaders decide, and followers comply. It is something altogether different to lead through moral persuasion, which honors the choice of others to follow. Top–down is still in play, but bottom–up and sideways are fast becoming just as important, placing a premium on moral authority. Consequently, effective New Normal leadership is less and less about making declarations and, increasingly, a persuasive process. This means that effective leadership may be practiced not only by Leaders, but also by member-leaders. Anyone capable of earning trust and establishing credibility is capable of moral persuasion.

Performance Shift #2: From the Few to the Many

Effective leadership in the New Normal is less and less about the charisma or competence of the few and increasingly about the collaborative effort of the many.

Old Normal Expectations and New Normal Realities

The Old Normal narrative assumes that a few Leaders armed with position power and the "right stuff"—drive, intelligence, a charismatic personality, and hyper-competence—best serve the organization. Organizations give this select group access to the levers of command and control and expect them to get results. In a predictable world of well-mannered change, this is, typically, sufficient to get the job done, at least in the short term.

The New Normal exposes the inherent weakness of this perspective. When confronted with massive uncertainty and rapid, discontinuous change, the Old Normal Leader has nothing to offer save a measure of formal authority and his or her personal assets. Although these may be substantial, the demands of effectiveness far outdistance the capabilities of any one individual Leader or small group of Leaders, no matter how talented. The best effort of the gifted few is insufficient. Nothing less than the collective strength of the organization—the talent and insight of many member-leaders—will suffice.

Consequently, in the New Normal, organizations are best served not by an elite few doing all the important work, but by many member-leaders collaborating to get important things accomplished. To collaborate is to "co-labor," and, therefore, to work in an interdependent fashion to achieve common ends. As Henton et al. (2004) put it, "We need flexible, innovative responses rooted in collaboration that meet real organization needs, rather than the simple top-down, 'mainframe,' one-size-fits-all models of the earlier Progressive era" (p. 44).

The New Normal Next Practice: Collaborative Engagement

Ibarra and Hansen (2011) define collaborative leadership as, "The capacity to engage people and groups outside one's formal control and inspire them to work toward common goals—despite differences in convictions, cultural values, and operating norms" (p. 73). Collaborative engagement is the process of forging productive partnerships that leverage the unique perspectives and diverse talent of many member-leaders to serve the welfare and progress of the organization.

Collaborative Engagement in Action

This new way of thinking about effective leadership is embodied in three simple, but powerful, principles: (1) *Each is valuable*; (2) *No one is sufficient;* and (3) *All are required for the enduring success of the organization.* Collaborative engagement is the practice of embracing, embodying, and extending these principles throughout the organization. As collaborative engagement typically begins and ends with the attitudes and behaviors of those with formal authority (although member-leaders must also participate), this section is focused on what Leaders must believe and do to extend this leadership practice throughout the organization.

Here is how collaborative engagement works.

First, Leaders embrace, embody, and extend the conviction that "each is valuable." New Normal Leaders do not see member-leaders as mere "worker bees," whose value resides only in their loyalty to Leaders and their agenda. Rather, they operate out of the deep conviction that vast, untapped leadership potential resides in many members—most of whom have no access to position power. McNamee (2004) observes, "In the New Normal, enterprises will increasingly recognize the value of individuals at all levels of the organization" (p. 59). This makes good sense, as sustainable effectiveness depends on the efforts of many motivated and talented members-leaders who are ready and willing to contribute to the welfare and progress of the organization.

Second, Leaders embrace, embody, and extend the conviction that "no one is sufficient." Recognizing their assets and liabilities, New Normal Leaders know they cannot do it all. They appreciate, firsthand, the impossibility of staying abreast of a rapidly changing external environment. They know the limits of their interpretive capacity in processing the vast amount of data and experience each day brings their way.

Third, Leaders embrace, embody, and extend the conviction that "all are required for the enduring success of the organization." If each is valuable and no one is sufficient, it follows that no qualified member is excluded from the leadership work. Collaborative engagement calls for the wide distribution of leadership opportunity up, down, and across the organization, with the maximum participation of members a part of everyday organizational life. Kouzes and Posner (1996) remind us, "Leadership is everyone's business" (p. 108).

This highlights the critical importance of distributing leadership responsibilities more broadly throughout the organization. Heifetz et al. (2009) state:

> Individual executives just don't have the personal capacity to sense and make sense of all the change swirling around them. They need to distribute leadership responsibility; replacing hierarchy and formal authority with organizational bandwidth, which draws on collective intelligence. Executives need to relax their sense of obligation to be all and do all and instead become comfortable sharing their burden with people operating in diverse functions and locations throughout the organization. (p. 68)

The principle of "all are required" is inconsistent with hoarding Leadership prerogatives by reserving the important information and consequential decisions for a select few. Although a Leader's presence may, indeed, loom large—they do not refrain from providing strategic direction or taking constructive action—they take pains to avoid casting a shadow over the efforts of members. Instead, Leaders serve as catalysts for widespread participation in the leadership work. In general terms, a catalyst acts as the stimulus to bring about or accelerate a result. In similar fashion, New Normal Leaders galvanize the collective strength of members, employing their position power to distribute leadership prerogatives and opportunities throughout the organization.

Organizations may differ with respect to how much of what kind of information gets shared with how many, or who gets invited to join

Leaders in strategic discussions. Whatever shape the Leader–member collaboration takes, the intention is the same—provide a maximum number of members ample opportunity and sufficient resources to join with Leaders in doing the leadership work.

Summary

As the familiar Old Normal leadership landscape is replaced by the New Normal wilderness, effective leadership is not only changing, it is evolving into something fundamentally different. A twenty-first century New Normal leadership narrative is fast replacing images of success grounded in charisma and technical–managerial competence. New Normal organizations are best served, not by an elite few doing all the important work, but by many member-leaders collaborating with Leaders to get important things accomplished. Collaboration is fast becoming a prominent feature of the New Normal landscape, a fundamental driver of organizational effectiveness

CHAPTER 5

Next Practices: Part II

Introduction

Three additional New Normal performance shifts have emerged, each necessitating an additional next leadership practice. Each is collaborative in nature and depends on the exercise of moral authority on the part of both Leaders and member-leaders.

Performance Shift # 3: From Certainty to Contingency

Effective leadership in the New Normal is less and less about predictive certainty and increasingly about making sense of circumstances as they arise and responding constructively.

Old Normal Expectations and New Normal Realities

Driven by a dislike of ambiguity and a preference for order, predictability, and control, organizations send Leaders on an illusory quest for final certainty. The Old Normal narrative picks up on this expectation, affirming that "good leaders" slay the dragon of uncertainty by anticipating events and protecting the organization from unwanted situations and negative outcomes.

The New Normal—marked by novelty and discontinuous change featuring a kaleidoscope of unpredictable factors and actors—makes this kind of leadership impossible. The next decade will, likely, feature a stomach-turning mix of economic roiling and unprecedented events. Uncontrollable and unexplainable dynamics will shape and reshape the landscape. Confusion will reach unprecedented levels. No Leader, no matter how talented, will be able to provide the organization with a sufficient Old Normal supply of predictability. In light of these realities, effective Leaders reject the idea that they serve the organization best by having all the right answers.

The New Normal Next Practice: Sensemaking

Although the terrain is marked by discontinuous change and perpetual novelty, this does not mean Leaders lapse into passivity. Instead, they practice "sensemaking." Organizational psychologist Karl Weick (1979) coined the term to describe the process of seeking to understand and explain, at least to a degree, the world around us (Drath & Paulus, 1994). Sense-makers reflect on the flow of past events, assess present realities, and interpret the "mess of the present." They help the organization understand complex, confusing, and ambiguous circumstances. This practice is also called "meaning making"—the process by which individuals and communities make sense of emerging change and give meaning to unfolding events (Gioia & Thomas, 1996).

Sensemaking is grounded in an understanding of the organization's external operating environment, coupled with deep insight into the situation at hand. Sensemaking is not about lightning bolts out of the blue, transcendent insights, or history-changing, "eureka moments." Rather, this practice places primary emphasis on the mundane process of fact gathering and keen observation such that the organization attains a thorough understanding of what is required for sustained success. Weick compared this process to mapmaking, as the one making sense then charts the terrain and gets a compass read to fix the location of the organization and point it true North.

Sensemaking in Action

As the leadership landscape becomes less and less predictable, Leaders who continue to operate in the Old Normal frame fall into three categories. First, risk-averse Leaders circle the wagons, suspend judgment, and avoid difficult decisions. Second, some Leaders shine the spotlight on technical fixes like reorganizations to provide themselves, and the organization, a sense of order and progress. Third, self-assured Leaders speak and act with an authoritative certainty, grounded more in their personality than in insight into the realities of the situation. They overestimate what they know—or think they know—and underestimate what they do not. Remember the presumption of de Lesseps.

The practice of sensemaking provides Leaders a new set of options for making responsible decisions in the context of uncertainty. As Heifetz et al. (2009) state, "People clamor for direction, while you are faced with a way forward that isn't at all obvious. Twists and turns are the only certainty. Yet you still have to lead" (p. 64).

First, New Normal Leaders normalize not knowing. Effective New Normal leadership places a premium on "coming clean" with the organization about the limitations imposed on Leaders and organizations in an uncertain world. Knowing that the present is unprecedented and that no one has been "here" before, Leaders refrain from projecting an aura of certainty. Final and authoritative answers are not theirs to give, and, therefore, they do not give the impression that they can use their superior intelligence, access to information, potent personality, or position of power to protect the organization from difficult issues and unpleasant surprises. Instead, they normalize uncertainty and ambiguity, and make it acceptable to be confused, perplexed, and baffled by circumstances and events.

Second, New Normal Leaders prompt a "first read" conversation. Although Leaders have given up on the idea of predictive certainty, this does not mean they allow the organization to wallow in helpless despair. Instead, they help the organization get a first read on the realities of the present by prompting a conversation around "what is happening and why." Leveraging the practice of collaborative engagement, Leaders join with member-leaders in identifying the potential risks and opportunities embedded in its present circumstances. After these are identified, they invite member-leaders to edit, amend, or disagree with these insights. This initial read on the situation may provide nothing more than provisional insight—a tentative foothold of understanding from which to grasp the critical elements of a situation. But, it is a start. Although the first read is rarely the final word, it begins the conversation and provides an initial compass read on the location of the organization and the possibilities for constructive action.

Third, New Normal Leaders leverage initial, provisional clarity to generate "substantial clarity." Substantial clarity, here, means sufficient clarity to take constructive, collective action. Weick (1979) calls this making "retrospective sense" of the present. Leaders join with member-leaders to discern the patterns emerging from circumstances as they unfold, and what this might mean for the present and future of the organization. This conversation helps create a conceptual map of the terrain, marking the relevant features of the operating environment, and giving the organization insight on where it stands and what next steps might be taken. This insight is extrapolated into an agenda for constructive action that prompts the organization to address its most pressing challenges, seize opportunity, and take preventative measures with respect to threats.

Substantial clarity is not to be confused with final clarity or authoritative certainty. Delphic pronouncements are out of order. As Robert Frost (1995) put it, the best we will get is "a momentary stay against confusion" (p. 777). But, that is a start. In a wilderness environment where confusion is the norm, knowing your location and getting a compass read on true North is of great value. Therefore, while Leaders and organizations will not achieve a MapQuest level of directional specificity, they can gain sufficient clarity to take the next step with a measure of confidence, although they have no way of knowing all the factors in play, or what the outcomes of their decisions might bring.

Fourth, New Normal Leaders practice a combination of active reflection and reflective action. Kiefer and Schlesinger (2010) coined the term "creaction" to describe taking "creation-oriented action" in the face of uncertainty. Leaders have to make tough decisions, and act with limited information and little or no idea of how things will turn out. Adjustment and readjustments are a way of life, with each round of reflection and action leading to another round of self-correction as the organization inches forward in an uncertain landscape.

Performance Shift # 4: From Making Promises to Telling the Truth

Effective leadership in the New Normal is less and less about promising results and increasingly about telling the truth.

Old Normal Expectations and New Normal Realities

In the Old Normal, "good leaders" set goals and accomplish them in accordance with a plan and timetable. Along the way, they keep the organization on "even keel"—meaning that almost everyone is reasonably happy and optimistic about the organization's progress. Old Normal Leaders are productive and uplifting. They uphold the party line that "things are good and getting better; that good results are our birthright, and no one can stop us." They infuse the organization with optimism and positive self-regard regardless of its capability or performance. Highlighting unpleasant realities is forbidden.

As we learned from de Lesseps, a wilderness is full of unpleasant surprises, and there is no guarantee of progress. The prospect of failure is a constant. The only certainty is difficulty, and no Leader or organization is exempt. Consequently, promising outcomes by a particular date is a recipe for disappointment. Keeping everyone happy is impossible. It is quite possible that some, perhaps many, will get discouraged or quit. In light of these realities, New Normal Leaders have given up on the idea that they serve the organization best by making bold promises, as in "I promise this outcome by this date," or worse, "I promise to keep you all happy."

The New Normal Next Practice: Exercising Candor

Although Leaders do not promise immediate results or contented people, they do deliver much by way of candor. The term candor comes from the Latin "*candeo*" meaning, "to be white," with the root *candere*, meaning, "to shine." The English word incandescent (as in a light bulb) is derived from this term. Candor carries the idea of innocence, purity, and sincerity and, thus, freedom from disguise or trickery. Candid people have an open and transparent way about them. They let the warm light of reality shine into conversations and decisions. They express their true thoughts and feelings without equivocation, dissimulation, or disguise. They are fair, honest, impartial, forthright, frank, and open with others, especially in the context of telling the truth about difficult matters.

Candor in Action

Of course, making promises is not inherently bad. The issue is what is promised. Although New Normal Leaders are reluctant to make promises with respect to performance outcomes, they do make and keep a solemn promise that they will deliver candor, that they will tell the truth with respect to the hard realities that touch on the welfare and progress of the organization, as well as what they and member-leaders can and cannot do about these realities, given their capabilities and human limitations. Candor creates a healthy "reality flow"—the unimpeded communication of important information, some of which is difficult to hear—throughout the organization. Heifetz (1994) notes effective leadership is primarily about "mobilizing people to tackle tough problems." Leaders serve the organization best when they direct its attention to its most important and difficult issues. As Leaders create the structures and expectations that support truth telling up, down, and across the organization, it prompts honest and constructive dialog around the organization's most difficult issues.

First, New Normal Leaders are candid about the harsh realities of the moment. In the wilderness, the hard truth is that difficulties abound and people are bound to get disappointed. In political parlance, the practice of candor disallows "spinning" or manipulating the facts in the service of self-interest—whether that is the furthering of one's agenda or the avoidance of negative information.

Second, New Normal Leaders are candid about the difficulties of progress. Organizations have little or no control over the external operating environment. No one can say, with certainty, how decisions will turn out or strategies will perform. The status quo stubbornly resists a makeover. Bad things happen to good organizations. The few things Leaders have control over—short-term goals, process improvements, budget allocation, job descriptions, reconfiguring teams, and so onmay help move the organization forward a little, but a better tomorrow cannot be organized or budgeted into existence.

Although it may appear counterintuitive, especially to those grounded in the Old Normal narrative, the widespread practice of candor is surprisingly refreshing and makes a powerful contribution to organizational effectiveness. Friedman (1995) notes that David Ben-Gurion, the first Prime Minister of Israel, believed facts were his "first constituency" (p. 271). Painfully aware of the grim geopolitical realities Israel faced in its early years as a nation, Ben-Gurion played the part of a "pragmatic idealist." He was an astute politician; nevertheless, he considered the people of Israel his "second constituency." As he saw it, his job as Prime Minister was to ask the nation to face the hard facts—his first constituency—and insure that the nation's collective experience was shaped by these unpleasant realities (Morris, 2008). If a Leader's "first constituency" is the mood, the sensibilities, or the short-term comfort of the organization—if they see their primary role as a "reality adjuster" who spins the facts to stave off anxiety and disappointment—they have committed nothing short of leadership malpractice.

Performance Shift # 5: From Solving Problems to Facing Dilemmas

Effective leadership in the New Normal is less and less about solving technical problems and Increasingly about facing adaptive problems, "wicked problems," and dilemmas.

Old Normal Expectations and New Normal Realities

The Old Normal narrative calls on Leaders to protect the organization from obstacles to progress, and when they do arise, to address them immediately and keep things running smoothly. This is not possible in a New Normal environment that serves up a steady diet of problems not amenable to technical solution. Problems come in four categories.

Technical or Tame Problems

Tame problems (Grint, 2010) are akin to Heifetz's (1994) technical problems. These problems have a limited degree of uncertainty and are solved through a "scientific approach"—expert diagnosis and analysis, and the application of proven processes. These problems may, indeed, be difficult and complicated; however, ultimately, they are amenable to solution by competent individuals with the authority, expertise, and experience to address the problem. These problems offer a consensual solution—there is agreement about the nature of the problem, and the "one-best-answer" is obvious to all (Rittel & Webber, 1973). Improving the efficiency of a manufacturing process, or reorganizating the organization to better serve customers are examples of technical problems.

Adaptive Problems

The New Normal landscape has its share of technical problems—organizations still need fixing; however, it is inhabited by a higher order version of difficulty in the form of adaptive problems. According to Heifetz (1994), adaptive problems reside in the gap between the present capacities of Leaders and/or member-leaders and the demands of reality at any given moment. Adaptive problems are, typically, the tip of the iceberg, symptomatic of a host of "soft issues," such as competing values, low morale, lack of trust, or disagreement around vision and strategic direction. This makes adaptive problems difficult to clearly frame, and impossible to solve once and for all.

Adaptive problems typically arise in novel situations, and require experimentation—learning new ways of interacting with one another and the world. These "new ways" may require deep and, sometimes, painful adjustments such as changing long-established habit patterns, valued priorities, widely held beliefs, and deeply embedded attitudes and behaviors—all exceedingly difficult to change. Changing organizational culture in response to opportuntiies or threats in the external operating environment, or repairing the trust between leaders and "rank and file" organization members are examples of adaptive problems.

Wicked Problems

Wicked problems are a permanent feature of the New Normal operating environment. These problems are deemed "wicked" because they are solution-resistant, aggressive, unpredictable, and immune to being managed or "tamed." Residing in open, complex systems with ambiguous causal connections, wicked problems are fraught with diagnostic difficulties and have no "one-best-answer." They are deeply complex, not merely complicated and multifaceted. They cannot be isolated from their immediate environment, solved, and returned without impacting the environment (Grint, p. 16).

Wicked problems have no "stopping rule"—there are no criteria that tell when the problem is solved. In this sense, wicked problems are not resolved, but rather, re-solved—solved over and over again (Rittel & Webber, 1973). The temporary solution to a wicked problem may cause even more problems as the initial "solution" generates a wave of unintended consequences. Every wicked problem is essentially unique—one of a kind. Therefore, a transfer of solutions from one wicked problem to another is ill-advised and, potentially, disastrous. Most public policy problems fall into this category, such as setting federal budget priorities, lowering the crime reate or eliminating poverty.

Dilemmas

A dilemma is a perplexing set of circumstances demanding a choice between two opposing and highly disagreeable alternatives. Dilemmas are permanent features of the New Normal landscape, confronting Leaders and organizations with problems that are difficult to untangle and which afford a limited number of alternatives—all of which have negative consequences. Dilemmas present two unpleasant alternatives demanding an "either–or" response. A difficult choice must be made—not to choose only prolongs the anxiety and possibly makes matters worse. In addition, no one knows how the choice will turn out. Leaders and organizations must place their bets and live with the negative consequences, whatever they may be. Whether to confront lagging financial performance by laying off employees or risk losing customers by raising prices is an example of a dilemma.

Technical problems may be solved once and for all; however, adaptive problems, wicked problems, and dilemmas are "solution resistant." There is no one, correct solution or final remedy. Rather, these problems require the organization to face up to unpleasant realities, make difficult choices, and live with the consequences. The solution to a technical problem is predictable in the sense that we can anticipate the new state of affairs resulting from solving the problem. However, no one knows what exactly the interaction with an adaptive problem, wicked problem, or dilemma might set into motion, except that it is likely to increase uncertainty and raise anxiety levels in the organization.

The New Normal Next Practice: Staying Solid

Although technical problems bring more than their share of stress and discomfort, adaptive and wicked problems as well as dilemmas generate significant stress and anxiety. This class of problem confronts the organization with an unpleasant reality—an obstacle in the form of an unsolvable problem or no-win situation bars the way to the future. The organization must make a difficult choice and, whatever the choice, it will unleash negative consequences. These difficult issues sap the energy of even the strongest people, robbing the organization of efficacy and enthusiasm and, in some cases, leaving it paralyzed in indecision.

Confronted with an adaptive or wicked problem or dilemma, Leaders and member-leaders must carry a double-burden. They must not only deal with their own anxiety—they are only human—but also with the negative emotions that flood the organization. Staying solid is the practice of monitoring and regulating one's anxiety level, staying in touch with the anxiety level of the organization, absorbing excess, unproductive "emotional heat," and providing practical ways for the organization to constructively manage its stress and disappointment.

Staying Solid in Action

Leaders must manage their own anxiety and leverage adaptive problems, wicked problems, and dilemmas as an opportunity for individual and collective learning and growth.

First, New Normal Leaders serve the organization best, not when they rescue it from "all-that-is-negative" or protect it from distress and discomfort, but when they invite it to courageously face its most pressing problems and dilemmas (Grint, 2010; Heifetz, 1994). Protection and rescue typically takes the form of redirecting the organization's attention from the unsolvable problem to a more manageable, technical problem. As Heifetz and Laurie (2001) state, "Followers want comfort, stability and solutions from their leaders. But that's babysitting. Real leaders ask hard questions and knock people out of their comfort zones. Then they manage the resulting distress" (p. 131). As the adaptive problem, wicked problem, or dilemma is not going away, the only constructive response is to face it head on—to identify it, to call it by name. This means inviting the organization to face difficult issues, make tough choices, and deal constructively with the consequences.

Second, New Normal Leaders provide the organization constructive help in dealing with emotional challenges inherent in addressing unsolvable problems. Although Leaders do not rescue the organization from hard realities and negative emotions, neither do they abandon it. They provide the organization a "crucible" to hold the "emotional heat" generated by the problem and make it at tolerable, even productive.

Crucibles are containers made of heat-resistant material capable of withstanding the exceedingly high temperatures required for melting or fusing metal. Of course, the container must have a melting point higher than the heat of the transformational process they contain. The idea of a crucible is a fitting metaphor for the leadership work of providing a "reliable container"—a solid and secure place in which the organization can constructively process the negative emotions generated by facing an adaptive problem, wicked problem, or dilemma.

New Normal Leaders act as stewards of the crucible as they regulate the "emotional temperature" of the organization, making sure that the heat is at "just right levels" to promote constructive engagement with the issue at hand. The challenge is to keep the collective temperature at what Heifetz and Linsky (2002) call a "productive level." Too much emotional heat, and the organization may go into a panic mode. Some may go into a fight mode and attack the bearer of bad news. Some may flee, leaving the organization for a more temperate climate. However, if the emotional climate is too cool, the organization may lack the constructive discontentedness and productive energy to work through the problem. They may choose to ignore unpleasant issues, fail to make tough decisions, and wait too long to make painful but necessary changes. Therefore, Leaders "keep their hands on the thermostat," turning up and lowering the heat as necessary (Heifetz et al., 2009).

The next chapter discusses two final New Normal performance shifts.

CHAPTER 6

Next Practices: Part III

Introduction

Two final New Normal performance shifts exist, each necessitating an additional next leadership practice. Each is collaborative in nature, and depends on the exercise of moral authority on the part of both Leaders and member-leaders.

Performance Shift #6: From the Learned to Learners

Effective leadership in the New Normal is less and less about being learned (technical mastery) and, increasingly, about being a learner.

Longshoreman and social commentator Eric Hoffer (1973) put it well: "In a time of drastic change it is the learners who inherit the future. The learned usually find themselves equipped to live in a world that no longer exists" (Aphorism 32). Learners adjust readily to all sorts of conditions. The learned do not think they need to and, therefore, do not.

Old Normal Expectations and New Normal Realities

The Old Normal narrative calls on Leaders to function as Hoffer's learned person. Leaders provide expert analysis of technical problems, use established models and decision rules to solve them, and bring performance improvements. This approach typically works well—provided the operating environment remains stable, yesterday's lessons continue to work, change remains well behaved, and problems remain amenable to solution by technical expertise.

There is nothing inherently wrong with a learned approach. Increased efficiency in vitally important areas is a good thing. Better processes and improved technology serve more customers, help more patients get cured faster, save time and money, and so on. However, the learned Leader is at a decided disadvantage in a New Normal operating environment that places a premium on learning agility.

As Toffler (1984) famously noted, anyone who wants to stay effective must be instructed in how to "learn, unlearn and relearn." Toffler (1984) cited Herman Gerjuoy:

> The new education must teach the individual how to classify and reclassify information, how to evaluate its veracity, how to change categories when necessary, how to move from the concrete to the abstract and back, how to look at problems from a new direction—how to teach himself. Tomorrow's illiterate will not be the man who can't read; he will be the man who has not learned how to learn. (p. 414)

These words carry added relevance in the twenty-first century. In times of rapid and discontinuous change, it is incumbent on Leaders to avail themselves of a rich flow of information, refresh their knowledge base, and, most important, correct faulty assumptions and adjust their cognitive maps. Technical expertise is still important. However, in the New Normal, the ability to gain new knowledge quickly, adjust one's perspective, leave behind outdated practices, and explore new possibilities for addressing new problems is even more important.

The New Normal Next Practice: Generative Learning

The New Normal requires an approach to learning that emphasizes the personal and collective capacity to thrive in dynamic and unpredictable environments. This practice is called *generative learning*. As the phrase implies, generative learning is about generating new knowledge, approaches, and perspectives, and, thus, enlarging one's capacity to address new problems as well as survive and thrive in novel and changing circumstances. This is Hoffer's learner—curious, teachable, and eager to engage the world in all its newness, ready to learn as a way of life, anytime, anyplace, from anyone, and to do it fast.

Generative Learning in Action

Individuals and organizations that practice generative learning seek to understand their world, not only to make it a more efficient place today, but also to develop new ways of thinking, discover new perspectives, and design new approaches to address the challenges and opportunities of an uncertain future.

First, New Normal Leaders and member-leaders distinguish technical learning challenges from generative learning challenges. There is nothing wrong with technical expertise; it is the "jacks or better to open" dictum for success in both Old Normal and New Normal contexts. Old roads leading to important destinations may need repair, or a new lane or two—a technical learning challenge. Moreover, the organization may need new roads in uncharted territories leading to new destinations—a generative learning challenge. However, Leaders and member-leaders must not adopt the technical perspective when, in fact, they are facing an adaptive problem, wicked problems, or a dilemma calling for a generative approach.

When confronted with an unprecedented challenge, the technically learned are predisposed to reframe it as a technical problem and search for a solution by using known routines and procedures. De Lesseps was technically learned but, decidedly, not a generative learner. Although generative learners recognize the importance of technical learning, they also recognize the futility of applying an old solution to a new problem. When faced with an unprecedented problem or novel circumstances, generative learners embrace the circumstance for what it really is—something entirely new that will require thinking in new ways and bringing a different set of capabilities to bear on the challenge.

Although experts may be consulted, they are employed as sounding boards to confirm or refute what the organization is already learning—technical experts are rarely the final word. Furthermore, although bodies of knowledge and important skill sets are mastered, these are not the only tools in the repertoire of the individual or organization. Curiosity and the quest for innovative and more effective approaches to dealing with novel problems may trump reliance on tried and true methods. Working models from other times and places are carefully studied—yesterday's lessons are not forgotten, but neither are they sacrosanct. Although blueprints for past success may, indeed, prove a valuable starting point for addressing today's new problems, they are held loosely. If validated, they may lead to a new round of technical learning. However, if they prove ineffective, they are jettisoned in favor of a search for new and better ways.

Second, generative learning asks Leaders and member-leaders to embrace its challenges and difficulties as opportunities for growth and increased effectiveness. Generative learning opportunities are likely to cause stress and anxiety, discomfort and dissatisfaction; however, low morale and negative attitudes often play a powerful role in alerting us to impending dangers and emerging opportunities for growth. New Normal organizations see disruption, change, and setbacks as an opportunity to address new problems from new perspectives, enlarge the organization's knowledge base, develop new competencies, and reflect anew on its values and assumptions.

Performance Shift # 7: From Short-Term Results to Sustained Progress

Effective leadership in the New Normal is less and less about one or a few extraordinary Leaders achieving short-term results and, increasingly, about sustained progress fueled by a New Normal-friendly culture.

Old Normal Expectations and New Normal Realities

The Old Normal narrative evaluates a Leader based on his or her track record of delivering short-term results. Leaders are expected to fix problems and achieve goals quickly. Many deliver, at least in the short term. The Leader's competency package may be just what the organization needs, given its unique challenges. If a crisis emerges, charismatic leaders are well suited to respond to the challenge. Mixed with sufficient formal authority and a little luck, and most talented Leaders can succeed for a while.

Nevertheless, short-term success is not enough. The New Normal demands sustainable performance, results over time, in good times and bad, as Leaders come and go. Although there is no sure-fire formula for sustained success in a rapidly changing world, one critical factor differentiates organizations that survive and thrive from those that wither and die. That factor is a "New Normal-friendly" organizational culture.

What Is Organizational Culture?

Organizational culture, according to Schein (1992) is "a pattern of shared basic assumptions that the group learned as it solved its problems of external adaptation and internal integration, that has worked well enough to be considered valid and, therefore, to be taught to new members as the correct way to perceive, think and feel in relation to those problems" (p. 12). It is the invisible environment in which we relate, learn, solve problems, decide, and engage the world. Culture is "the way things really are around here"—how the organization operates on an average day without thinking about it.

Culture functions like DNA—a hidden, genetic code and growth blueprint that shapes the collective character of the organization as well as its behaviors and practices. An organization's culture scripts its member to think, act, and relate in particular ways, and supports these attitudes and behaviors through its social architecture—features of the organizational landscape such as stories, policies, procedures, systems, rewards, and ceremonies that reinforce normative behavior.

The New Normal Next Practice: Culture-Shaping

The supreme challenge and highest contribution of a Leader is to shape organizational culture. Schein (1992) notes, "The dynamic process of culture creation and management are the essence of leadership and make one realize that leadership and culture are two sides of the same coin" (p. 1). Leaders serve as cultural architects, designing and helping to build a "New Normal-friendly" organization—an organization uniquely suited to survive and thrive amid the rigors of the twenty-first-century operating environment.

Culture-Shaping in Action

Organizational culture is malleable to a degree, especially when it faces crises, challenges, and new opportunities—staples of the New Normal. Leaders shape culture through what Schein (1992) calls "culture embedding mechanisms." Schein identifies six primary embedding mechanisms Leaders leverage to shape organizational culture: (1) What Leaders pay attention to, measure, and control; (2) How Leaders react to critical incidents and organizational crises; (3) Observed criteria by which Leaders allocate scarce resources; (4) Deliberate role modeling, teaching, and coaching; (5) Observed criteria by which Leaders allocate rewards and status; and (6) Observed criteria by which Leaders recruit, select, promote, retire, and excommunicate organizational members (*underlined L's are by the present author*, p. 231).

In addition to these culture-shaping mechanisms, Leaders employ simple rules to shape a New Normal-friendly culture. Simple rules are the distilled essence, the practical, operational embodiment of the identity, ruling ideas, purpose, mission, and core values of the organization. They are the organization's DNA or building blocks, its genetic code—the non-negotiable principles and values that shape and inform the daily activities of the organization. A simple rule is expressed as the combination of an ethical mandate and operating directive that guides and shapes the choices and behaviors of everyone in the organization, as in: "Always act in this manner because it is the right thing to do, the best thing to do, the most important thing to do." Simple rules must be woven into the daily life and work routines of the organization, and explicitly connected to formal aspects of organizational life such as hiring, promotion, rewards and recognition, and budgeting. (Specific New Normal simple rules are discussed in the Roles section.)

Summary

Old Normal expectations are colliding with New Normal realities, putting Leaders, member-leaders, and organizations on notice. Leading effectively in the twenty-first century calls for a radically different approach from previous decades and, consequently, a different set of personal and collective assets. Figure 6.1 lists seven New Normal performance shifts and the accompanying "next practices."

Performance Shifts	Next Practices
#1: From Formal Authority to Moral Authority	Moral Persuasion
#2: From the Few to the Many	Collaborative Engagement
#3: From Certainty to Contingency	Sensemaking
#4: From Promising Results to Telling the Truth	Candor
#5: From Solving Problems to Facing Dilemmas	Staying Solid
#6: From the Learned to Learners	Generative Learning
#7: From Short-Term Results to Sustained Progress	Shaping Culture

Figure 6.1 Performance shifts and next practices.

CHAPTER 7

Ancient Assets for the Twenty-First Century

Introduction

While effective Leaders and member-leaders manifest a wide range of attitudes and behaviors, the same stable core configuration of cognitive, moral, and emotional capacity sustains leadership performance in the New Normal. The list of necessary qualities that support New Normal next practices is remarkably short—a sense of larger purpose, wisdom, humility, integrity, courage, and emotional maturity. This suite of capacities goes by a variety of names in the leadership literature—substance, character, and inner strength. Contemporary authors note that effective leaders manifest "fierce resolve" and "humility" (Collins, 2001), "moral courage" (Kidder, 2006), "psychological presence" (Kahn, 1992, p. 322), and "integrity" and "character" (Cloud, 2006).

Contemporary leadership theorists and practitioners are increasingly comfortable calling these assets by their ancient name—virtue. As the editors of *Fast Company* (2003) put it, "The New Normal... calls for a steadfast approach to business that reinforces the cardinal virtues of honesty, integrity, and authenticity." Virtue is a catalog of the inner strengths—the conceptual, moral, and emotional assets required to effectively engage the New Normal world and meet its demands for sustained success. These patterns of attitude, behavior, and relationship are grounded, not in personality or technical–managerial competence, but rather, they are an expression of the deep dispositions and moral character of the individual.

A Brief History of Virtue

Plato (428–347 BC) and Aristotle (384–322 BC) created much of our vocabulary of virtue. Specifically, they embraced prudence (practical wisdom), justice (fairness), fortitude (courage), and temperance (moderation) as the moral bonds of civic life. The other source of virtue language is Judeo-Christian, especially the virtues of faith, hope, and love emphasized by St. Paul. Thomas Aquinas (1225–1274) integrated the four Greek virtues with these "theological virtues" and called them "cardinal virtues." The term cardinal comes from the Latin *cardo*, meaning a "hinge," and, thus, the fixed moral point on which all other virtue turns. These seven virtues flowed together into a moral amalgam that shaped theological, educational, and civic life in Western Europe for almost 15 centuries. Furthermore, empirical research indicates that these virtues carry global appeal beyond the West (Peterson & Seligman, 2004). Bass and Steidlmeier (1999) state, "An approach to ethics based upon moral character and virtue enjoys an extraordinarily broad cross-cultural base in terms of the 'framing narratives' that guide ethical discourse in cultural settings as diverse as Western and Confucian traditions" (p. 193).

For the ancient Greeks and early Christians, virtue was no mere philosophical consideration. Rather, virtue was understood in terms of actions that were visible and of practical benefit to others. The Greeks viewed virtue as a concrete moral force—the capacity to do something "good" and to keep doing it over time. Our term ethics comes from the Greek *ethos*, meaning habit. The English term virtue, from which we derive our terms virile and valor, comes from the Latin *virtus* meaning "strength." Virtue is cognitive, moral, and emotional strength placed in service of others—the community, organization, customers, or the world at large.

Virtue is not a product of birth. It is not a function of personality. It is not a gift bestowed on a privileged few. Although virtue is not a "workshop skill" picked up in a few hours, it is, indeed, "learnable"— the goal being to ingrain these attitudes and dispositions such that they become moral reflexes, governing our intellect, will and emotions, decisions, actions, and relationships. Thus understood, virtue is accessible to anyone willing to work at developing these habits over time.

Virtue Is Back: Detour and Resurgence

The public conversation around the importance of virtue ended abruptly, early in the twentieth century, when Gordon Allport, the one-time president of the American Psychological Association and one of the most influential psychologists of the last century, almost single-handedly banished the terms "character" and "virtue" from academic discourse (Nicholson, 1998). Allport (1921, 1927) correctly recognized that character and virtue are value-laden concepts and, thus—by his way of thinking—a "messy business." As he put it, morality introduces an "extra and uncertain variable" into the empirical study of personality. Accordingly, he replaced the idea of moral character with the concept of value-neutral "traits of character" or "personality characteristics." Allport (1927) argued that human behavior was best understood as a manifestation of the individual's "habit system," composed of traits that prompted certain kinds of behaviors. Because character was a value-laden construct, it was relegated to the realm of philosophers and religious leaders, whereas the researchers focused on the study of personality traits—amiability, conscientiousness, and extraversion, to name a few—to the neglect of virtue and moral character.

As empirical social science was banishing virtue from its vocabulary, moral philosophers—especially those devoted to the study of virtue ethics—kept the concept of virtue alive. Anscombe (1958) called for a return to an Aristotelian approach to such ideas as "good" and "bad," human nature, motives, moral character, virtue, and human flourishing. Her ideas served as a stimulus for the work of MacIntyre (1984), Hursthouse (2001), and Foot (2003). Virtue ethics is alive and well in religious traditions, and has recently found traction in works on business ethics (Maitland, 1997; Boatright, 2000; Rae & Wong, 2004).

In 1998, a watershed moment occurred in the field of psychology when University of Pennsylvania professor Martin Seligman delivered his presidential address to the American Psychological Association. Seligman's speech launched the positive psychology movement that seeks to empirically study the conditions under which human flourishing takes place. The movement places emphasis on human strengths, such as optimism, courage, future-mindedness, hope, faith, and honesty. Seligman et al. (2005) call these human strengths "virtues," in effect, reversing almost seven decades of value-neutral language in the field (Peterson & Seligman, 2004).

The recent literature is consistent with this renewed emphasis on virtue, arguing that leadership is an inherently ethical pursuit. Effective leaders adhere to high ethical standards and behave in ways congruent with those standards (Parry & Proctor-Thomson, 2002). Moral integrity—conceptualized as a character of uncorrupted virtue (Montefiore & Vines, 1999)—and leadership performance are inseparably bound in the eyes of followers (Kouzes & Posner, 1993; Engelbrecht et al., 2005). The leadership characteristics most valued by followers, as well as other stakeholders, are honesty, integrity, and truthfulness (Kouzes & Posner,

1993). Ethical behavior on the part of leaders contributes to employee commitment and satisfaction, and attracts and retains the best employees (Trevino et al., 2000). Integrity, on the part of leaders, fosters trust and "good citizenship" behaviors on the part of employees that, in turn, contribute to the effectiveness of the organization (Organ & Ryan, 1995). Additionally, virtue drives each of the next leadership practices we discussed in the previous three chapters.

Moral Persuasion and Virtue

Moral persuasion is neither a "workshop skill" based primarily on technical–managerial competence, although written and oral communication is valuable, nor a function of a personality. Rather, this next practice draws upon a suite of assets that transcend one's personality and technical–managerial competence. Specifically, it takes *courage* and *love* to practice moral persuasion.

Courage

Courage is the inner strength to advance or endure in the face of hardship, emotional turmoil, physical harm, loss of reputation, finances, health, position, and even life itself.

Courage and Credibility
Credibility is one's earned reputation for trustworthiness. The English term *credible* comes from the Latin *credibilis* and *credere*, from which we get our English word *creed*. A creed is a body of information, set of beliefs, principles, or affirmations put forth to be believed, trusted, and applied. In like manner, a credible individual is someone who can be believed and trusted to do the right thing for others, even in circumstances where acting in one's self-interest would be understandable—an act of courage. Credibility is earned and, with it, the right to engage others in moral persuasion, when individuals demonstrate they can be trusted to seek the interests of others even in circumstances when self-interest is put in jeopardy.

The assigning of credibility to an individual is based not on his or her placement on the organizational chart, but rather, on their track record in earning and holding trust—trust does not materialize out of thin air. When a Leader or member-leader honors the trust placed in them, the initial loan of credibility invested in them by others bears interest and results in the granting of more credibility. However, this loan of trust can be called back when the individual abuses that trust by acting in an untrustworthy, self-serving manner. Those who invested trust in them respond by removing themselves from the individual's scope of personal influence, rendering moral persuasion impossible.

Love

Those who possess formal power are faced with the daily decision of whether to use their power to defend and expand their position and privilege or to serve the best interests of others. The virtue of love protects against the self-serving use of power. Love, sometimes called altruism, is behavior intended to benefit others without the expectation of external rewards, including reciprocation from those who benefit from the loving actions. Love includes the concept of respect, in that, to love a person means to esteem them and hold them in high regard, to show them consideration, and, thereby, to cultivate an awareness and understanding of them as individuals. To love and respect someone means to consider them a person of value and consequence, and, thus, to give appropriate consideration to their values, feelings, and concerns.

Love is fundamental to the practice of moral persuasion. The most persuasive person is the one with the earned reputation for valuing the interests of others. We are more likely to be persuaded by a person we think genuinely cares for us and looks out for our best interests. Aristotle (2006) observed, "There are three things which inspire confidence in the orator's own character—the three, namely, that induce us to believe a thing apart from any proof of it: good sense, good moral character, and goodwill" (p. 55). Aristotle called this "kindness," which is goodwill expressed by helping others in need and expecting nothing in return by way of material compensation or personal advantage.

Collaborative Engagement and Virtue

Collaborative engagement cannot be learned in a half-day workshop, although skills amenable to learning in a workshop setting such as active listening, delegating, and discerning talent are valuable. Rather, this next practice draws upon a suite of assets that transcend one's personality and technical–managerial competence. Specifically, it takes the full range of virtue, with special emphasis on prudence, justice, and temperance, to practice collaborative engagement.

Prudence

Prudence is a combination of foresight, humility, and rationality, put in service of "the good." Collaborative engagement picks up on the humility dimension of prudence. Humility is not a disempowering sense of smallness. Rather, it is a deep sense of one's unique contribution, one's limitations, and the need to work with others to make a lasting difference. Humble individuals have an accurate, but not understated, assessment of their abilities and achievements, and an equally accurate, but not overstated, sense of their limitations and weaknesses. Humble people recognize their limits and seek to learn from others. They are open-mindedly realistic and, therefore, recognize the diverse and complex nature of reality and, thus, the need to collaborate with others to get important things accomplished.

Consequently, humble people do not need to minimize the contribution of others, distort information, or reinterpret experience for the purpose of defending oneself, or presenting the self in a dishonest, inaccurate, and self-elevating manner. They do not have to put others down to lift themselves up. Humble people assertively express their gifts and abilities, but they do so in a manner that respects others and gives them the same opportunity. They are open to input, even critique, and stand ready to make adjustments to their leadership, even if these adjustments are personally painful.

Justice

Justice embodies the ideas of fairness, equality, equity, and proportionality, especially in one's day-to-day dealings with "neighbors." Justice involves the willingness to take into account the rights, concerns, and feelings of others. It is the moral habit of securing for others what is "rightfully due" to them. Compte-Sponville (2001) calls justice "equals without egos" (p. 72), in that, it makes irrelevant the discrepancies in power, intelligence, and social standing.

Sustained effectiveness in the New Normal depends on high levels of participation from a diverse range of people. This, in turn, depends on the exercise of justice to create a harmonious, properly ordered, respectful, and "fair" place in which all that have a stake in the organization are free to fully contribute to its welfare and progress. Just Leaders see to it that no member of the organization usurps the rightful place and contribution of others, and that everyone who has a stake in the organization is given appropriate access to resources, information, and opportunities such that they can contribute to the full extent of their ability.

Temperance

Temperance is the inner discipline of self-restraint, the strength to say "no" to harmful drives, impulses, and the inordinate desire for comfort, self-interest, and pleasure. The practice of temperance is an exercise in self-discipline—an active self-defense of one's inner, moral order from that which would enslave us to act in accordance with base desires and short-term interests. "Temperance," says Compte-Sponville (2001), "is that moderation which allows us to be masters of our pleasure instead of becoming its slave" (p. 39). Collaborative engagement depends on the capacity to say "no" to the abuse or hoarding of power, and to say "yes" to the appropriate sharing of power and resources.

Sensemaking and Virtue

Sensemaking is not a "workshop skill," although skills amenable to workshop training such as strategic analysis, planning, and problem solving are valuable. Rather, this next practice demands the exercise of faith and prudence.

Faith

Faith is fidelity to a larger purpose or narrative worthy of allegiance. This story serves as the interpretive framework for seeing beyond the mess, noise, and fog of any given moment to create a sense of shared meaning throughout the organization. Drawing from faith, Leaders and member-leaders set the moral trajectory of the organization by connecting its daily life and circumstances to this larger story that provides substantial clarity and context for any given moment in the life of the organization.

Prudence

Sensemaking depends on the virtue of prudence. The human capacity to interpret reality is limited and skewed. Prudence, at least partially, corrects for this. Prudence sees. It is the virtue of realism, practical discernment, objectivity, and insight, especially in unexpected or unprecedented circumstances. It grasps the full context of a situation, both circumstances and people—what is actually happening, as well as how individuals and groups are likely to interpret the situation and respond. Prudence specializes in "reading" situations in order to get a sense of what the circumstances might mean and how the organization might constructively respond.

Candor and Virtue

Candor cannot be learned in a workshop setting, although skills such as assertive communication, conflict management, and negotiating are valuable. Rather, this next practice draws upon a suite of assets that transcend one's personality and technical–managerial competence. Specifically, it takes courage to practice candor.

Courage

Candor—speaking in a truthful, fair, and forthright manner—is an exercise in courage. Courage is only found where there is the genuine possibility of loss—loss of friends, reputation, status, power, possessions, or, at the extremes, freedom or life. Courage is necessary to win the inner battle over human frailty and the temptation to choose silence and security over transparency and honesty, to shave the truth when it minimizes the risk to one's interests. It takes courage to take the initiative to speak in spite of the risk that it may not be well received—to tell the truth even when it is unpopular.

Summary

Candor is an expression of one's inner habits and dispositions—specifically, one's courage. Lacking courage, the practice of candor may be undermined by fear and self-protection. In a leadership landscape full of risk and failure, disappointment and difficulty, no amount of charisma or technical–managerial competence will compensate for this deficiency.

Generative Learning and Virtue

Generative learning cannot be mastered in a half-day training session, although skills such as information gathering and managing innovation are valuable. Instead, it takes wisdom and courage, especially emotional courage, to practice generative learning.

Prudence (Wisdom)

Wisdom is a necessity in times of rapid and discontinuous change, where a premium is placed on critical thinking, creative problem solving, and the capacity to adjust and adapt to new information. It takes wisdom to stay effective in novel situations, none of which call for prepackaged responses based on formal rules.

Courage

Effectiveness in the New Normal depends not on the leader's present level of competence, but on his or her capacity to stay in the learning process. This takes courage, especially of the emotional variety. The New Normal confronts Leaders and member-leaders with disorienting circumstances. This puts everyone in a state of disequilibrium—off balance and uncertain where to go or what to do next.

This confronts Leaders and member-leaders with a New Normal learning paradox. Jarvis (1992) observes, "The paradox is that if harmony is fully established, there can be no learning situation" (p. 83). The good news is that the New Normal is a rich learning environment. The challenging news is that this rich learning environment exacts a high price in the form of the fear of failure, and, thus, demands corresponding levels of courage to stay in the learning process.

It takes courage to face up to the deep disjuncture between the demands of the New Normal and one's present knowledge, experience, and capabilities. It takes courage to take on new learning challenges, even as it makes us look like foolish novices. It takes courage to look reality in the face and lean into, instead of shrinking back from, its corrective messages. It takes courage to ask for help, change one's mind, and admit error when presented with evidence that challenges or overrules our opinions and convictions. It takes courage to admit we do not know what is coming next and embrace the emotionally vulnerable state of "perpetual unpreparedness" and, with it, the prospect of failure.

Staying Solid and Virtue

Staying solid is not learned in a training session or two, although skills like self-awareness and crisis management can be taught in this setting. Rather, this next practice draws upon a suite of assets that transcends one's personality and technical–managerial competence. Specifically, it takes faith, hope, and temperance (self-control) to practice staying solid.

Faith

A clear and compelling purpose—a larger transcendent story beyond self-interest—provides the emotional scripting to properly interpret and constructively respond to difficulty and delay, obstacles and adversity—daily occurrences in the New Normal.

Hope

Hope is an expectation of a future good, mingled with the understanding that this good is never guaranteed and significant obstacles stand in the way of its fulfillment. It is steadfast confidence mixed with a realistic sense of contingency. Hope is manifested in the tension between the painful realities of an inadequate or unacceptable today—where expectations are yet to be realized—and the anticipation of a better tomorrow when these expectations are substantially fulfilled.

Hope is essential in a New Normal operating environment. There may be little or no evidence of progress despite the best efforts of Leaders. The sacrificial efforts of member-leaders may be rewarded only with further delay and difficulty. As the organization lives through months and years marked by the discrepancy between effort expended and outcomes achieved, energy flags and morale falters. It takes hope to constructively manage one's own disappointment, anxiety, and discouragement and retain sufficient positive emotional energy to help others do the same.

Temperance

Temperance is strength of character grounded in self-mastery. "Having strength of character means having the capacity to do what is right and avoid what is wrong. Self-control when applied to adaptive or virtuous goals, is essentially that capacity" (Baumeister & Exline, 2000). On the positive side, self-mastery is the strength to say "yes" to the opportunity to love and do the right thing in the face of difficulty, loss, and pain. Conversely, it is the strength to say "no" to the impulse and inclination to act selfishly, to remain indifferent and passive, and to do the easy thing instead of the right thing. It takes temperance to say "no" to the temptation to quit when adaptive problems, wicked problems, and dilemmas bar the way to the future.

Shaping Culture and Virtue

Shaping culture is not a technical workshop skill, although skills such as hiring and staffing, building effective teams, organizing and managing processes and systems, and monitoring organizational performance are valuable assets. Rather, it takes the full range of virtue—faith, hope, love, prudence, justice, courage, and temperance—to practice shaping culture.

Faith

It takes faith to shape a New Normal-friendly organization. Faith is akin to fidelity, which signifies an honored agreement or bond of trust that binds Leaders and member-leaders together to a special purpose—a larger story that calls upon all in the organization to risk and sacrifice on behalf of one another and those the organization intends to serve. Without faith, there is no "why" and, thus, no larger story to promote and sustain collaboration and mutual sacrifice. Instead, the organization is likely to be awash in corroding cynicism and paralyzing anxiety, its collective life devolving into a random sequence of isolated actions that mean nothing and take it nowhere. Without faith, there is no basis for long-term loyalty, only contractual arrangements, reducing the organization to a temporary collection of individuals with short-term agendas motivated by self-interest.

Hope

It takes hope to shape an organization that genuinely believes its best days are yet to come, and that its hard work and sacrifice are worth the effort. Without hope, collective, sacrificial effort is not possible. Hoffer (1951) observed, "The self-sacrifice involved in mutual sharing and co-operative action is impossible without hope. When today is all there is, we grab all we can and hold on ... On the other hand, when everything is ahead and yet to come, we find it easy to share all we have and to forgo advantages within our grasp" (p. 68).

Love

It takes love to shape an organization that generously gives of its resources to seek the benefit of others. The demonstration of love by Leaders and member-leaders fosters trust, facilitates shared commitment to the organization's goals, and motivates exceptional levels of performance.

Prudence

It takes prudence to shape an organization that seizes opportunity, guards against threats, and stays effective in novel and shifting terrain.

Justice

It takes justice to shape an organization with high levels of participation and collaborative effort from a diverse range of member-leaders. Justice guides Leaders and member-leaders in shaping a fair and respectful place in which all who have a stake in the organization have access to resources and information, together with the opportunity to unleash their talent, gifts, and strengths to contribute to its welfare and progress.

Courage

It takes courage to shape an organization where members explore, discover, self-correct, and take on new learning challenges. It takes courage to embark on this journey and sustain progress when no one has all the right answers or knows how things will turn out.

Temperance

It takes temperance to resist the pressure to seek one's own comfort and interests, or succumb to negative emotions.

Charisma, Competence, and Twenty-First-Century Leadership Effectiveness

The historic significance of heroic–charismatic leadership is undeniable. Charismatic individuals have inspired entire nations and brought hope to millions. At times, they have changed the course of history. Given the dynamism of the New Normal, it is likely that crises will increase in number and intensity. Charismatic Leaders, at their best in a crisis, will continue to play a significant part in our organizations.

Nevertheless, charisma must be embedded in virtue if it is to serve the best interests of others. Carson (1995) notes that Martin Luther King recognized his personal charisma and rhetorical powers—although significant—were, nevertheless, insufficient to lead the civil rights movement. "King used charisma as a tool for mobilizing black communities, but he always used it in the context of other forms of intellectual and political leadership suited to a movement containing many strong leaders" (p. 320). King understood that substantive change flows from the collective action of many, and not just an elite few.

Moreover, the contribution of the technical–managerial approach to leadership theory and practice is undeniable. This approach to

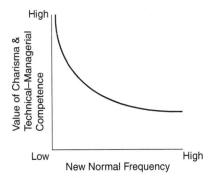

Figure 7.1 The diminishing value of charisma and technical–managerial competence.

organizational effectiveness has created countless jobs and raised the standard of living for millions. Organizations will confront technical problems into the indefinite future. Budgets must still be met, and processes run efficiently. However, virtue—understood as an expression of cognitive, moral, and emotional competence—must guide and shape the expression of technical–managerial competence if these assets are to serve the welfare and progress of the organization.

Although charisma and technical–managerial competence remain valuable twenty-first-century leadership assets, if honored above virtue or seen as a substitute for it, these assets will create conditions for leadership failure—remember de Lesseps. Figure 7.1 depicts the decreasing value of charisma and technical-managerial competence as the New Normal increases in intensity.

However, these are potentially powerful assets, as they are informed and shaped by the exercise of virtue. Hamel (2012) notes, "Like nuclear fission, self-interest works only as long as there's a containment vessel—a set of ethical principles that ensures enlightened self-interest doesn't melt down into unbridled selfishness. Unfortunately, the groundwater of business is now heavily contaminated with the runoff from morally blinkered egomania" (p. 6). Virtue is the containment vessel, the moral energy and sustenance for the practice of "enlightened self-interest," and the safeguard against "unbridled selfishness."

Summary

The drivers of disruptive change—globalization, rapid technological development, and hypercompetition have reached an unprecedented level of scope and intensity, and show no signs of slowing down. The value of charisma and technical–managerial competence is fast diminishing as New Normal realities increasingly shape the operating environment, and situations calling exclusively for the application of these assets grow fewer by the day. Barton et al. (2012) wrote:

> It is often said that the principles of great leadership are timeless, or based on immutable truths. But when we meet with the men and women who run the world's largest organizations, what we hear with increasing frequency is how different everything feels from just a decade ago. Leaders tell us they are operating in a bewildering new environment in which little is certain, the tempo is quicker, and the dynamics more complex. They worry that it is impossible for chief executives to stay on top of the things they need to know to do their job. Some admit they feel overwhelmed.

William Gibson famously noted, "The future is already here—it's just not very evenly distributed." The New Normal has already arrived, and it will continue to arrive, expanding in scope and intensity. Participation is mandatory—it serves up no polite invitations. It rewards and punishes with ferocious consistency. It honors collaboration, but rejects the go-it-alone efforts of the best and brightest. It rewards learners, but ignores the learned. It respects moral authority, but cares not a bit for an individual's location on the organizational chart. Position power,

	Virtue Assets						
	Faith	Hope	Love	Prudence (Wisdom)	Justice	Courage	Temperance
Moral Authority			X			X	
Collaborative Engagement				X	X		X
Sensemaking	X			X			
Candor						X	
Staying Solid	X	X					X
Generative Learning				X		X	
Shaping Culture	X	X	X	X	X	X	X

Figure 7.2 Next practices and virtue assets.

charisma, and technical–managerial competence, although helpful, are inadequate to meet the leadership challenges of the New Normal. In the second decade of the twenty-first century, virtue is fast replacing these assets as the primary driver of effective leadership.

Figure 7.2 lists New Normal "next practices" and the corresponding virtue-asset required for each.

SECTION III

The 4R Model of Leadership: Relationships

This section introduces the framework of the 4R model of Leadership and explores the Relationships component of the model. The Relationships component of the model replaces Old Normal images of success with a fresh vision of effective leadership as virtue-based influence.

CHAPTER 8

The 4R Model of Leadership

Introduction

The New Normal has arrived, exposing the Old Normal leadership narrative and its supporting myths as inadequate. The Old Normal narrative must be replaced with a New Normal leadership narrative supported by a fresh set of images and vocabulary better suited to address the conceptual, moral, and emotional challenges of the twenty-first century. This calls for a shift in emphasis from Old Normal "best practices" that draw on an elite Leader's charisma and technical–managerial competence to New Normal "next practices" grounded in virtue-based collaboration. The 4R model provides the conceptual framework to support this shift.

Introducing the 4R Model of Leadership

The 4R model provides a simple framework for conceptualizing effective leadership practice in the New Normal. The model pictures the critical features of the leadership terrain—the challenges and opportunities leaders are likely to encounter—and organizes them in four categories: (1) Relationships—the virtue-based personal assets that support all New Normal next practices; (2) Roles—the work of shaping a New Normal-friendly organizational culture; (3) Responsibilities—the doing or practitioner side of leading; and (4) Results—the work of monitoring and sustaining organizational performance. The 4R model depicts how these variables interact with one another, placing primary emphasis on the exercise of virtue (Relationships) as the driving force of effective New Normal leadership (see Figure 8.1).

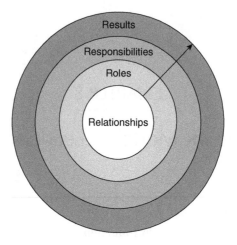

Figure 8.1 4R model overview.

Relationships

The Relationships component of the 4R model pictures a fundamental feature, perhaps the most important feature of the New Normal landscape—the critical connection between the exercise of virtue and the effective implementation of New Normal next practices through a collaborative effort. Virtue refers to the individual and collective strengths that enable Leaders and member-leaders to work together and get important things accomplished in difficult circumstances. As we have discussed, the New Normal operating environment is exceptionally challenging—confusing, unpredictable, and full of cognitive, moral, and emotional demands. Moreover, the internal life of most organizations offers its own set of challenges. Even the best organizations are less than ideal places, populated by Leaders and members susceptible to fear, discouragement, selfishness, and moral lapses. In these conditions, sustainable effectiveness demands inner strength and moral muscle, depths of faith and hope, courage and wisdom not only from those in positions of formal authority, but also from many members. The Relationships component of the model addresses this "virtue necessity." As the often-quoted opening line of Tolstoy's *Anna Karenina* goes, "Happy families are all alike; every unhappy family is unhappy in its own way." Similarly, those who lead effectively in the New Normal share a few foundational assets, a seamless configuration of cognitive, moral, and emotional strength that transcends personality and technical–managerial competence. The Relationships component of the model identifies and explores this suite of virtue. It is composed of four discrete, but interrelated, constellations of virtuous attitude and behavior that are the driving force of effective New Normal leadership. These virtue configurations connect the historic, cardinal virtues (faith, hope, and love; prudence (wisdom), justice, courage, and temperance) to personal characteristics identified in the leadership literature as critical to effective leadership practice (elaborated in chapter 9). In the spirit of simplicity, Relationships highlight the *sine qua non* of leadership capacity—the essential assets; the rudimentary, primal elements; the irreducible minimum without which the effective practice of New Normal leadership is unlikely, if not impossible—not what some Leaders and members might possess, but what all who lead well must possess.

The virtue configurations are (1) Dynamic Determination, (2) Intellectual Flexibility, (3) Courageous Character, and (4) Emotional Maturity. Each configuration identifies a set of cognitive, moral, and emotional strengths required to meet the demands of effectiveness in the New Normal operating environment. For the purpose of memory, the naming and sequencing of these configurations is presented as the acrostic "DICE." The image of dice is a reminder that an organization "rolls the dice" and bets its future on the quality of its Leaders and member-leaders.

The cumulative expression of the DICE configuration is called collaborative quotient (CQ), which is the capacity to effectively implement the next practice of collaborative engagement. CQ refers to an individual's collaborative capacity, the ability to spin a web of partnerships characterized by shared purpose and mutual trust. The model designates CQ as the "+1" factor. In other words, high CQ is what you get when an individual functions with sufficiently high levels of Dynamic Determination, Intellectual Flexibility, Courageous Character, and Emotional Maturity. DICE + 1, then, represents the full range of attitudes and behaviors required to lead effectively in the New Normal, with CQ featured as foundational to sustained New Normal leadership effectiveness.

Placing virtue-based Relationships at the core of the 4R model counters the myths of charisma and technical–managerial competence, reminding Leaders and member-leaders that—although personality and technical skill often play a part in the success of the organization, they are rarely adequate and never determinative. Gifted, determined, and intelligent people lacking in virtue may deliver the goods for a time.

However, they will not serve the collective good in the long run. Rather, individuals and organizations that excel in developing and exercising virtue are most likely to thrive in the decades ahead.

The exercise of virtue could be termed a "charisma and competence of the ordinary." By this, it is meant that even the most "ordinary" individual that practices virtue, not just an elite few, will earn a reputation as a capable, winsome, even inspirational person. This emphasis on virtue offers a more hopeful alternative as well as a more realistic assessment of what it takes to lead effectively in the New Normal.

Roles

The 4R model pictures a second critical feature of the New Normal leadership terrain—the challenge of shaping an organization capable of thriving in harsh and changing conditions. The model pictures effective leadership as a virtue-driven, collaborative endeavor (Relationships) lived out in an organizational context (Roles).

The model presents five distinct, but interrelated, Roles. Each Role is designated according to a grid with an "Others" and "Us" axis, and a "Today" and "Tomorrow" axis (see Figure 8.2). The resulting framework identifies four leadership Roles: an "Others–Tomorrow" Role (Direction Setter), an "Others–Today" Role (Ambassador), an "Us–Today" Role (Coach), and an "Us–Tomorrow" Role (Learner). The model pictures a fifth synthesizing Role, the Steward, which integrates the concerns and obligations of each of the previous four Roles. Each Role is presented as: (1) a critical dimension of organizational life that merits the attention of Leaders and members-leaders as well as the investment of

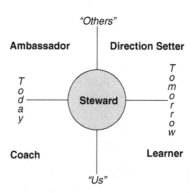

Figure 8.2 Roles overview.

organizational resources; (2) the organizational context in which the collaborative efforts (Relationships) of Leaders and member-leaders are expressed; and, (3) a point of culture-shaping leverage.

Furthermore, each Role serves as an organizing metaphor, a window of insight and a lens that brings into focus the fundamental obligations of Leaders and member-leaders to the organization. The sum of these obligations is that of shaping and sustaining a New Normal-friendly culture. Leaders and member-leaders collaborate as cultural architects, designing and building the kind of organization capable of succeeding over time in the twenty-first century. Accordingly, each Role has embedded in it a culture-shaping script that prompts Leaders and member-leaders to draw from their fund of DICE + 1 and work together to shape a New Normal-friendly organization.

In order to provide an accurate, large-scale map of the New Normal terrain, the Roles category does not clutter the conceptual landscape with every conceivable, formal role some Leaders and member-leaders might play (CEO, vice president, general manager, division head, etc). Rather, the model pictures the five Roles all Leaders and member-leaders must play to shape an organization likely to survive and thrive in the New Normal.

Roles depicts the connection between two critically important features of the New Normal leadership terrain: (1) The necessity of virtue-driven, collaborative effort between Leaders and member-leaders (Relationships); and (2) The creation, sustenance, and extension of an organization of moral vision and sustainable excellence. The Roles category provides a new vocabulary, a language of leadership supported by fresh images and powerful metaphors that readily connect with the lived experience of leaders as they explore the leadership challenges and opportunities in their corner of the New Normal landscape. Roles help the organization regulate its attention by highlighting those aspects of organizational life—the activities, interactions, and processes important enough to merit the time and attention of Leaders and member-leaders as well as the investment of its resources.

Responsibilities

The Responsibilities category depicts a third essential feature of the New Normal landscape, effective leadership practice—the implementation of leadership or leadership as a verb. The model pictures the work of leading (Responsibilities) as a seamless configuration of virtue-driven, collaborative behaviors (Relationships) lived out in each Role. These

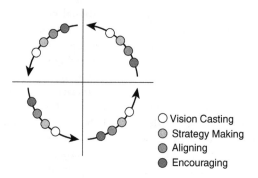

Figure 8.3 Responsibilities overview.

behaviors serve as a catalyst for personal and collective transformation in keeping with the directional imperatives of the organization.

The model pictures Leaders and member-leaders: (1) drawing from a fund of virtue to forge collaborative partnerships (Relationships); (2) stepping into each corner of the organization to shape its culture (Roles); and (3) practicing four leadership behaviors—each with a distinctive New Normal twist—vital to the work of bringing substantive change and lasting benefit to the world (Responsibilities). The Responsibilities are: (1) Vision Casting; (2) Strategy Making; (3) Aligning; and (4) Encouraging. As with Relationships and Roles, the Responsibilities category is not a catchall list of every important activity some Leaders and member-leaders might perform. Rather, it depicts the essential activities all Leaders and member-leaders must do if the organization is to deliver on its promises to the world (see Figure 8.3).

Results

The Results component of the model identifies the last prominent feature of the New Normal landscape—durable performance in a harsh environment. The Results category highlights the critical connection between performance feedback and sustained effectiveness in the New Normal. Results capture the logic and progression of the 4R model. Valued outcomes are accomplished over time (Results) when Leaders and member-leaders draw from a fund of virtue to collaborate (Relationships) in shaping a New Normal-friendly culture (Roles), and join together to engage in essential leadership practices that bring substantive change in accordance with the directional imperatives of the organization (Responsibilities).

The 4R Model and Twenty-First-Century Leadership

The 4R model supports effective twenty-first century leadership practice in three ways. First, the model provides an easy-to-understand-and-apply framework grounded in an accessible version of effective leadership. The model replaces Old Normal images of success with a virtue-based approach to leadership effectiveness, putting effective leadership practice within the reach of "ordinary" individuals and not just an exceptional few with the "right stuff" by Old Normal standards. The DICE + 1 components of Relationships organize and present the leadership research in a memorable format—the DICE + 1 acrostic is almost impossible to forget.

Second, the model provides a tool to navigate the New Normal terrain—a topographic map highlighting the critical features of the New Normal landscape, including the realities and demands, opportunities and challenges faced by organizations. Through the lens of the model, Leaders and member-leaders are provided an accurate compass read, a ready reference point, a place to stand and gain perspective on the leadership journey.

Third, the model provides a developmental blueprint for "ordinary" individuals to become the kind of people that organizations need to survive and thrive in twenty-first century. The model serves as a rich source of feedback, providing a framework for observing, understanding, and profiting from one's leadership experience as well as the experience of others. The model invites individuals to take a reflective stance amid the performance of leadership; to put their experience on the line, test their assumptions as to what constitutes effective leadership, and engage others in dialogue at the intersection of their daily leadership challenges and the framework of the model. Developmental progress is validated. The downside of the acting out of Old Normal patterns is exposed, blind spots are revealed, and performance issues are brought to light.

Summary

Drawing from each component "R," the model presents a clear, integrated picture of effective leadership in the New Normal. It reminds Leaders and member-leaders that sustainable effectiveness is driven by personal and collective virtue (Relationships), and enhanced or diminished by organizational culture (Roles). Requisite leadership behaviors (Responsibilities) are a collaborative practice—not the purview of an elite few. The Results process keeps the organization tuned in to reality. It strengthens the organization at its virtuous core (Relationships), producing cultural dispositions (Roles), and enhancing leadership behaviors (Responsibilities) that help the organization survive and thrive in the New Normal.

Looking Ahead

The next five chapters explore each dimension of the DICE + 1 virtue mix. Four foundational principles govern the process of learning the virtues discussed in these chapters.

Principle #1: Motivation

To identify the virtues is simply to name the attitudes and behaviors that life demands of anyone aspiring to live well and do well over time, and contribute to the welfare and progress of a community or organization. As such, virtue is not so much a "should" or "ought" as it is a "given" or "must." To learn virtue, one must conclude that reality demands these attitudes and behaviors, that this demand is legitimate and reasonable, and demands my best effort. As Plato put it, developing virtue requires "taking pains" (1956). The acquisition of virtue is a "tedious and uphill road" (1968). What the ancients called *velleity*—a passing whim, slight wish, or good intention—will not suffice. Virtue must be deeply desired and pursued with intentionality and rigor. Like the acquisition of muscle strength, the development of virtue is a slow, difficult, but ultimately, doable process requiring discipline and strenuous effort.

Principle #2: Exemplars

To learn a virtue, one must have a good idea of what it looks like in a real-life situation. Toward this end, each chapter highlights an exemplar—an individual who manifests a particular virtue to a high degree and, thus, provides a clear and compelling picture of virtue in action. Whereas bookish definitions are helpful, the power and practicality of virtue is best demonstrated in individuals who, despite human frailty, lived in a virtuous manner in difficult circumstances. These individuals remind us that the exercise of virtue is the essence of our humanity and the fabric of community life. They demonstrate that virtue has instrumental value—virtue worked in, and through, them on behalf of others in the particulars of time and place. In this, exemplars provide tangible proof that, although right choices are difficult, they are not impossible, and that it is, indeed, possible for any and all to join with them in living well, even when it is inconvenient or demands sacrifice.

Principle #3: Exercise and Evaluation

Virtue must be practiced. "Practice" in this sense means investing significant attention and energy in evaluating one's performance in living out a particular virtue. This involves honestly facing the demands of reality, identifying one's performance, for better or worse, in meeting these demands, and taking constructive steps to make concrete improvements in attitude and action.

Principle #4: Friends and Feedback

We cannot learn virtue alone. Aristotle compared the acquisition of virtue to learning to play an instrument. It requires not only dedication and practice, but also a friend, coach, or teacher who knows how to play and gives feedback. Learning virtue requires the encouragement, practical help, and constructive feedback of others, especially those who themselves are in the process of learning it.

CHAPTER 9

Dynamic Determination

Introduction

In the New Normal, nothing good comes easy or fast. Goals are elusive, circumstances unpredictable, and choices difficult. Failure is a constant companion—those who lead may give their best, even sacrificial effort, only to fall short. Many lose heart in the face of disappointment and delay. Doubt and skepticism, fear and frustration, and anxiety and ambivalence abound. In this operating environment, the virtue-mix of faith, hope, prudence, and courage found in Dynamic Determination is at a premium.

Defined

Dynamic Determination is a cluster of virtuous attitudes and behaviors, a constellation of cognitive and moral capacities that draws from the virtues of faith, hope, prudence, and courage. These virtues supply the inner strength to initiate action in the face of obstacles, to not shrink back in the face of resistance, and to sustain constructive activity in the face of adversity. Dynamic Determination is the strength to act and keep acting in pursuit of noble ends, especially in the face of obstacles and opposition. It is the capacity to stand firm when opposed, to stay on course when deterred, and to sustain progress when impeded. Notably, that the Greek word *dunamis*, which means power, gives us our English words "dynamic" and "dynamo." Individuals with Dynamic Determination possess the power—the inner strength—to constructively engage and shape the world in accordance with their purpose, mission, and values.

What It Is Not

Dynamic Determination is not raw ambition in pursuit of self-serving, grandiose ends. It is not the will to achieve. It is not the obsessive pursuit of activity or the frenetic energy of a "type A" personality.

Dimensions

Dynamic Determination is a configuration of virtue—a suite of attitudes and behaviors manifested as "strength for others." It is composed of seven virtue strands.

1. Purpose is akin to faith. It is a deep and abiding sense of transcendent meaning that connects the individual to a larger story with plot, script, and movement toward valued ends. Purpose ignites our innate "telic orientation"—we all want and need a motivating force beyond self-interest—and sets the individual on a course of energetic striving toward noble ends.

2. Passion is purpose-generated energy—the strength to engage and shape the world in accord with one's purpose. The term "passion"" has its roots in the Greek term *pathos*, denoting pain and suffering. The idea of passion is bound inextricably to suffering in service of a noble end. Passion ignites the will, energizes the emotions, and sets the individual in motion to pursue a larger, noble purpose, especially in the face of difficulty.

3. Prudence is the wise, judicious, and effective investment of one's energy and resources to accomplish valued ends.

4. Prioritizing is wisely identifying the few things that matter, in light of one's purpose.

5. Proactivity is the disposition to act decisively to accomplish one's priorities.

6. Persistence is the inner strength to finish what one starts in spite of obstacles and adversity.

7. Peace is the practice of inner contentment and the discipline of replenishment. Peace highlights the fact that Dynamic Determination is a virtue-mix and not an obsessive, anxious pursuit of results.

Described

People fueled by Dynamic Determination are caught up in a larger, noble purpose beyond self-interest that emboldens them to act and persevere in the face of adversity. They take on life in a robust and imperturbable manner. They overcome obstacles, and sustain effort in the face of overwhelming odds. They are full of positive energy and vitality for accomplishment. They show up when others leave, act when others do not, and refuse to quit when others do. They stay the course, and finish the race.

Demonstrated

William Wilberforce was born on August 24, 1759, and died on July 29, 1833. For over four decades, Wilberforce led the charge to abolish the slave trade in Great Britain. His life is a shining example of Dynamic Determination.

In the eighteenth century, the British created the world's most brutally efficient slave system, and earned the dubious distinction of being the world's leading slave-trading nation. Between 1700 and 1810, British merchants transported almost three million Africans across the Atlantic to work in British-owned plantations in the West Indies. Appalling conditions aboard the slave ships killed many before they arrived. Some committed suicide during the journey.

Slavery was one of Great Britain's most profitable industries, and was firmly embedded in the British economic and political system. Owners of the slave plantations returned to Great Britain and used their profits to purchase vast estates as well as seats in Parliament. However, to the average Briton, slavery was a hidden scandal—the firsthand toll in human misery that was comfortably out of sight.

Wilberforce was an unlikely man to take on the vested interests of the most powerful nation on Earth. He stood only 5 feet tall. By all accounts, he was homely and physically frail, prone to bouts of fatigue, and debilitating illness—most likely, ulcerative colitis. Nevertheless, he was a dynamic speaker with vitality for life, a keen mind, and great powers of persuasion. In 1780, at the age of 21, he won a prestigious seat in Parliament. Scottish lawyer and essayist James Boswell listened to one of his speeches on the campaign trail and commented: "I saw what seemed to be a mere shrimp mount about the table, but as I listened the shrimp grew and grew and became a whale."

In 1784–1785, Wilberforce went through a reflective, spiritual process that resulted in his conversion to Christianity. On a trip through Europe, Wilberforce borrowed a book—*The Rise and Progress of Religion of the Soul*, by Philip Doddridge (writer of the Hymn, *Oh Happy*

Day)—from a friend. As Wilberforce read the book and studied the Scriptures, he experienced, in his words, a "great change" in his life that gave him a deep sense of larger, transcendent purpose.

In 1787, at the suggestion of his friend, Prime Minister William Pitt the Younger, Wilberforce was approached with the opportunity to become the parliamentary voice for the British abolition movement. Soon after his meeting with Pitt, on October 28, 1787, 28-year-old Wilberforce entered this notation in his personal journal. "God Almighty has set before me two great objects, the suppression of the Slave Trade and the Reformation of Manners." Wilberforce, knowing his personal limitations, wrote: "I feel the great importance of the subject and I think myself unequal to the task allotted to me." Despite these doubts, Wilberforce agreed to take up the cause.

Wilberforce was not the first to take on the slave trade, and he did not take it on by himself. A national network of talented and dedicated men and women supported him. The Society of Friends (Quakers) in Britain had presented a petition to Parliament in 1783, and, in 1787, had helped form the Society for the Abolition of the Slave Trade. However, it was Wilberforce who put his personal reputation and political future on the line, as it fell to him to carry the banner in Parliament and provide public, legislative leadership for the cause of abolition.

Initially, Wilberforce naively assumed that the forces aligned with the slave trade would see the wrong of their ways and grant the cause a quick victory. Instead, Wilberforce was opposed by some of England's most powerful people, including planters, merchants, ship owners, authors, and poets, and even King George III. National hero Admiral Lord Nelson, a longtime friend and supporter of planters in the West Indies, wrote from his flagship, *Victory*, that he would fight for the rights of plantation owners "while I have an arm to fight in their defense (Nelson lost his right arm at the battle of Santa Cruz) or a tongue to launch my voice against the damnable doctrine of Wilberforce and his hypocritical allies." Byron satirized Wilberforce in his epic poem, *Don Juan*.

The engine of his staying power was his passionate conviction that all people were equal in God's sight, and that the institution of slavery was inherently evil. Wilberforce researched the slave trade and was introduced, in great detail, to its inhumanity. He would, later, tell the House of Commons, "So enormous, so dreadful, so irremediable did the trade's wickedness appear that my own mind was completely made up for abolition. Let the consequences be what they would, I from this time determined that I would never rest until I had effected its abolition."

The agent for Jamaican plantation owners in Great Britain recognized the unusual perseverance of Wilberforce. He warned his planter allies, "It is necessary to watch him (Wilberforce) as he is blessed with a very sufficient quantity of that Enthusiastic Spirit, which so far from yielding that it grows more vigorous from blows." The agent was a good judge of character. Animated by a noble purpose and his crystal-clear set of priorities, Wilberforce manifested remarkable perseverance.

For 20 years, Wilberforce campaigned tirelessly for a legislated end to the slave trade. He introduced the Abolition Bill in Parliament almost every year in the decade of the 1790s, but to no avail. When he presented his first Abolition Bill in 1791, it was easily defeated by 163 votes to 88. Stiff resistance from the West India interests defeated the bill year after year. To further complicate matters and slow down the progress of the abolition movement, the British public was focused on the outbreak of war with France and, therefore, lost enthusiasm for the cause of abolition. Some abolitionists lost heart entirely and withdrew from the campaign.

The stress and strain took its toll on Wilberforce. He entertained thoughts of retiring from Parliament and avoiding the exhausting process of campaigning for re-election. John Newton (a former slave trader and writer of the hymn *Amazing Grace*) was instrumental in encouraging Wilberforce to stay the course.

In 1797, 1798, and 1799, his annual motion for abolition was defeated. In 1800 and 1801, his motion for abolition was deferred by Parliament in anticipation of a general conference of European powers with respect to continuing the war against Napoleon. No progress was made in 1802. In 1803, Wilberforce's motion was postponed because Great Britain expected an invasion from Napoleon's France.

Wilberforce persevered. A small victory came in 1805 when the House of Commons passed legislation that made it unlawful for any British subject to transport slaves. The House of Lords, however, blocked the measure.

In February 1806, a new administration—the Whig government of Lord Grenville and Foreign Secretary Charles Fox—was formed, which strongly opposed the slave trade. Fox and Wilberforce teamed up to pass legislation in the House of Commons, and Grenville persuaded the House of Lords to accept the measure.

February 23, 1807 was an unforgettable moment in Parliament. Wilberforce's perennial motion was debated. Most of the speeches supported abolition. Solicitor-General, Sir Samuel Romilly, gave an eloquent speech against the slave trade and in favor of Wilberforce's legislation.

Romilly concluded with an emotional tribute to Wilberforce, and the House of Commons broke into an uncharacteristic show of emotion reserved for great occasions as they stood, turned to Wilberforce, and gave him three rousing "hurrahs." Wilberforce, overwhelmed with this display of support and personal affirmation, sat with his head in his hands and wept.

The Abolition of the Slave Trade bill passed the House of Commons 114–15, and the House of Lords 41–20. The Abolition Act received the Royal Assent and became the law of the land on March 25, 1807. Historian J. M. Trevelyan, described the passing of abolition legislation as "one of the turning events in the history of the world."

Nevertheless, the fight to eradicate slavery in the British Empire was far from over. Forty-seven-year-old Wilberforce had come only half-way to completing his life mission. He faced another 26 years of struggle to rid the British Empire of the institution of slavery, as only the transportation of slaves was illegal. Over half a million slaves remained on plantations in the West Indies. Wilberforce and his allies knew that the only way to stop slavery was to make the possession of slaves illegal.

In 1825, 66 years old, Wilberforce resigned from the House of Commons. Wilberforce was resting at home on Friday, July 26, 1833, when he heard the House of Commons had passed the Abolition of Slavery bill. On Saturday, he took a turn for the worse, and died on Monday. "Thank God," said Wilberforce, "that I have lived to witness a day in which England is willing to give twenty millions sterling for the Abolition of Slavery." The next year, over 800,000 slaves throughout the British Empire were set free. Biographer John Pollock (1977) called Wilberforce "a man who changed his times" and "who made goodness fashionable" (see Pollock, 1977; Belmonte, 2002; Metaxas, 2007).

Lessons

Wilberforce is an exemplar of Dynamic Determination, providing a clear and compelling demonstration of this virtue configuration in action. We learn five lessons.

First, noble purpose unleashes the energy required to engage and shape the world. Wilberforce was what Fernandez-Araoz (2014) calls a "high potential" person with "the right kind of motivation...A fierce commitment to excel in the pursuit of unselfish goals. High potentials have great ambition and want to leave their mark, but they also aspire to big, collective goals, show deep personal humility, and invest in getting better at everything they do" (p. 51). Guinness (1998) calls Wilberforce an "Entrepreneur of life. This is the person who assumes responsibility for a creative task, not as an assigned role, a routine function, or an inherited duty, but as a venture of faith, including risk and danger, in order to bring into the world something new and profitable to mankind" (p. x).

His purpose became his imperative, serving as an integrating and stabilizing force, activating his whole person, intellect, will, and emotions to meet the demands of each day. As Emmons (1999) states, "A person with a congruent goal system experiences vitality and satisfaction with life; thus, he or she is better able to deal with stress effectively and to perceive daily life events as challenges and opportunities rather than as threats" (p. 117). Loehr and Schwartz (2001) call this "spiritual capacity," which refers to "The energy that is unleashed by tapping into one's deepest values and defining a strong sense of purpose. This capacity, we have found, serves as sustenance in the face of adversity and a powerful source of motivation, focus, determination and resilience" (p. 127).

Second, effective lives are marked by clear priorities. Wilberforce exemplified the "physics of personal focus." Like a laser beam, the greater the focus, the greater the energy released. British political philosopher Isaiah Berlin described this perspective as the difference between the hedgehog and the fox. The hedgehog knows one big thing. The fox knows many little things. Wilberforce knew the few big things that mattered.

Third, prudent action—not good intentions—carries the day. Wilberforce embodied a rare combination of high purpose and practical realism. He believed that the world was oblivious to good intentions and naïve hopes. The forces behind slavery would only get stronger, the practice only more deeply embedded in British life—regardless of the impassioned pleas of opponents. He knew he must, therefore, act wisely and decisively to shape the world in accordance with his purpose.

Fourth, persistence is required in all great undertakings. Wilberforce was a man of invincible determination. He acted over the decades, but with no promise of immediate or ultimate success. When he began his legislative efforts, he could not have known it would take more than 20 years of strenuous effort and exhausting conflict in Parliament to abolish the slave trade. Moreover, he could not have anticipated it would take an additional 26 years to emancipate existing slaves.

Fifth, inner peace is essential to sustained effort. Wilberforce manifested a rare, paradoxical mix of passionate intensity and inner peace. Typically, passion destroys peace, leading to a life of ragged intensity. Or peace undermines passion, leading to complacency. The virtue-mix of faith, hope, courage, and prudence found in Dynamic Determination avoids the extremes. Wilberforce manifested a serene striving and a carefree, but not careless, attitude toward progress in his mission. He understood the difference between his vision for change and what was beyond his power to control. He did what he could, and did not waste energy fretting about what remained to be accomplished.

Desirability for Leading in the New Normal

Although the challenges and opportunities encountered by Wilberforce are unique to his time and place, the twenty-first-century operating environment calls for the same faith, hope, courage, and prudence modeled by Wilberforce.

Faith, Hope, and Transcendent Purpose

In classical Greek literature, faith is akin to fidelity, which signifies an honored agreement or bond of trust. Faith binds people together around a special purpose, which sets the organization on a moral trajectory and provides good and compelling reason to risk and sacrifice. This virtue-mix is a requirement in the New Normal, where progress, if it comes at all, often arrives in bits and pieces. Sacrificial effort may be rewarded with difficulty and delay. As the organization lives through months and years marked by the discrepancy between effort expended and outcomes achieved, energy flags and morale falters. The journey proves to be longer and more difficult than first anticipated. These challenges place a premium on individuals and organizations fueled by faith. Hildebrand (1955) observed, "Strong lives are motivated by dynamic purposes; lesser ones exist on wishes and inclinations. The most glowing successes are but the reflections of an inner fire" (p. 96).

Hope is an expectation of a future good mingled with the understanding that this good is never guaranteed, and that the obstacles are many to its fulfillment. It is steadfast confidence, mixed with a realistic sense of contingency. Snyder (1991) found that "high hope" individuals have: (1) a greater number of goals across various arenas of life; (2) select more difficult goals; and (3) see their goals in a more challenging and positive manner. People with low hope, predictably, are associated with the opposite attitudes—fewer, easier goals and a negative stance toward present difficulties. Low-hope individuals settle for mediocrity, low energy, and low morale. Individuals and organizations animated by hope do not allow the painful realities of today to obscure their vision for a better tomorrow; however, neither do they allow the expectation of a better tomorrow to disconnect them from the harsh realities of today. Rather, they live in the tension, infusing the organization with the deep conviction that every day is pulsing with potential for progress, as well as the understanding that progress will not come easily.

Passion Born of Noble Purpose

Suffering, in its many forms—confusion, anxiety, disappointment, and loss—is a given of the New Normal. In this environment, passion born of noble purpose—the capacity to suffer for a worthy end—is at a premium. The first obligation of a New Normal Leader is to make sure his or her "inner fire"—the source of sustained, constructive action—is burning. The second obligation is to help others do the same. Burns (1978) reflected, "Where nothing is felt, nothing matters... The leader's fundamental act is to induce people to be aware or conscious of what they feel—to feel their true needs so strongly, to define their values so meaningfully, that they can be moved to purposeful action" (p. 44).

Setting Priorities

The uncertainty and ambiguity of the New Normal place a premium on setting clear goals and investing resources wisely to secure them. Leaders and member-leaders deal with a steady stream of difficult decisions, typically, without adequate information. Without the framework of a larger purpose and clear priorities, it is likely the attention of the Leaders and member-leaders will be hijacked by a mix of fragmented and disconnected pursuits, leading to a flurry of activity without progress toward valued ends. In this operating environment, the focus that comes from clear priorities—a few, critically important things that must happen—is a competitive advantage.

Being Proactive

It is understandable when individuals procrastinate, succumb to complacency, waver in indecision, stay on the sidelines, and play it safe. Leaders and member-leaders must overrule this natural impulse. Kouzes and Posner (1996) state, "Leaders don't wait" (p. 101). In the New Normal, procrastination is dangerous, sometimes deadly. Ironically, procrastination is not passive. It is a clear choice, a vote for the Present over the possible, the way things are over the way things could and should be.

Wilberforce knew that, if left alone, things get worse. Consequently, it is necessary to act in the imperfect Present rather than wait for an ideal Future free from problems and constraints. Newspaper columnist Art Buchwald (2006) put it well. "So, whether it's the best of times or the worst of times, it's all the time you've got."

Practicing Peace

New Normal Leaders and member-leaders care deeply about results—they are not careless about their obligations. However, they also know it is not always in their power to make good things happen on schedule. They manage this tension by staying focused, giving their best effort each day, taking rest as they need it, and coming back for more tomorrow.

Summary

The exercise of Dynamic Determination is a fundamental necessity when difficulty and unpredictability is way of life, and when staying the course means the difference between success and failure. Although the exercise of Dynamic Determination does not ensure success in every endeavor, sustained effectiveness is impossible without it. Its expression gives individuals and organizations a chance to succeed. Its absence spells certain failure.

CHAPTER 10

Intellectual Flexibility

Introduction

Unprecedented and ever-changing circumstances mark an average day in the New Normal. In an operating environment marked by volatility, uncertainty, complexity, and ambiguity, where sound decisions must be made in situations wherein no rulebook exists and technical–managerial competence is of limited help, the virtue of prudence found in Intellectual Flexibility is at a premium.

Defined

Intellectual Flexibility is a configuration of virtue, a constellation of cognitive, moral, and emotional capacity that draws from prudence and its derivatives—wisdom and humility. The English term "wisdom" is derived from the Indo-European root *weid* and the Latin *videre* meaning "to see." If Dynamic Determination is about engaging and shaping the world, Intellectual Flexibility is about seeing the world—people, circumstances, events, and interactions—such that, based on what is seen, the world is constructively engaged. Intellectual Flexibility is the cognitive and moral capacity to see clearly, accurately, and comprehensively so that one lives in accordance with what one sees. The opposite of Intellectual Flexibility is foolish, prideful inflexibility and, with it, closed-mindedness, narrowness, and rigidity that traps the individual in his or her assumptive framework, diminishes one's perceptual range, and, thereby, renders the individual short-sighted or blind, with consequent ineffectiveness in interactions with people and circumstances.

Intellectual Flexibility includes both the practical and transcendent dimensions of wisdom. Practical wisdom involves the application of "reflective judgment" about the important, but uncertain, matters of life and human affairs (Sternberg, 1990). Practical intelligence is the capacity to see patterns, similarities, and distinctions in order to solve problems associated with attaining one's goals. This kind of intelligence is "a set of abilities that permits an individual to solve problems or fashion products that are of consequence in a particular cultural setting" (Walters & Gardner, 1986, p. 164). It includes the traditional idea of intelligence, but goes beyond it to include broader, cognitive as well as moral and emotional capacities such as humility, creativity, curiosity and open-mindedness, love of learning, breadth and depth of perspective, and sensitivity to the perspective and needs of others.

Transcendent wisdom is expertise in the meaning and conduct of life. It features "being able to see and appreciate the deep significance of whatever occurs... appreciating the ramifications of each thing or event for the various dimensions of reality, knowing and understanding not merely the proximate goods but the ultimate ones, and seeing the world in this light" (Nozick, 1989, p. 276). Transcendent wisdom is the capacity to make proper sense of the world, take stock of one's life and circumstances in ways that offer perspective, meaning, and insight into oneself and others. Transcendent wisdom knows what matters in the larger scheme of things, and how to live accordingly: to set one's priorities in accord with one's larger purpose and to live daily in light of them. Sternberg (2000) sums up the idea of transcendent wisdom as life-perspective. "Wisdom," he writes, "is involved when practical intelligence is applied to maximizing not just one's own or someone else's self interest, but rather a balance of various self-interests (intrapersonal) with the interests of others (intrapersonal) and of other aspects of the context in which one lives (extrapersonal), such as one's city or country or environment or even God (p. 638).

What It Is Not

Intellectual Flexibility is not about being shrewd, "book-smart," or having a high intelligence quotient (IQ).

Dimensions

Intellectual Flexibility is composed of four virtue strands.

Seeing the Whole: Synoptic Seeing

Intellectual Flexibility is the capacity to see and substantially comprehend "the whole picture," whether that of an individual, circumstance, interaction, organization, or the world. This is synoptic seeing. Synoptic means, "to view together," and, thus, refers to getting a panoramic perspective on matters. For instance, synoptic meteorology is a branch of that science that studies atmospheric and weather conditions, as they exist simultaneously over a broad area, for the purpose of forecasting the weather. This branch of meteorology deals with all the variables that make up the global weather picture, high- and low-pressure systems and weather fronts, to ascertain how these variables work together to create large-scale, macro-weather patterns—for instance, how an arctic high-pressure weather system might influence the weather in Atlanta.

Similarly, Intellectual Flexibility is the capacity to see how systems interact with other systems. For instance, this perceptive capacity is necessary for seeing how the interactions between people or groups might contribute to the relational "weather patterns" of organizational life, or understanding how the global economy, or political environment at a state or federal level, is relevant to a particular business decision.

Seeing the Interconnectedness of a Particular System: System Seeing

Synoptic seeing is about understanding how systems interact with other systems. System seeing is about understanding how a particular system works with respect to its interdependent parts. A system is a complex unit formed of interdependent and interactive parts, all of which serve a common purpose. Intellectual Flexibility is the capacity to see these points of systemic interconnectedness and appreciate their power of these connections to impact individuals and organizations. This may include the complex web of interpersonal connections that constitute the social fabric of the organization, as well as the operational facets of the organization—human and financial resources, strategic direction, information sharing, and decision-making.

Seeing the People (Including Ourselves) in the Whole: Social Seeing

Intellectual Flexibility includes the capacity to see important features of the social landscape, and to be sensitive to context and perspective—both one's own and others—in order to understand the social, moral, and interpersonal implications of our actions and decisions.

Living in Accord With What One Sees

As the Chinese proverb goes, "Ninety percent of what we see lies behind our own eyes." Each of us wears a lens that colors our world with a unique perspective. Although allowing us to see some things clearly, this lens also distorts our perceptive capabilities. Intellectual Flexibility is the moral capacity to adjust for one's lens—to admit one's perceptual limitations, embrace feedback, and learn from personal experience, including one's mistakes, as well as the insights and experiences of others. This often means making adjustments to one's assumptive framework—worldview, beliefs, values, attitudes, and behaviors—such that the best choice is made in the service of the best ends. As such, Intellectual Flexibility is a matter of mind and heart—an exercise in both practical and transcendent wisdom.

Described

Knowing the dynamic complexity of life, and knowing one's personal limitations, those with Intellectual Flexibility practice a "disciplined open-mindedness." They listen to all sides of a matter and make decisions based on the demands of effectiveness, and not in defense of their assumptions or ego. They are voracious learners, insatiably curious, and ready to explore and discover. They see the world as it is, and not as they suppose it or wish it to be. They believe that changing one's mind in the face of new evidence is not a sign of weakness, but of strength. They give advice and take advice, knowing that the former is premised on the later. They stay effective in a variety of situations, none of which is exactly alike, and few of which call for "pre-packaged" responses based on formal rules.

Demonstrated

Roald Amundsen was the first person to walk to the South Pole. His life is a case study in the application of Intellectual Flexibility. In contrast, the lack of Intellectual Flexibility on the part of his competitor to reach the South Pole, Captain Robert Scott, led to his death and the deaths of all who accompanied him.

Amundsen's childhood hero was British explorer Sir John Franklin. Franklin had died four decades earlier trying to locate the Northwest Passage—a sea route around the north of Canada linking the Atlantic and Pacific. Amundsen wanted to emulate Franklin in every way—except for getting lost and freezing to death. By the time he was a teenager, Amundsen had settled on his aim in life, which was to become a successful arctic explorer.

Amundsen learned all he could about Franklin's expedition, especially the factors that contributed to his failure. Amundsen learned that success in Arctic exploration is a simple two-step process. First, successful arctic explorers achieved their stated goal. Second, they returned to tell the story. Failures did not return, and unless they kept a good diary (as did Scott), their story was never told.

Amundsen went to work preparing to succeed as an arctic explorer, combining an unusually high level of personal focus—on par with that of Wilberforce—with an unusually keen practical wisdom. Amundsen ordered his days to prepare himself mentally and physically for the rigors of arctic exploration. He took up soccer and cross-country skiing to increase his physical endurance. In the winters, he slept with his bedroom window open to acclimate to the frigid cold. He studied math, knowing it was the foundation for navigation, a skill required to be a ship's captain—a requirement to lead Arctic expeditions. Amundsen anticipated how "small things" added up to future success.

After 6 years of rigorous preparation, at 20 years of age, Amundsen undertook his first Arctic adventure. It was almost his last. With a college friend, he attempted to become the first person to cross-country ski across the 75-mile high plain north of Oslo. After running out of food, getting lost in a blizzard, and almost freezing to death, Amundsen and his friend turned back, barely making it to safety. A year later, they learned that they had stopped only a few hundred feet from their final destination, a farmhouse obscured by the blizzard. Chastened by this experience and knowing that such a failure would be fatal on an Arctic expedition, Amundsen accelerated his regimen of preparation.

Knowing he had to become a ship captain if he was to lead an Arctic expedition, Amundsen signed on as a seaman aboard the *Belgica*, on an expedition to study weather conditions in the Antarctic. The ship was blown off course and trapped in an ice flow for over a year. The crew barely survived.

Twice wiser, Amundsen devised a 4-year plan to study math, astronomy, and magnetic sciences. His goal was to gather a crew and lead an expedition to retrace Franklin's steps to find the still undiscovered Northwest Passage. It took him and his crew three Arctic winters of hardship, always on the brink of disaster, but on August 26, 1905, Amundsen became the first person to sail from the Atlantic to the Pacific through the Northwest Passage.

Amundsen, next, set his sights on the still unconquered North Pole. However, he was too late. In September 1909, American explorer Commander Robert Peary reached the North Pole by foot (a claim since disputed). Amundsen was disappointed, but turned his attention to the last Arctic frontier—the South Pole. British explorer, Captain Robert Scott did the same. It was June of 1910, and the race was on.

Amundsen's years of preparation and experience, along with his keen ability to envision how small, seemingly insignificant details added up to secure a larger goal, led him to approach the expedition quite differently than Scott. Amundsen reached the Bay of Whales on the Antarctic continent on January 11, 1911. On the journey, he spent considerable time doing topographical research, and mapped a shorter route to the Pole than Scott. Amundsen chose what, at first, appeared an overly cautious approach. For the next 9 months, Amundsen's crew made short trips to the interior continent to set up supply depots spaced 70 miles apart. Scott saw no reason for such a time-consuming project.

On October 19, 1911, in the warmth of the southern spring, Amundsen and his crew broke camp and set off for the South Pole in four sleds pulled by 52 husky dogs. Scott had chosen Siberian ponies and newly invented motor sledges. It soon became evident that the ponies could not stand the severe cold and workload. All of them had to be shot in a matter of days. Within the first week, the sledges failed in the wet and cold. They were abandoned, and Scott's men had to pull the sleds the entire way. With their supplies spread out over his route, Amundsen's dogs and crew pulled a much lighter load and made better time over a shorter distance.

To make matters more difficult for Scott, he made an unfortunate choice of clothing—heavy wool instead of the reindeer wool Amundsen had seen worn by the Eskimos he encountered on his Northwest Passage expedition.

On December 14, 1911, Amundsen's crew reached the end of their 1,860-mile journey—the South Pole. They marked the spot with a tent, the Norwegian flag, and a note of condolence for Scott. A disappointed Scott read the note 5 weeks later on January 17, 1912.

On the return trip, Scott and four of his crew died of starvation and exposure just 9 miles from their supply station. Amundsen and his crew, with ample supplies and healthy dogs, made it back to their supply ship safely.

The race between Amundsen and Scott captured the world's attention. Upon his return to Norway, Amundsen was asked to explain how he won the race with Scott. Amundsen responded with these famous words. "Victory awaits those who have everything in order. People call this luck" (see Huntford, 2010; King, 1999; Bown, 2012).

Lessons

Amundsen is an exemplar of Intellectual Flexibility, providing a clear and compelling demonstration of this virtue configuration in action. We learn five lessons.

First, wisdom is less about flashes of brilliant insight, and more about knowing what to do next in light of larger aims, combined with the discipline to do it. Once Amundsen decided to become a polar explorer, he immediately got to work, knowing that his high aim would be achieved only through strenuous, daily effort, and that success comes in small, daily portions that add up to larger successes over the decades. For over a decade, Amundsen carefully planned and prepared each day with a view to achieving his larger aim. Although it is impossible to fully prepare for the unprecedented, Amundsen did all he could. He established an ambitious learning agenda and did the seemingly "small" things that make a big difference—like learning math and sleeping with his window open in winter. His Arctic success was secured in the days, months, and years of careful planning, preparation, experimentation, and learning. As novelist Louis L' Amour (1985) reflected, "Victory is won not in miles but in inches. Win a little, now hold your ground, and later win a little more" (p. 261).

Second, panoramic vision (synoptic seeing) is essential in complex, unprecedented tasks. Amundsen appreciated the full range of variables critical to Arctic exploration, the big picture as well as the seemingly insignificant details that meant the difference between success and disaster—math, the expertise of a sea captain, rigorous physical training, supply chain logistics, the right clothing and equipment, and a doable but rigorous travel regimen. Amundsen translated these variables into a plan of action, and executed the plan amid fluid circumstances that required constant adjustment to the plan.

Third, prudence, humility, and a teachable attitude are crucial ingredients in taking on novel challenges. Knowing the unprecedented nature of his journey and the likelihood of unpleasant surprises along the way, and recognizing the limits of his experience, Amundsen listened and learned from others. In this, he possessed a reflective capacity for self-questioning that tempered his strong ego with humility, and guarded against a descent into arrogance and rigidity. He tested his assumptions, embraced feedback, changed his mind when necessary, and based his decisions on solid evidence—dogs over ponies, supply chain logistics over heroic efforts.

Fourth, successful endeavors in novel circumstances require anticipating the needs of the future and practicing the discipline of delayed gratification. As the African proverb goes, "Dig the well before you are thirsty." Amundsen's chain of supply stations was central to his success. This was hard work with no immediate reward—setting up the stations brought him no closer to the South Pole. In fact, this task cost precious time in the race with Scott, and took enormous physical effort. Amundsen committed himself to this strategy as a prudent safeguard against starvation, as well as a competitive advantage in terms of his sled dogs and men carrying less weight. He refused the course of action that appeared less difficult, get started and carry your own supplies, and which promised immediate payoff, getting closer to the South Pole, although it gave Scott a head start. Scott fell victim to "specious rewards"—less than optimal, immediate outcomes (Ainslie, 2001). Although Scott's approach required less work, it ultimately cost the lives of him and his men—a breach of transcendent wisdom.

Summary

Amundsen embraced the lessons of the past and made each day count toward his longer term goal. He engaged the realities of the present, knew what to do next, and exercised the discipline to do it as well as the humility to self-correct and keep learning in the process.

Desirability for Leading in the New Normal

Although the challenges and opportunities encountered by Amundsen are unique to his time and place, the twenty-first-century operating environment calls for the same exercise of prudence. Specifically, Intellectual Flexibility is the driver of two next practices—sensemaking and generative learning.

Sensemaking

Sensemaking is required in situations where decisive action must be taken, but no "rulebook" or decision model exists to guide the way. Bartz (2009) notes that making sense in the chaos is at a premium in New Normal times. "They want someone to tell them what it all means. These are wonderful opportunities for leadership. Employees, investors, customers and business partners are heartened by executives who can sift through the avalanche of opinion and clearly communicate what matters—and what doesn't—to the enterprise" (p. 128).

Sensemaking Requires Thinking Ahead. The term prudence is related to the Latin *providentia*, which means foresight. Sensemaking is a forward-looking practice, anticipating whether a course of action will achieve a particular valued end, and appreciating the future state that one's decisions and actions will likely cause. Chanda Kochhar, managing director and CEO of India's ICICI Bank, observes:

> Coping with a more volatile environment is a challenge common to many leaders. At ICICI, we constantly survey the horizon to anticipate that next big change. Scenario planning has always been important, but these days change can come so much more quickly. So we are always asking "what if." What if the currency moves by 5 percent in two days? What if the stock market moves by 10 percent in two days? What would be the impact on our customers? Our people? What are the steps we would have to take? You have to be ready to react at any moment. (Chandler, 2012)

Sensemaking Requires Systemic Thinking. In a highly interdependent, complex environment, dealing with problems in isolation from other problems is naïve and dangerous, as it fails to appreciate the law of unintended consequences—the many "bounces" that a single decision or interaction can have. Kanter (1996) states:

> Trying to lead while the system itself is being reshaped puts a premium on brains: to imagine possibilities outside of conventional categories, to envision actions that cross traditional boundaries, to anticipate repercussions and take advantage of interdependencies, to make new connections or invent new combinations. Those who lack the mental flexibility to think across boundaries will find it harder and harder to hold their own, let alone prosper. (p. 98)

Kanter's reference to "brains" is not about high IQ, but rather the wisdom and humility found in Intellectual Flexibility.

Generative Learning

The mix of wisdom and humility found in Intellectual Flexibility is a necessity in times of rapid and discontinuous change, where a premium is placed on generative learning—critical thinking, creative problem solving, and a willingness to adjust and adapt to new information.

Humility is associated with better information processing and problem solving (Weiss & Knight, 1980). Kotter (1997) calls this the "untrapped mind" (p. 206). Mark Frissora, CEO of Hertz, observes, "Most people, including CEOs, have too much pride. Pride gets in the way of what we call TOM—Total Open Mind—which is our shorthand for an entrepreneurial, innovation orientation. We say, 'No pride allowed. If you're not in TOM mode, we can't have this conversation'" (Frissora and Kirkland, 2013).

Summary

Intellectual Flexibility is a fundamental necessity when unpredictability is way of life, and learning quickly is the difference between success and failure. The capacity to gain new knowledge quickly, to adjust one's perspective, adapt one's approach, leave behind outdated practices, and explore new possibilities for addressing new problems brings Leaders, member-leaders, and entire organizations a decided competitive advantage. As Amundsen demonstrated, the only way to prepare for the unexpected is to cultivate a humble and teachable attitude that fuels continuous learning. This is less about being "book smart" and more about being wise.

CHAPTER 11

Courageous Character

Introduction

We live in cynical times when it comes to trusting distant voices, especially those associated with authority. The last decade has seen a precipitous decline in trust in our public institutions and leaders. Economic contractions and major scandal have driven this trust deficit. From Wall Street to Main Street, public leaders and institutions are failing at an alarming rate.

One of the best indicators of public trust is The National Leadership Index (NLI), conducted by the Center for Public Leadership at the Harvard Kennedy School (Rosenthal, 2012). The 2012 NLI is the eighth annual measurement of public attitudes toward the leadership of 13 sectors of American life: Military, Medical, Nonprofit & Charity, Supreme Court, Local Government, Business, Religious, Education, Executive Branch, State Government, News Media, Congress, and Wall Street. With the 2012 Presidential election approaching, Americans reported a slight increase in confidence in public leaders for only the second time since 2005 (Pittinsky et al., 2005). However, the news was not altogether encouraging, as 69 percent of Americans think we are currently facing a leadership crisis (Rosenthal, 2012). For the second consecutive year, only two sectors—military and medical leadership—received above-average confidence scores. Ratings for the remaining 11 sectors remained or fell into the below-average range. Confidence in public sectors critical to America's strength and strategic direction remain dangerously low. Congress scored the least amount of confidence of the 13 sectors, dropping below Wall Street. Leadership in the educational sector is fifth from last. Owens (2012) reports that America's confidence in Wall Street, banks, and financial institutions has plummeted since the economic downturn of 2008.

In this operating environment, the virtue-mix of love and courage found in Courageous Character is at a premium.

Defined

Courageous Character is a cluster of attitudes and behaviors that draw from the virtues of love and courage. In this sense, it is "sound" or virtuous character put in the service of others. Sound character is closely related to the idea of moral integrity and moral courage. Integrity comes from the Latin *integras*, meaning "whole" and "sound." The idea of integrity carries the sense of something or someone possessing the power of purity and the strength of wholeness. It is helpful to think of integrity as a larger category of moral attributes such as honesty, authenticity, trustworthiness, responsibility, and transparency.

Aristotle thought of virtue as a state of character—deeply seated moral dispositions with a bent toward moral excellence; a habit pattern of choices and interactions that are fittingly and fully human. We call this state "moral integrity"—the "structural state" of a well-integrated person, one who has organized the various aspects of his or her person around a coherent and morally praiseworthy sense of identity, values, and loyalties and, consequently, in word and deed, consistently seeks the welfare of others. Moral integrity means that an individual is not tainted or infected with impurities in the form of inner dispositions or inclinations that weaken one's relational capacities.

Aristotle contrasted the virtuous person with the "many-colored and changeable" person or, in modern parlance, a duplicitous individual. The duplicitous person is "two faced" in that they knowingly present themselves as one kind of person, with one set of attitudes, intentions, words, and behaviors whereas embracing the opposite.

Summary

Courageous Character is a decisive trajectory of the heart, a fixed and stable disposition, the settled orientation of one's worldview and values, desires, and affections that is expressed as a particular kind of life—a pattern of choice and action reflecting moral courage, integrity, and love.

Values, Character, and Virtue

Although these terms are often used interchangeably, it is best to think of them as related but distinct ideas. Values are the moral standards by which a person judges the quality of his or her life, relationships, and work. The idea of a value is morally neutral. Everyone has values, for better or worse. Hitler had values—Arian supremacy. And Mother Teresa had values—the inherent dignity and worth of the individual. Therefore, it is technically accurate—although confusing—to say that Hitler and Mother Teresa were "value-driven individuals." This renders the term nearly meaningless.

The English word "character" is from the Greek *kharax*, the term for a pointed stake and, thus, something that makes a distinctive mark or indentation. The word came to be associated with an embosser or stamp for making a coin and, correspondingly, to the distinctive marking on the coin made by the stamp to indicate the type and value of the coin. The term was expanded to mean that which our culture, family, experiences, and choices have deeply imprinted and embedded into us by way of a distinctive "mark." In this sense, character is the imprint that life makes on us and, thus, what defines our inner condition, shapes the deep, dispositional grooves of our personality, the contours of our inner person. It is the sum total of the peculiar traits and distinctive and essential qualities or attributes that sets us apart from others and marks us as individuals.

Our character is more than our experience—the imprint life makes on us. Furthermore, our character is powerfully shaped by our response to our experience. In this sense, character is self-determined. It is the self we shape through our choices and actions, our attitudes and responses to life over time. It is the person we make of ourselves, for better or worse, the self-erected structure of our personhood.

A person's character is a dynamic arrangement of values, beliefs, and convictions in constant interaction with one's circumstances. Character is what we are predisposed to do habitually, ratified by our choices to act and interact in a particular manner. Our worldview, the choices we make, the communities to which we belong, how we relate to others, what we risk, what we suffer and lose, and how we respond to these experiences determine the shape of our character.

Understood in this sense, Hitler and Mother Teresa possessed character, but of a radically different sort. To say that Hitler and Mother Teresa "had character" is, again, to render the term meaningless.

Virtue speaks to a particular set of values—faith, hope, love, wisdom, justice, courage, and self-control put in the service of noble ends and the welfare of others. Virtue rejects worldviews, beliefs, and values that script individuals to act selfishly, to seek ends at the expense of others, and to undermine community life. Yes, there is an unavoidable "right" and "wrong" here. Virtue does what is "right"—it respects others and seeks their welfare, at times, at the risk of one's own. Virtue stands in distinction to what is "wrong"—to debase, disrespect, or dehumanize others in pursuit of selfish ends.

Character refers to the personality structure in which values operate. A virtuous set of values is a distinctive pattern of attitude and behavior operating in one's character structure—the moral content and trajectory of one's character, but not the character itself. In this sense, virtues are those values and moral habits that befit human character, develop human character into what it ought to be, and shape the pattern of a life lived in accord with that character. Hitler had a character structure defined by corrupt values and self-serving ends. Mother Teresa possessed a character shaped by virtuous values.

Summary

Values and character are morally neutral ideas. Virtue is not. "Sound character" is the deep disposition to act in accord with virtuous values—those patterns of behavior that befit a genuine human being, strengthening the individual to act in a humane manner—to seek the welfare of others even when it places one's interests at risk. Virtuous character is what is meant by "sound " or "strong" character. In contrast, an "unsound" or "weak" character lacks virtuous moral content and, consequently, treats others in an indifferent or inhumane manner, as objects of one's self-interest.

What It Is Not

It is inadequate to understand Courageous Character as the mere absence of vice or avoiding doing wrong. Rather, it is the active presence of virtue—concrete deeds that accomplish what is right and noble.

Dimensions

Courageous Character is a configuration of virtue—a suite of attitudes and behaviors manifested as strength for others. Courageous Character in manifested in three strands of attitude and behavior: (1) Love—the capacity to pursue the best for others, to seek their welfare even when it places one's own at risk; (2) Courage—the strength to put something one values at risk in service of a noble end.; and (3) Moral integrity— the strength to live in accord with what one values, to live as one, whole, and morally healthy person, even and especially when a price tag is attached. Courageous Character, then, is the capacity to live one's life as an authentic human being who seeks one's neighbor's welfare even at the risk of loss.

Described

The person with Courageous Character discerns what is right and proper to serve the welfare of others and acts in accordance with what is right, in spite of fear or self-interest. The person with Courageous Character seeks the best for others in the pressure of the moment, when the demonstration of love carries with it a valid threat of personal loss.

Demonstrated

Rescuers: Portraits of Moral Courage in the Holocaust by Block and Drucker (1992), recounts the heroic efforts of 105 people from 11 nations that fell under the Nazi occupation of Europe from 1939 to 1945. The authors identify the participant categories of the Jewish Holocaust, commonly named persecutors (Nazis), victims (Jews), and bystanders (the passive citizens of Europe who looked the other way during the Holocaust). The book highlights a fourth category of participants—the rescuers. The rescuers were those who, in sharp contrast to their passive countrymen, refused to look away as their neighbors were being led away to the killing camps. Instead, they risked their lives to hide the Jews from the Nazis. The rescuers ranged from those who saved one life, to famous examples such as Raoul Wallenberg, who may have saved as many as 100,000 Jews, as well as the entire French mountain village of Le Chambon, which, under the leadership of a local minister Andre Trocme and his wife Magda, sheltered over 5,000 Jews.

Aiding Jews was an invitation to personal tragedy and even collective disaster. The Germans regularly published lists of Polish citizens who were executed for various "crimes" against the Nazis, with many executed for harboring Jews. The two families that hid Anne Frank were arrested, with one man spending 8 months in a forced labor camp. The entire Polish village of Huta Pienacka was burned to the ground with its inhabitants trapped inside, men, women, children, and even the animals, in the winter of 1944 for giving shelter to 100 Jews living in the surrounding forest.

The rescuers chose to disregard these grim realities. Block and Drucker found in the rescuers a humble and unassuming group who consistently protested that what they did was natural and even ordinary.

They denied the exceptional quality of their actions, claiming they were simply doing what anyone would do.

Nechama Tec (1986) pursued the question of what set the rescuers apart from their fellow citizens. Tec's findings based on interviews with Polish rescuers are strikingly similar to those of Block and Drucker. The rescuers refused to be called "heroes." However, Tec found they did manifest a crucial difference from their peers. The rescuers spoke of a sense of being propelled by their values and conscience, and living by a moral imperative to help others even in the face of risk and, incredibly, the censure and disdain of their neighbors. Janka Polanska saved 10 Jews by hiding them in her small apartment. She reflected, "I have to be at peace with myself, what others think about me is not important. It is my own conscience that I must please and not the opinion of others" (p. 161).

Tec theorized that these life-risking acts were a natural and obvious duty to the rescuers, but only because their actions flowed out of an ingrained value structure—a set of deep dispositions and moral habits reflecting a higher moral law, developed over the decades as they performed relatively simple and risk-free good deeds. "In case after case," Tec writes, "there is a long history of giving aid before the war" (p. 189). The rescuers lived by the simple moral imperative that anyone in need deserved help. They visited the sick, collected books for poor students, even took care of stray animals. Tec concludes, "They just got into the habit of doing good. If they hadn't perceived the pattern as natural, they might have been paralyzed into inaction." When the crisis moment arrived and Jews showed up at their door asking to be hidden from the Gestapo, the rescuers did not perceive themselves as being faced with a momentous decision that called upon them to act out of character. They simply lived out their values in one more expression of a deep and abiding commitment to help others in need.

Lessons

The rescuers are exemplars of Courageous Character, providing a clear and compelling demonstration of this virtue configuration in action. We learn five lessons.

First, moral courage—and, in the case of the rescuers, physical courage—unleashes the other virtues. C. S. Lewis (2009) noted, "Courage is not simply *one* of the virtues, but the form of every virtue at the testing point, which means, at the point of highest reality. A chastity or honesty, or mercy, which yields to danger will be chaste or honest or merciful only on conditions. Pilate was merciful till it became risky" (pp. 161–162). The moral and physical courage of the rescuers allowed them to preserve their personal integrity by loving their neighbor at great personal risk. Without courage, their love would have gone unexpressed.

Second, small, daily choices make a big difference. Goodness in mundane and "private" moments served as the proving ground for the expression of goodness in a moment of crisis. Little could the rescuers have known that a stray dog fed, a book sacrificially purchased, or an inconvenient hospital visit to a sick neighbor would prepare them for a day of moral crisis when they were asked to risk their lives to live out these same values. In this sense, virtuous character is not forged in crisis. It is revealed in crisis. It is forged day-by-day, decision-by-decision. When the public occasion arose, the rescuers simply did what was necessary to continue being themselves. They refused to divide their private self from their public life, knowing that, if they gave in to evil, they would become co-conspirators in their own diminishment as human beings.

Third, courage is not the absence of fear, but rather, knowing what to fear. The rescuers remind us that fear and courage are not mutually exclusive and, in fact, commonly coexist. Courage is not the lack of fear, but in knowing fear and not allowing it to force us into complicity with evil, or to be kept by fear from the pursuit of the good. Polish rescuer Felicja Zapolska observed, "In general, those who helped were sensitive people who tried to overcome their fears. Everyone was afraid. Do not believe if someone tells you that they were not afraid because it has to be a lie" (p. 169). Although the rescuers feared for their lives and the lives of their family and friends, they feared even more the greatest enemy of the soul—the divided and fragmented self that believes one set of values in private but lives by a more convenient set of values in public.

Fourth, the exercise of virtue is often difficult. Virtue is a corrective feature of human experience that speaks to the capacity to act in a manner differently from what might be expected, given our proclivity to seek security and comfort, and avoid risk and adversity. Therefore, we are not surprised that the rescuer's behavior stood in stark contrast to what they might have understandably chosen to do—take the easier way of their contemporaries—if they lacked love and courage.

Fifth, although our character is deeply personal, it is never private in consequence. Character is embedded deep within us, but it is expressed "between us" and "among us." Although character is shaped outside the glare of public scrutiny—delivering a book to a shut in—the expression of character is a matter of public consequence. For the rescuers, character determined how they responded when neighbors knocked on their door in the middle of the night.

Summary

Few of us will occupy the same size or shaped stage as the rescuers. Our daily choices and mundane acts are likely to go unnoticed and unappreciated. However, no rescuer could have imagined that their seemingly insignificant daily choices would matter so greatly in the moment of crisis. *Middlemarch* (2003) is a nineteenth-century novel by George Eliot (the pen name of Mary Ann Evans). Eliot offers a sympathetic look at unknown and simple people living lives of quiet dignity. She ends the book with these powerful words. "For the growing good of the world is partly dependent on unhistoric acts; and that things are not so ill with you and me as they might have been, is half owing to the number who lived faithfully a hidden life, and rest in unvisited tombs" (p. 838).

Each generation is indebted in ways it will never know to the quiet courage of those in preceding generations who did the right thing day after day and, in so doing, laid the foundation for the "growing good of the world."

Desirability for Leading in the New Normal

Although the challenges and opportunities encountered by the rescuers are unique to that time and place, the same courage and love they modeled is an indispensible asset in the New Normal. Specifically, Courageous Character is the driver of two New Normal next practices—moral persuasion and candor.

Love, Courage, and Moral Persuasion

It takes a mix of courage and love to earn the trust necessary to practice moral persuasion. Courage, love, and trust are inextricably bound. The demonstration of altruism (another term for love) is associated with higher levels of trust-based relationships between leaders and followers, and aids mutual commitment to the organization's goals, as well as exceptional levels of performance (Engelbrecht, 2002). We are willing to trust someone when we have made a positive assessment of his or her sincerity, selfless motivation, reliability, and track record in doing the right thing on behalf of others, even at the expense of one's self-interest. In the case of those with formal authority, trust is built when Leaders refrain from using power for personal gain but, instead, use it in socially constructive ways and demonstrate care and consideration for others—it takes love to use power appropriately (Engelbrecht et al., 2005; Bass & Steidlmeier, 1999). As love is expressed without ulterior motives or the expectation of something in return, others deem these individuals worthy of trust, extending their moral authority and supporting the next practice of moral persuasion.

If that trust is abused, credibility built up over the decades can disappear in a day. In the case of Leaders, although they may continue to hold formal power, their personal influence is diminished, and the exercise of moral persuasion is undermined. This has disastrous consequences in the New Normal, where the need to trust is accentuated in times of uncertainty, insecurity, high risk, and weak performance (Lau & Liden, 2008). As organizations face greater adversity and uncertainty, a sense of vulnerability increases, and trust in credible leaders is seen as increasingly important (Burke et al., 2007). In a world where nothing can be predicted, love and courage is at a premium.

Love, Courage, and Candor

Courageous Character is necessary in the New Normal, where Leaders and member-leaders are, daily, called upon to win the inner battle over human frailty, vulnerability, and the understandable temptation to choose security and self-interest over the risk and sacrifice of the wilderness journey. "Without courage," writes Compte-Sponville (2001) "we cannot hold out against the worst in ourselves and others" (p. 50). It takes courage to exercise candor—to deliver difficult-to-hear news, make tough decisions, and act when others hesitate in the face of uncertainty and risk—permanent features of the New Normal leadership landscape. Lacking courage, when adversity strikes, the individual is likely to capitulate to their fears and protect their reputation, secure their privileges and comfort, and seek the course of action that will afford them the least difficulty—a recipe for failure in the New Normal.

Summary

Love and courage are critical assets in the New Normal operating environment where the trust deficit is a daily reality, and the exercise of moral authority and candor are often the difference between success and failure. A deep sense of moral obligation to secure the welfare of others is fundamental to leadership effectiveness in a densely networked global economy, where it is increasingly difficult to make decisions devoid of moral consequence, and the ramifications of one's decisions reverberate from one end of the world to the other at the speed of light. In the decades ahead, the only way to do well in the long run is to courageously seek the good of others in the short run.

CHAPTER 12

Emotional Maturity

Introduction

The myth of the exceptional leader glamorizes the work of leading, talking about it in terms of inspiring messages and creative breakthroughs. Although true at times, leading in the New Normal brings more than its share of stress, disappointments, and frustrations. Disruptive change, uncertainty, and the anxiety these produce are likely to increase in the decades ahead. Those who lead must understand the emotional drivers of individual and collective performance—the hopes and fears, aspirations, and concerns of others. In this context, leading is less about rational analysis—although this is still important—and more about relational realities, placing a premium on the virtue-mix of faith, hope, and temperance (self-control) found in Emotional Maturity.

Defined

Emotional Maturity is a cluster of virtuous attitudes and behaviors that draw from the virtues of faith, hope, and temperance. Emotional Maturity is the capacity to steward one's gifts and talents such that they are expressed in the service of others, especially with respect to understanding their needs and concerns, rather than being diminished by the deficiencies and vagaries of one's emotional life, in particular, one's self-centeredness and emotional reactivity.

What It Is Not

Emotional Maturity is not the same as emotional wellbeing. Emotional wellbeing is a temporary, "surface trait," meaning that it comes as goes as situations vary. Emotional Maturity is a deep trait or "source trait," meaning that it is stable and sustainable even in adverse circumstances. Emotional wellbeing rises or falls as circumstances change; Emotional Maturity is an enduring pattern of attitude and behavior with cross-situational consistency.

Dimensions

Emotional Maturity is a configuration of virtue—a suite of attitudes and behaviors manifested as strength for others. Emotional Maturity is expressed in a 5-fold configuration of attitude and behavior.

Emotional Recognition and Regulation

Emotional recognition and regulation is the capacity to constructively manage one's emotional life as opposed to relinquishing control of one's inner landscape to negative emotions. Emotionally mature people possess the inner strength to control their emotional life, to "catch themselves" before responding to negative circumstances with maladaptive attitudes and behaviors—withdrawal, anger, fear, and anxiety. Emotionally mature individuals possess "locus of control," which is the inner sense that one is in charge of his or her feelings and behavior and, therefore, is not subject to external forces undermining one's best intentions. Consequently, emotionally mature people are not passive victims of circumstance.

Emotional Resilience

Emotional resilience is the strength to rebound from loss or failure. Resilience is derived from the Latin term *resilire*, meaning "to bounce or spring back." Emotionally mature people possess the strength and durability to absorb the stress, shocks, and pressures of daily life, to endure in hard times, to be stretched momentarily, but then to regain one's emotional equilibrium.

Emotional Realism

Emotional realism is the dual capacity to accurately appraise one's strengths and limitations, as well as accurately read the emotional content of situations. Emotionally mature people exhibit high levels of perceptual clarity and correspondence, meaning that their subjective experience matches the objective world. They operate out of a stable, secure, and accurate sense of self. They are not overly pessimistic or unrealistically hopeful.

Emotional Responsibility

Emotional responsibility is the capacity to take ownership and accountability for one's attitudes and actions. Emotionally mature people accept the consequences of their decisions, and refrain from making excuses or blaming others.

Emotional Resonance

The English word resonance is derived from the Latin *resonantia*, meaning "an echo." Emotional resonance is the act of "echoing"—picking up and repeating emotional content. As such, it is the capacity to accurately read emotional cues and give voice to the emotions and needs of others. Emotionally mature people connect with others and interact with them in a manner appropriate to their situation and need.

Described

Emotionally mature people do not engage in self-destructive behavior. They manage stress and control their moods. They avoid self-pity and resentment. Although they experience negative emotions, they maintain their emotional equilibrium. Because they have substantially settled issues of power, identity, and esteem, they are relatively free from self-preoccupation and, thus, capable of taking the spotlight off of themselves to serve others. They are "givers" not "takers."

Demonstrated

Amanda Berry Smith is a shining example of Emotional Maturity demonstrated in the most difficult of circumstances.

Smith was born a slave in Maryland on January 23, 1837. At the deathbed request of the daughter of her owner, her family was granted the status of a "free colored people." Smith's father moved the family to Pennsylvania where they lived and worked on the land of a wealthy farm owner.

At the age of 13, Smith and her brother walked 5 miles each way to attend white school. They left school after 2 weeks, discouraged by the long walk and the chilly reception by the teacher and other students. Smith would amass less than 1 year of formal schooling in her lifetime.

In September 1854, at the age of 17, Smith married Calvin Divine. It was a short and stormy marriage. Divine was likely an alcoholic. Their first child died in infancy. Their second, a daughter Mazie, survived to adulthood. At the onset of the Civil War, Divine enlisted in the Union Army. He went south to fight, and was never heard from again. Smith, now in her early 20s, found herself a widow and single mother, faced with grinding poverty.

In 1856, Smith experienced a religious conversion that would set the trajectory of her personal and professional life for the next 50 years. In 1864, she met and married James Smith, a local pastor in Philadelphia. He was a teamster by trade and, therefore, at least in Smith's eyes, an "established man." A year later, she gave birth to a girl, Nell. Six weeks later, Nell "was taken sick with a summer complaint" and died.

When the Civil War ended in 1865, Smith and her husband moved to New York City where James worked as a hotel waiter. New York was a place of both financial opportunity and grinding poverty. It was not a friendly place for Blacks, and was well known for its southern sympathies during the Civil War and its violence against Blacks after the war.

Smith worked as a live-in maid and boarded Mazie with strangers. When she became pregnant with her fourth child, her employer asked her to move out for fear that she would not be able to continue working her long hours, and not be able to pay the rent. In September of 1866, Smith gave birth to her fourth child, Thomas Henry.

James shifted from job to job, and proved to be an unreliable provider. Three weeks after the birth of Thomas Henry, Smith moved in to a damp, cold, basement apartment, two blocks from Washington Square. She later moved upstairs, but the unhealthy climate in the basement aggravated the severe arthritis and chronic respiratory ailments that would plague her the rest of her life.

Like thousands of Black women of her generation, Smith assumed the role of a washerwoman, taking in laundry and cleaning the homes of wealthy white families. This meant a life of unrelenting toil and undiminished drudgery. She worked 18 hours a day washing and ironing, sometimes falling asleep on her feet. The poor living conditions and relentless schedule contributed to the deaths of her two infant sons, Thomas Henry and William Henry. Thomas Henry died 8 months after his birth from tubercular meningitis. On August 1, 1867, Smith gave birth to her fifth child, William Henry. At 10 months of age, he died from bronchitis. She was scarcely able to make the funeral arrangements. James, then suffering from stomach cancer, did not offer to help. An acquaintance gave her $20 for the funeral. James died 5 months later.

At 30, Smith found herself twice widowed, and had buried four infant children. She was desperately poor, caught up in a grinding work schedule, and suffered from severe arthritis and chronic respiratory ailments. Moreover, she was the sole financial and emotional support for her only surviving child, Mazie.

Smith found the inner emotional strength to deal with her adversity through involvement at the Green Street ME Church. Her involvement with this all-White congregation laid the foundation for her next 50 years. Smith proved to be a powerful teacher and preacher, and became well known among Black Methodists and White churches in New York City. Smith, manifesting remarkable resilience, bounced back from personal tragedy and set her sights on the next chapter of her life.

In the late nineteenth century, large outdoor gatherings known as camp meetings were an integral part of American life. These meetings fostered an inclusive spirit, attracting large, diverse crowds from all walks of life, rich and poor, men and women, and Black, White, and Native American.

Smith attended a camp meeting in October 1870 as a participant. She was introduced to several White leaders of the movement, and immediately impressed them as a person of strength and spiritual power. These meetings were a perfect venue to showcase her gifts as a speaker and singer. Invitations to speak at Black and White churches and camp meetings poured in, and Smith began the grueling life of a traveling speaker.

Far from alleviating her adversity, her newfound prominence brought new adversity in the form of public criticism. Ironically, many women—both Black and White—due, in part, to her unusual dress, criticized her. Smith refused to wear the typical expensive outfits most other women wore to religious meetings and, instead, wore the plain, distinctive dress of Quakers, which conflicted with the style and status sensibilities of contemporary women.

Furthermore, Smith faced tremendous racial pressure. She was a Black woman who interacted daily with Blacks and Whites, males and females alike. This brought her a double dose of resentment. She had to overcome a life-long sense of racial inferiority and fear of White people, when, all the while, she was ridiculed and rejected by some Whites.

Moreover, Smith faced withering criticism from Blacks for taking her place next to Whites in public settings. She was accused of abandoning her own people, who, Black critics argued, needed her more than Whites, in favor of access to the White world and the status and financial gain associated with it. Faced with the daily choice of whether to arrange her life to avoid humiliating encounters with racist Whites by associating mainly with Blacks, or to work with both Blacks and Whites, Smith, operating from a stable and secure sense of her own identity and values, chose the difficult path of "both–and." Although she spoke in many Black churches, she also continued to speak in White churches and Camp meetings. Further, she rose to prominence in White organizations like the Women's Christian Temperance Union (WCTU).

After achieving national notoriety as a public speaker, Smith caught the eye of influential British women who convinced her to come to England. In 1878, Smith traveled to Liverpool, England, to begin the next phase of her life—12 years devoted to missions work in Europe, India, and Liberia.

The work in Liberia presented its own version of adversity. Travel was difficult and dangerous. Many Liberians struggled with alcohol abuse (liquor imports from Great Britain and the United States undermined the educational work done by missionaries and, in some regions, liquor was used as currency). Smith was sharply criticized by fellow missionaries for spending too much time with Liberian Black settlers from America, while ignoring the native Liberians. She continued to struggle with chronic respiratory problems and arthritis and came down with malaria. Smith persevered. Drawing from deep reserves of emotional strength, she participated in the opening of 16 mission stations, all of them for the indigenous people of Liberia.

Smith returned to America in 1889, worn out by travel. Her colleagues considered her "well advanced on the down-hill side of life." Friends expected her to retire from public life. However, Smith was not finished.

The last chapter of Smith's life was devoted to building an orphanage for Black children in Harvey, Illinois. Harvey was a planned temperance community 20 miles south of Chicago, and became the home base for progressive movements, including the Equal Suffrage Association and the WCTU. It was an ideal place for Smith to set up an orphanage.

Smith devoted 4 years to travel and fund appeals on behalf of the orphanage. In addition, she donated the proceeds from her autobiography to the fund development effort. On June 28, 1899, the orphanage opened debt free with an endowment of $300. Despite her best efforts, the home continued to struggle financially. Smith spent most of her time on the road, continuing her speaking at temperance meetings and raising money for the orphanage. As she put it, "I almost stagger under the great load."

By 1910, the institution had grown to 30 children and was supported by donations from individuals and by a newspaper, *The Helper*, published by Smith. Although she had assembled an impressive Trustee Board and competent staff, the home continued to have financial problems. Bouts of arthritis, respiratory problems, and the daily pressures of overseeing the home eventually took their toll. On November 15, 1912, her failing health forced her to retire. At the age of 76, Smith moved to Sebring, Florida. In January 1915, she suffered a stroke and died on February 25, 1915, of a cerebral thrombosis (Smith, 1893; Israel, 1998).

Lessons

Smith is an exemplar of Emotional Maturity, providing a clear and compelling demonstration of this virtue configuration in action. We learn three lessons.

First, faith and hope found in Emotional Maturity are the source of resilience. A clear and compelling purpose—a larger transcendent story—provides the emotional scripting to properly interpret and constructively respond to adverse and even tragic circumstances. Resilient people are able to cope with negative emotions, but without the dulling effect of coping by denial. Prompted by a "redemptive sequence script," they are infused with the will to endure adversity, and supplied the emotional resources to bounce back. Less resilient people typically lack such a script. When faced with failure or adversity, they become easily upset and emotionally overwhelmed, and focus their limited and diminishing emotional energy on devising and implementing coping strategies that shield a fragile and vulnerable self from painful realities. They become self-absorbed and withdraw into a protective shell to shield themselves from adversity. They live a small and defensive life, with little or no capacity for meeting difficult challenges (Baumeister, 1991; Coutu, 2002; McAdams, 1993, 2001; McAdams et al., 1997).

Smith demonstrated remarkable resilience in the face of overwhelming adversity, bouncing back, time and again, from crushing disappointments. Where others might understandably find good reason to quit, she found sufficient reason to persevere, fueled by faith – her profound sense of larger, transcendent purpose. This purpose connected the particulars of her daily life, including adversity, to a larger, coherent story line, with plot, movement, and a substantially satisfying ending. Her purpose shed positive light on the negative events of her present, providing the framework to constructively interpret her suffering, as well as the emotional resources to transcend adversity. Smith was robust, the term coming from the Latin meaning "oaken," "hard," and "strong." She exhibited what Bennis and Thomas (2002) call "adaptive capacity."

Second, as the saying goes, "Life is 10 percent what happens to you, and 90 percent how you respond." Smith made full use of the 90 percent. She manifested emotional hardiness, which is "a constellation of personality characteristics that function as a resistance resource in the encounter with stressful life events" (Kobasa et al., 1982, p. 169). Her life is reminder that emotional strength comes not from "without" in the form of positive circumstances, but from "within" in the form of one's emotional resources. Smith suffered greatly but never gave in to despair or became a prisoner of the moment. Although she was not in a position to vanquish the external enemies of racism or sexism and could not change her difficult personal circumstances, she possessed the emotional strength to rise above adversity and personal tragedy and leave her mark on four continents, touching the lives of tens of thousands of people. Psychiatrist Victor Frankl (1959) spoke of this attitude after being imprisoned in a Nazi concentration camp in World War II. "Everything can be taken from a man but one thing: the last of the human freedoms—to chose one's attitude in any given set of circumstances, to choose one's own way" (p. 89).

The distinction between Emotional Maturity and emotional wellbeing is helpful in understanding Smith's power to cope with adversity. On numerous occasions, Smith was temporarily overcome by adversity. Her emotional wellbeing was undoubtedly low at these times. However, she possessed sufficient Emotional Maturity to deal with these setbacks, and regain a positive and constructive stance toward life.

Third, Emotionally Mature people take responsibility for their own words and actions, and let others do the same. Smith manifested extraordinary levels of self-control, refusing to lash out against her critics. Secure in her convictions, she was not easily intimidated by criticism. She refused to take the easy way out and capitulate to the demands of others.

Desirability for Leading in the New Normal

Although the personal and public challenges faced by Smith are unique to her time and place, leading in the twenty-first century calls for the exercise of the same faith, hope, and temperance. Specifically, Emotional Maturity is the driver of the New Normal next practice, "staying solid."

The New Normal operating environment is harsh to the extreme, featuring a steady dose of disappointment, failure, and unpleasant realities. The internal life of the organization offers no respite from these external forces as organizations often reflect and, at times, magnify the turbulence of the New Normal, serving as incubators of anxiety, confusion, cynicism, conflict, and mistrust.

This confronts Leaders and member-leaders with a daunting set of expectations. Organizations expect their Leaders (and member-leaders) to be a stable and positive presence in the face of stress and change; to thrive in adversity, to find new and adaptive courses of action, usually in the face of problems, difficulty, and dilemmas; to exercise sensitivity to the needs of others; to stay realistically hopeful amid difficult situations; to sustain hope and infuse the organization with positive energy, even as others grow weary and lose heart. In other words, organizations expect Leaders (and member-leaders) to exhibit Emotional Maturity, to "stay solid" rather than succumb to emotional reactivity, and to help others do the same.

Each component of Emotional Maturity contributes to the next practice of staying solid.

Emotional Recognition and Regulation

It is imperative for Leaders and member-leaders to recognize negative emotions when they occur, appreciate how these feelings impact their leadership, and manage the negative feelings instead of being overwhelmed by them. This strength enables them to remain calm in stressful situations and weather adversity without being swept away by emotional reactivity, and to manage mood swings that might rob them of sound judgment. Frederic Oudea, Societe Generale's chairman and CEO reflects on how effective twenty-first-century Leaders respond in times of crisis. "Here the key was, first, at a personal level, to remain calm, manage your stress, and avoid creating useless turbulence by establishing a solid process to help the team and organization themselves to make the right decisions at the right time" (Oudea and Kirkland, 2013).

Emotional Resilience

Emotional resilience is the "motivational force within everyone that drives them to grow through adversity and disruption"—an average day in the New Normal (Richardson, 2002, p. 307). It is imperative that Leaders and member-leaders recover their emotional vitality and optimism in the face of stress and adversity, that they bounce back from difficulty and setbacks with sufficient emotional reserves left over to stay the course and help others do the same. Noting the catastrophic events of this century—9/11, Katrina, the problems in the Fukushima Nuclear reactors following the tsunami in Japan, and the failures of financial institutions in the fall of 2008—Michael Useem, a professor at Wharton, observes, "The leadership qualities of standing strong, coming back from adversity, being focused on a better place ahead even if it looks terrible now all those features or those facets we tend to sum up on the world 'resilience.' These are the vital elements of the last couple years for anybody with responsibility for just about any thing in the private sector" (Javetski, 2012).

Resilient people practice what Maddi (2002, 2005) calls "transformational coping." Transformational coping is focused on cultivating a learning response versus a controlling response to stress, adversity, and failure—daily occurrences in the New Normal. Resilient people—Maddi calls them "stress hardy"—are not primarily concerned with controlling life so as to avoid negative outcomes. People who need to control things tend to see failure as disaster. Maddi counsels that, if we seek to control life and avoid stress, we will reduce our life to the size of postage stamp. In contrast, emotionally resilient people view adversity in a broader context as an occasion for learning. Setbacks are life lessons designed to teach us how to do better next time. Consequently, emotionally hardy people do not put much effort into avoiding stressful circumstances. Rather, they see adversity, and even failure, as a prompt to deep learning—an asset in the New Normal operating environment.

Emotional Realism

Emotionally mature people are capable of assimilating heavy doses of the reality—daily fare in the New Normal. They anchor their attitudes and actions in the real world—one marked by unpleasant facts, distressing problems, and unsolvable dilemmas. They neither deny negative circumstances or feelings, nor do they allow their feelings, whether negative or positive, to cloud their judgment and distort their picture of reality.

Bar-On (2002) calls the ability to stay anchored to the real world "reality testing." People with realism make a conscious attempt to authenticate the accuracy of their feelings and insights. They seek verification for what is happening in the social and circumstantial realm. They search for objective evidence to confirm or disprove their assumptions and perceptions. Realistic people see and accept the reality of a difficult situation, reframe the situation, and put the negatives in the best light, taking active steps to do whatever they can do. Those who lack realism are prone to maladaptive coping mechanisms such as substance abuse, denial, and disengagement or distancing oneself from problems. Consequently, they render themselves incapable of constructively responding to stress and adversity (Scheier and Carver, 1992).

Emotional Responsibility

Taking responsibility for outcomes is especially important in the New Normal, where Leaders report an ever widening "performance gap"—the difference between what the organization expects of them and what they have in their power to deliver by way of demonstrable progress. If not handled properly, the performance gap may create a cycle of blame, with Leaders on the receiving end. McNamee (2004) observes, "Like so many other areas of the New Normal, your ability to succeed is inextricably linked with your willingness to assume personal responsibility" (p. 40). Knowing it is impossible to blame others and, at the same time, improve one's performance, emotionally mature leaders take personal responsibility for their judgments and the outcomes of their decisions, and embrace constructive feedback.

Emotional Resonance

Emotionally mature people respect the power of negative emotions—daily fare in the New Normal—to distract, diminish, and, at times, debilitate others. When he was in jail, Nelson Mandela and his fellow prisoners were allowed to watch documentary movies. His favorites featured the great naval battles of World War II. One film showed newsreel footage on the sinking of the British battleship H. M. S. Prince of Wales by the Japanese. The Prince of Wales and her crew had played host to a historic meeting between Winston Churchill and Franklin Roosevelt in the early days of World War II, and Churchill personally knew many of the officers and crewmen. The newsreel showed a brief image of Churchill weeping after he had heard the news of the loss of the ship and most of her crew. Mandela (1994) reflected, "The image stayed in my memory a long time, and demonstrated to me that there are times when a leader can show sorrow in public, and that it will not diminish him in the eyes of his people" (p. 501).

Emotionally mature people are sympathetic, knowing firsthand what it means to confront despair and discouragement. They listen in a manner that communicates to others that they are "for" them and "with" them in the realities of their experience, struggles, and disappointment. This caring and supportive environment is a competitive advantage in difficult and uncertain times.

Summary

The faith, hope, and temperance that fuel Emotional Maturity are at a premium in the twenty-first century. "In an age when crisis is the new normal, global organizations need leaders who are able to act quickly and calmly amid chaos" (Barton et al., 2012). Emotional Maturity is a fundamental necessity when the journey is difficult and disappointing; when it is easy to grow weary and lose heart; and when those leading must deal with their own distress and disappointment and have enough positive energy left over to address the needs of others.

CHAPTER 13

Collaborative Quotient

Introduction

In the New Normal, no Leader—no matter how talented—can go it alone. The strength of many, not just a few, is required to secure the welfare and progress of the organization. This requires a high level of collaborative capability. A collaborative approach to leadership does not mean Leaders abstain from exercising their technical–managerial competence and charisma. Rather, it means they employ what charisma and competence they possess as a catalyst to release the collective strength of the organization—the diverse talent and unique perspective of many.

Defined

To collaborate is to "co-labor" and, therefore, to work in an interdependent fashion to achieve common ends. Collaborative Quotient (CQ) is the capacity to do so. CQ is a "composite virtue," the integrated expression of the DICE configuration of virtue, with each virtue serving to strengthen the individual to co-labor with a variety of people in a variety of situations. In the language of the 4R Model, CQ is what you get when Dynamic Determination, Intellectual Flexibility, Courageous Character, and Emotional Maturity operate in sync and synergy, deepening one's capacity to forge relationships of high trust and mutual respect in the pursuit of valued ends.

Collaborative Quotient is not a workshop skill, although there are technical–managerial competencies that must be learned (negotiation skills and active listening). Rather, it is the expression of virtue-driven leadership. CQ is an honest and humble strength in that it embraces the reality that no one person—no matter how talented—can go it alone. It is a generous strength that does not control, dominate, or repel others, but rather, invites others who are also strong to the leadership mix. It is a just strength that calls for the equitable distribution of leadership prerogatives, based not on self-interest or formal position, but on the capacity of others to contribute to the welfare and progress of the organization.

What It Is Not

Collaborative Quotient is not about networking or building alliances, although these are important skills.

Dimensions

The dimensions of CQ are the components of the DICE configuration—Dynamic Determination, Intellectual Flexibility, Courageous Character, and Emotional Maturity. As such, CQ draws from the full range of virtue that contributes to each DICE component.

Dynamic Determination provides clarity around purpose and, thus, the context for collaboration. Intellectual Flexibility expands one's collaborative range, as it wisely seeks the input and perspective of others. Collaboration is an exercise in trust and, thus, works only when grounded in Courageous Character. Emotionally Mature individuals embrace the contribution of others, as they do not need to put others down to lift themselves up.

Described

Malcolm Forbes noted, "People who matter are most aware that everyone else does, too." People with high CQ are strong leaders in their own right, but keenly aware that others may be also. They are assertive—they know who they are and what they want—but inclusive, honoring the perspective and talent of others who also know who they are and what they want. With this in mind, they initiate and sustain constructive relationships with a wide variety of mature adults in a wide range of settings.

Demonstrated

From 1990 to 1994, two political adversaries, Nelson Mandela and F. W. de Klerk, forged a political coalition that dismantled the Apartheid system of government in South African, replacing it with universal suffrage, democratic institutions, and, eventually, Black majority rule. Their partnership is a study in how two radically different men with divergent personal and political histories achieved fundamental change that most thought necessary, but few believed possible (Glad and Blanton, 1997).

De Klerk was an elite Afrikaner—descendents of Dutch settlers—and a leader in the ruling White National Party (NP). From 1984 to 1989, as the Education Minister, de Klerk presided over the segregation of the public school system. Like his father, Mandela was groomed to be a counselor to the King of Thembu. Instead, he lived the majority of his adult life, ages 44 to 71, as a political prisoner.

The NP made Apartheid the law of the land in South African in 1948. Apartheid called for "separation of services" such as separate drinking fountains and restrooms, but also included laws prohibiting Blacks from participating in higher education and forced Blacks to live in regions called "homelands." Apartheid and its racist, cultural mandate was deeply embedded in every aspect of South African life, with the ruling NP, as well as some Blacks (Inkatha) loyal to the NP, deeply invested in its perpetuation (Glad and Blanton, 1997; Sampson, 2000; Mandela, 1994).

Mandela and de Klerk faced an overwhelmingly complex task fraught with personal and political risk. Their shared objective was nothing short of transforming an entire society without destroying it—or themselves—in the process. Both men had to persuade radical and violent elements in their own camp that the change process must happen in a peaceful and orderly manner. Each had to maintain his political influence and moral authority within his respective political organization while moving forward to embrace radical reforms that diverged from the vested interests of many in his party.

Mandela's challenge was to persuade Blacks they should remain patient with the pace and product of his negotiations with de Klerk—always slower and less than what they had good reason to believe they deserved. Mandela was well aware it made no sense to destroy the country in the process of freeing it. If Whites fled in the face of Black majority rule, it would devastate the nation. He knew he must find the "middle ground between White fears and Black hope" (Mandela, 1994, p. 568).

De Klerk faced the contentious and uphill task of persuading the minority White population that giving up privileged status was in their self-interest. Similar to Mandela, he served constituencies that regarded negotiations as a sign of weakness and betrayal of their political principles. Along with Mandela, he embraced a higher principle when driving the negotiations—neither side could win by force of arms without intolerable loss of life.

In 1987 and 1988, South Africa was in upheaval. Violence was pervasive as the ANC mounted a military struggle to oppose White rule, and the government responded with tanks and riot police. On July 5, 1989, Mandela met with President P. W. Botha (De Klerk's predecessor) for a "courtesy call." Although the meeting was not a breakthrough in negotiations, the NP had, in Mandela's words, "crossed the Rubicon."

A month later, Botha resigned as president. De Klerk, elected NP leader in February 1989, assumed control of the government. He immediately called for a new constitution that included concessions to non-Whites, ordered the release of political prisoners, and allowed the ANC to hold a massive rally. He began to systematically dismantle the legal building blocks of Apartheid, beginning with the repeal of the Reservation of Separate Amenities Act of 1953 that called for segregated parks, buses, libraries, restrooms, and other public facilities.

On December 13, 1989, de Klerk and Mandela met to discuss the possibility of power sharing—a radical move by de Klerk that earned him sharp criticism from NP members. On February 2, 1990, in the traditional opening speech before Parliament, de Klerk announced his plans to dismantle Apartheid that included lifting the ban on the ANC and previously illegal political opposition groups, and mandated the immediate release of Mandela from prison. De Klerk's speech ended with these words:

> History has placed a tremendous responsibility on the shoulders of this country's leadership, namely the responsibility of moving the country away from the current course of conflict and confrontation . . . The hopes of millions of South Africans is fixed on us. The future of Africa depends on us. We dare not waver or fail.

Archbishop Desmond Tutu declared that the speech "took his breath away." "It's incredible," said Tutu. "Give him credit. Give him credit. I do."

On February 9, 1990, Mandela was released. The same day, 50,000 people came to Cape Town to hear him speak. Mandela (1994) told the crowd he was not the messiah, but an "ordinary man who had become a leader because of extraordinary circumstances" (p. 566).

De Klerk capitalized on the momentum to drive legislative change. In April 1990, government and ANC officials met to discuss the guidelines for the negotiating process that would lead to a transitional government and new constitution. As the negotiations moved forward, events threatened to halt the process. On May 26, 1990, approximately 60,000 White protesters rallied against de Klerk's reforms. The next month, 11 Whites were arrested in a plot to assassinate Mandela and de Klerk in the hopes of prompting an overthrow of de Klerk's government and stopping the reform process.

On December 20, 1991, the 18 months of preliminary talks came to a close, and substantive negotiations began. Called CODESA—the Convention for a Democratic South Africa—the talks focused on free and universal elections, a new constitution, a constituent assembly and a transitional government. The talks started hopefully. A representative for the NP apologized for Apartheid. De Klerk spoke of the need for a transitional government. In addition, Mandela noted that progress in South Africa "had at last become irreversible."

On May 15, 1992, after a 4-month interval, negotiations started again. Known as CODESA 2, the talks focused on the nature and composition of a transition government, an interim constitution, general elections, and a new legislature. However, the parties had great difficulty coming to terms on a timetable, the nature of the transition government, and the composition of the new legislature. In Mandela's opinion, "the prospects for agreement looked bleak. What we disagreed about was threatening all that we had agreed upon" (Mandela, p. 602).

Again, events intruded on the process, placing the negotiations in further jeopardy. The ANC planned "rolling mass action" to demonstrate that Blacks would not wait indefinitely for reform. The mass action consisted of strikes, demonstrations, and boycotts that would culminate in a 2-day national strike. Before the national strike, Inkatha–ANC violence erupted. De Klerk's government was charged with incompetence and complicity in the Black on Black violence. According to Mandela (1994) "I found this to be the last straw, and my patience snapped. The government was blocking the negotiations and at the same time waging a covert war against our people. Why then were we continuing to talk with them?" (pp. 603–604).

Mandela instructed the ANC to suspend talks with the government. Many wanted to take up arms, but Mandela asked them to focus their negative emotions on the mass actions in the next months, and to refrain from violence. De Klerk asked for a face-to-face meeting with Mandela that Mandela denied, saying, "I felt such a meeting would suggest that we had something to talk about, and at the time we did not" (Mandela, p. 604).

On August 3 and 4, 1992, four million workers stayed home. This mass action, as well as continued violence, prompted de Klerk and Mandela to return to the negotiating table. On September 26, 1992, they met for an official summit that produced the *Record of Understanding*—a document that laid the groundwork for the negotiations that followed. The government agreed to accept a single, elected constitutional assembly that would adopt a new constitution and serve as a transitional legislature for the new government.

In February 1993, the government and ANC announced their agreement around a 5-year transitional government of national unity, a multiparty cabinet, and the creation of a transitional executive council. The country remained fragile, and sporadic violence continued. Nevertheless, negotiations moved forward and peaceful change prevailed. As Mandela (1994) reflected, "We were truly on the threshold of a new era" (p. 611).

National elections were set for April 1994. In a televised debate, Mandela was harsh in his criticism of the NP. However, Mandela ended with these words. "The exchanges between Mr. de Klerk and me should not obscure one important fact. I think we are a shining example to the entire world of people drawn from different racial groups who have a common loyalty, a common love, to their common country..." Mandela looked directly at de Klerk and said, "We are going to face the problem of this country together." Mandela reached over to take his hand and said, "I am proud to hold your hand for us to go forward" (Mandela, 1994, p. 617).

The elections led to the reversal of the formal leadership roles of Mandela and De Klerk. The ANC polled 62 percent of the vote and won 252 of the 400 seats in the National Assembly. Mandela was chosen the first Black president of South Africa, and de Klerk became Deputy President of the coalition government, and the leader of the main opposition party, his NP.

Mandela won the 1993 Nobel Peace Prize jointly with de Klerk. Mandela used his acceptance speech to cast a vision for the future of a just and equitable South Africa, and to pay tribute to de Klerk:

> He had the courage to admit that a terrible wrong had been done to our country and people through the imposition of the system of Apartheid. He had the foresight to understand and accept that all the people of South Africa, through negotiations and as equal participants in the process, together determine what they want to make of their future.

In Mandela (1994) words, "To make peace with an enemy one must work with that enemy, and that enemy becomes one's partner" (p. 612).

Lessons

The unlikely partnership of Mandela and de Klerk is a shining example of CQ, providing a clear and compelling demonstration of this virtue configuration in action. We learn five lessons.

First, the virtue configuration found in Dynamic Determination is fundamental to successful collaboration. Mandela viewed himself as an actor in a coherent narrative rich in moral reference points that provided him a script for daily living. As he stood convicted of high treason as a young man, Mandela (1994) summed up his life-mission.

> During my lifetime I have dedicated myself to this struggle of the African people. I have fought against White domination, and I have fought against black domination. I have cherished the ideal of a democratic and free society in which all persons live together in harmony and with equal opportunities. It is an ideal which I hope to live for and to achieve. But if needs be, it is an ideal for which I am prepared to die. (p. 322)

Mandela saw himself as a participant in a larger historic story that called upon him to serve others in a noble cause. His daily prison activities, whether crushing rocks or sewing, were part of a larger quest for human dignity. When Mandela was freed, he picked up where he had left off, describing his life mission as one "to liberate the oppressed and the oppressor both" (Mandela, 1994, p. 624).

Along with Wilberforce, Mandela and de Klerk were "entrepreneurs of life." They assumed responsibility for a creative task, not as an assigned role, but as a venture of faith. They stayed the course, as their shared purpose kept them returning to the negotiation table in spite of setbacks and differences.

Second, the virtue configuration found in Intellectual Flexibility is fundamental to successful collaboration. Mandela and de Klerk were unusually perceptive men with the mental flexibility to thrive in a historically unprecedented, ill-defined, novel, and complex social and political environment. Each possessed deep insight into the underlying systemic patterns that shaped the culture and politics of South Africa. Each understood the salient issues of the day, and possessed a keen sense of the dynamic and shifting political and social landscape that shaped their partnership, as well as the problems and pitfalls inherent in bringing their shared vision to fruition.

Third, the virtue configuration found in Courageous Character is fundamental to successful collaboration. It is unfair to compare the conditions under which De Klerk's character was forged with those of Mandela. Mandela's character was hard-earned in unusually severe conditions during his 27-year imprisonment. Mandela (1994) reflected, "Prison was a kind of crucible that tested a man's character. Some men, under the pressure of incarceration, showed true mettle, while others revealed themselves as less than what they had appeared to be" (p. 455).

Although less extreme, De Klerk's character was forged in a political struggle with his own NP leadership. De Klerk demonstrated moral courage as he broke with many in his party in negotiating with the ANC and, ultimately, by relinquishing the political power of the NP. Mandela displayed moral courage as well as physical couarage as he battled the Apartheid system, and simultaneously dealt with criticism from those in his own ANC party, who publicly questioned his commitment to the Black cause.

The partnership between Mandela and de Klerk depended on the moral integrity, trustworthiness and courage of both men. Each risked his reputation and put his life on the line, literally, to make the partnership work. Each took on the critics in his own political party, kept promises that angered many in their power base, and led the country to a place where many, both Blacks and Whites, did not want to go.

Furthermore, each man entrusted his political destiny to the personal and public integrity of the other. Mandela relied on the integrity of de Klerk to sustain his political credibility with the ANC. If de Klerk failed to keep his promises, Mandela would lose his standing with his political base as a trusted negotiator. The same applied to de Klerk. By the end of the negotiation process, even White South Africans came to trust Mandela, and de Klerk's Black critics came to respect his commitment to turn over power in a peaceful and orderly way.

Fourth, the virtue configuration found in Emotional Maturity is fundamental to successful collaboration. The negotiation process— emotionally draining and marked by episodes of anger and disappointment—called on each man to exercise self-control. Both managed their anger and disappointment and kept a relatively even keel. Neither succumbed to despair or prolonged bouts of resentment. Both men remained cordial, refusing to allow their political differences to degenerate into vindictive, personal battles.

	Faith	Hope	Love	Wisdom	Justice	Courage	Temperance
Dynamic Determination	X	X		X		X	
Intellectual Flexibility				X			
Courageous Character			X			X	
Emotional Maturity	X	X					X
Collaborative Quotient	X	X	X	X	X	X	X

Figure 13.1 DICE + 1 & virtue.

When their tempers flared, they did not let their emotions cloud their vision for a better South Africa or derail the negotiation process. Mandela learned to control his fiery temper and adopted, instead, a more rational and calculated approach to dealing with apartheid. In an incredible act of self-control and personal civility, on the day of his release from Robben Island prison, Mandela delayed his freedom for one final hour to have a last meal with his jailers.

Fifth, the full range of virtue is fundamental to successful collaboration (see Figure 13.1). Each man demonstrated a rare mix of hope and realism, self-sacrifice, and generosity. Each combined the head of a cool realist with the heart of a man passionately engaged on a mission of historic consequence. Each was cooperative without being compliant. Each passionately defended his convictions. However, each recognized that the other was equally convinced with respect to his political agenda that often conflicted with theirs. Although neither man was "conflict avoidant," neither sought confrontation. Neither man sought to dominate the other, nor allowed the other to dominate him. Each was assertive without being ascendant, full of aspiration for South Africa, but not ambitious for personal gain.

Perhaps most impressive, each man exercised the temperance and self-control required to deal constructively with issues of power and self-interest. It would have been understandable if de Klerk had held on to political power and refused a partnership with Mandela, knowing that a successful partnership meant relinquishing political power. It would have been understandable if Mandela had chosen retribution over partnership, knowing that a successful partnership meant political reconciliation. However, both chose, instead, to submit self-interest to the higher end of seeking the welfare of South Africa.

Each withstood the temptation to act out of their deepest fears, strongest desires, or most pressing needs. American moral philosopher Harry Frankfurt (1998) calls such individuals "wantons"—an unrestrained and undisciplined person, given to act in accord with the impulse of the moment, with no view to the consequences for themselves or others. Overwhelmed by emotional need and the temptations of power, the wanton is rendered powerless to act with prudence, justice, and courage.

Heifetz and Linsky (2002) note, "We all have hungers, expressions of our normal human needs. But sometimes those hungers disrupt our capacity to act wisely or purposefully... these hungers may be so strong that they render us constantly vulnerable" (p. 71). Daniel Vasella, CEO of Swiss drug company Novartis, notes:

> ... You have to able to resist seduction. If I look at all the reasons leaders fall, it usually the soft factors. I talk to my team about seductions that come with taking on a leadership role. There are many forms: Sexual seduction, money, praise. You need to be aware of how you can be seduced in order to be able to resist and keep your integrity. (Kirkland, 2012b)

Each man kept his integrity intact. Neither was seduced by power. Neither man gave himself over to emotional reactivity. Neither succumbed to the temptation to choose security and self-interest over the welfare of the nation.

Summary

The DICE configuration of virtue is a helpful framework for evaluating the chances for success in any collaborative endeavor. We want to forge partnerships with those who share our sense of larger purpose and who are capable of staying the course to accomplish valued ends (Dynamic Determination). We want them to be humble, wise and able to see our point of view (Intellectual Flexibility). We want them to be trustworthy, able to do the right thing for others even when it is not the easy thing for them (Courageous Character). We want partners who take responsibility for their emotional life and connect with us (Emotional Maturity). However, who among us wants to engage in a partnership of any kind with a person motivated primarily by self-interest, who quits at the first sign of trouble; a rigid know-it-all, incapable of seeing life from the perspective of others; someone who cannot be trusted; someone who flies off the handle and blames others? In other words, an effective partnership of any kind works only when both parties operate from a sufficient fund of DICE.

Desirability for Leading in the New Normal

Although the moral and global context of their partnership is unique, the twenty-first-century operating environment places enormous value on the kind of productive partnership modeled by Mandela and de Klerk. The most gifted Leader accomplishes nothing of enduring value alone. Collaborative partnerships must be forged that access the unique perspective and diverse talent of others. Each is valuable. No one is sufficient. All are required for the enduring success of the organization.

Collaborative Quotient is an indispensible New Normal asset. Collaboration is not just a wise assessment of one's strengths and limitations. It is not merely a pragmatic accommodation to the need of the moment. Rather, it is fundamentally necessary for survival in the richly networked, highly interdependent New Normal landscape. No Leader stands alone or functions in isolation. They are embedded in an interdependent social network where nothing of immediate importance or lasting significance gets done through the efforts of one or a few. As Ibarra and Hansen (2011) note, "Facebook, Twitter, LinkedIn, video-conferencing, and a host of other technologies have put connectivity on steroids and enabled new forms of collaboration that would have been impossible a short while ago. Many executives realize that they need a new playbook for this hyperconnected environment" (p. 70).

Furthermore, collaborative organizations possess a competitive advantage in the New Normal operating environment. If you have one, it is unlikely a competitor will go out and duplicate it. Ibarra and Hansen (2011) note:

> Research has consistently shown that diverse teams produce better results, provided they are well led. The ability to bring together people from different backgrounds, disciplines, cultures, and generations and leverage all they have to offer, therefore, is a must-have for leaders. (p. 71)

Collaborative engagement is a fundamental necessity in tackling large and complex endeavors, where no individual—no matter his or her level of talent or formal authority—is adequate to get the job done, on an average day in the New Normal.

Summary

The most valuable leadership asset in the New Normal is not charisma or competence, but rather, CQ—the capacity to spin a web of partnerships characterized by shared purpose and mutual trust. A high CQ is not what some effective New Normal Leaders or member-leaders might display some of the time. Rather, it is what every effective Leader and member-leader must display all of the time. CQ is THE trait of leadership consequence. It is the perennial success factor, the *sine qua non* of sustained leadership effectiveness.

SECTION IV

The 4R Model: Roles

The twenty-first-century leadership challenge is to create and sustain organizations fit for the future—organizations that not only survive but thrive in an inhospitable environment, the kind of organization deserving of the loyalty of customers and the commitment, even the sacrifice of members. New Normal Leaders and member-leaders serve as cultural architects, designing and building "New Normal-friendly organizations." This section explores five leadership Roles that help shape an organization fit for the twenty-first century.

CHAPTER 14

The Direction Setter Role

New Normal organizations need a keen sense of strategic clarity around some basic questions: What difference must we make in the world? Do we know and practice what is core and non-negotiable? Is there a seamless connection between what we promise to the world, and how we conduct our day-to-day organizational life? The Direction Setter Role addresses these critical questions (see Figure 14.1).

The Mandate and Simple Rule

The mandate of the Direction Setter Role is for Leaders to collaborate with member-leaders to accomplish the following: (1) Identify and/or clarify the directional imperatives of the organization—its purpose, mission, and core values and (2) Foster a cultural climate of strategic clarity and missional integrity, such that the organization lives in daily accord with its directional imperatives and keeps its promises to the world.

The Direction Setter Role is the foundation and focal point of the culture-shaping process. It is the first Role among equals, the master script for the Learner, Ambassador, and Coach Roles. The Direction Setter focuses the organization's attention on integrating its directional imperatives with the vital concerns of each of the other Roles. It explicitly names those the organization must benefit (Ambassador). It provides the framework and criterion for developing the next generation of leaders (Coach). In addition, it serves as a framework for identifying its learning agenda (Learner).

The mandate of the Direction Setter Role is to foster an organizational culture of strategic clarity and missional integrity. This work seeks to embed one simple rule into the fabric of daily, organizational

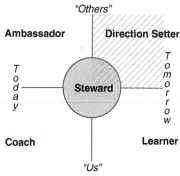

Figure 14.1 Direction Setter Role.

life: we exist to keep our promises to the world. This means every aspect of organization life—how the organization connects with others (Ambassador Role), what it is learning (Learner Role), and how it selects and develops leaders (Coach Role)—is in accord with its mission.

What It Is Not

The Direction Setter Role is not about setting big goals, "wordsmithing" tag lines or mottos, or showcasing a Leader's charisma and vision in pursuit of self-serving, grandiose agendas.

The Script

Each Role calls for Leaders and member leaders to follow a script—a written set of instructions that serve as behavioral prompts to engage in the formidable task of building a New Normal-friendly organization. Toward the end of shaping a culture of strategic clarity and missional integrity, the Direction Setter focuses the attention and resources of the organization on three script lines, which serve as points of culture-shaping leverage.

Script Line #1: Suit Up and Collaborate

Direction Setters suit up by way of "putting on" the DICE + 1 configuration (Collaboration Quotient) that is required to collaborate effectively in the culture-shaping process. Identifying directional imperatives is difficult, collaborative work. It does not come from the pronouncement of one or a few Leaders. It requires more than the technical expertise and careful calculations of strategic planning specialists. Rather, it demands the best effort of the entire organization from the grassroots up.

Script Line #2: Champion the Role

Direction Setters serve as champions of directional clarity and organizational integrity. Direction Setters invite the organization to join in the process of clarifying and living out its purpose, mission, and values in concrete ways in every aspect of organizational life. If the organization is to stay effective in fulfilling its promises to the world and expanding the scope of its influence, it is imperative that all members are clear about its strategic intent, and work daily to support it and communicate it. Although the proverbial buck stops with Leaders for initiating and sustaining the process to insure strategic clarity and organizational integrity, the day-to-day work of insuring a close connection between the directional imperatives of the organization and its everyday life must be distributed throughout the organization. From the "grass roots" to established Leaders, almost everyone is a champion for "inhabiting our values and keeping our promises to the world." This is, ultimately, a matter of collective integrity. If the organization is to live in accord with its directional imperatives, its Leaders and member-leaders must value and participate in this Role.

Script Line #3: Show Up, Pay Attention, and Ask Good Questions

Leaders and member-leaders show up in the Direction Setter Role, communicating through their investment of time and attention the importance of directional clarity and collective integrity. "Showing up" may look different from day to day—setting strategic direction for the organization, clarifying the mission to members, and evaluating the performance of the organization in light of its directional imperatives. This front-line experience gives Direction Setters an appreciation for every aspect of organizational life that contributes to shaping a culture of strategic clarity and collective integrity, and provides the framework for rigorous, in-depth, constructive conversations around the organization's performance in keeping its promises to the world.

Following the Script: Suit Up and Collaborate

The Direction Setter Role demands a sufficiently high level of CQ on the part of all who participate. Direction Setters draw from Dynamic

Determination to infuse the organization with faith in its larger purpose, hope to sustain its progress, and the courage to persevere in achieving valued ends in the face of difficulty. Drawing from Intellectual Flexibility, Direction Setters prompt the organization to see and seize opportunity, and make wise decisions on the investment of its resources. Drawing from Courageous Character, Direction Setters call the organization to do the right thing even if it is not the easy thing, in order to inhabit its values and keep its promises to the world.

Following the Script: Champion Strategic Clarity and Missional Integrity

Direction Setters deal in "directional imperatives"—the "identity-conferring commitments" that embody what the organization is, what it stands for, and aspires to be.

These consist of: (1) purpose, (2) mission, and (3) core values. The business and consulting literature uses a variety of definitions for these terms and, therefore, it is important to provide a clear definition for each.

Purpose

The Direction Setter clarifies the organization's purpose. Purpose is the North Star of the organization, its directional constant or "true North." Purpose does not specify a destination—you do not arrive at Polaris—but the star does provide a reliable compass setting. In organizational life, purpose sets the moral and strategic trajectory of the organization over the decades, its *telos* and *summum bonum* (highest good). Purpose is the organization's fundamental reason for existence, its *raison d'être*. Purpose speaks to the identity of the organization that transcends time and place and individual Leaders.

The identification of purpose gives voice to the heart and soul of the organization, its collective passion, driving center, and energizing core. It is the answer to the questions, "Why do we exist?" "What Big Thing are we living for?" "What is our Grand Aim, our Ultimate Concern?" In the language of virtue, purpose is an exercise in faith and hope. In the language of story, purpose is the narrative platform, the meta-narrative or master story that connects the particulars of daily organizational life with a larger, coherent story with plot and script, meaning and movement. This story tells the organization who it is, why it exists, and what important work it must do in the world.

Mission

The Direction Setter clarifies the mission of the organization. Mission can be defined as "a sending out to perform a special duty." The mission is a more specific statement of the organization's purpose—its special duty in light of its larger purpose. If the purpose defines what the organization is living for, the mission specifies what it is shooting for.

A mission statement typically answers two sets of questions: (1) What must we specifically do; and (2) For what specific group of people will we do it? In this, the mission statement is a promise to the world to do something of specific benefit for a designated group of "others."

Mission Is a Resounding "Yes"

The mission is a declaration of what the organization is uniquely qualified and passionately committed to offer to the world. It is an affirmation that the organization has competencies and resources that can meet the needs of others; it is a resounding "yes" to the world that it has something of unique and enduring value to offer.

Mission Is a Firm "No"

Embedded in the mission is also a negation, a firm "no" in response to many other "good things" that the organization might do. The mission specifies what vitally crucial things the organization will pay attention to, to the exclusion of other important matters; what it will invest its time, attention, and resources in to the exclusion of other pressing needs and important concerns that are best left to other organizations to address.

Core Values

The Direction Setter clarifies the core values of the organization. Core values are the principles or standards that determine what is right, worthwhile, or desirable. Core values are the passionate and enduring belief that particular patterns of attitude and action are not merely preferable, but essential.

Core values serve as the normative glue of the organization, guiding principles that powerfully shape its collective, daily behavior. Core values script the way power and prerogatives are distributed, how people are treated, and how important matters are decided and work gets done.

Core values are pervasive. Members embody these values regardless of the position they hold, the duties they perform, or the rewards they receive for doing them.

Core values are the moral metabolism of the organization, the collective habits of the heart, the deep-seated affections that shape the collective character of the organization. Core values provide the living, ethical criteria by which the organization makes important decisions on its investment of time, energy, and resources, discriminates between worthy and unworthy goals and outcomes, and evaluates the quality of its collective life and work in the world.

Core values tell the organization what is always important. They are sacred and inviolable, never negotiated or compromised. Core values are what the organization intentionally prizes and pursues, what all its members always do no matter what. They are "How we act and relate because of who we are," "What we do because it is right and therefore always worth doing." In this, core values are not a means to an end. Rather, inhabiting core values may, at times, place the organization at a competitive disadvantage.

Core values powerfully influence the collective behavior of the organization, scripting the way power and prerogatives are distributed, how people are treated, how important matters are discussed, and how decisions are made and work gets done. De Pree (1989) observes, "What we believe precedes policy and practice" (p. 26).

Following the Script: Show Up, Pay Attention, and Ask Good Questions

Direction Setters help shape a culture of strategic clarity and missional integrity by asking questions that matter. These questions are designed to prompt a candid, friendly, and constructive conversation around its performance in inhabiting its values and fulfilling its promises to the world.

Purpose

What are we living for? Why do we exist as an organization? What would the world lose if we ceased to exist? What puts a smile on our face, fire in our belly, and steel in our backbone?

Mission

What are we shooting for? What promises have we made—are we making—to the world? What will we do, specifically, for whom, specifically?

What benefit do we bring to whom? What distinctive competencies define our contribution to the world? What is it of unique and enduring value that we offer to the world? What, specifically, is our core, non-negotiable "service offering" or "value proposition?" What are we so deeply committed to that we will invest our time and energy, our sacrificial effort to make sure it happens, no matter what?

Core Values

What are we standing for? How do we relate and behave on our best days? What attitudes and behaviors are non-negotiable? What will we never compromise and, if need be, risk and sacrifice in honoring? How will we measure the quality of our collective journey? What is our shared criterion for decision-making?

When It Works: Toward a Culture of Strategic Clarity and Missional Integrity

When the Direction Setter Role is played well, the organization becomes increasingly typified by strategic clarity and deep integrity around its directional imperatives, and benefits in four ways.

First, the organization becomes increasingly "future-other oriented." Embracing the truth that the organization does not exist for itself, Leaders, member-leaders, and almost everyone is infused with a compelling sense of moral purpose and an ethos of service, a growing sense that the organization exists to benefit others and must keep its promises to them into the indefinite future.

Second, the directional imperatives provide a shared strategic focus and criterion for the investment of organizational resources. As the German proverb goes, "The main thing is to keep the main thing the main thing." A clear and shared set of directional imperatives helps the organization distinguish between vital necessity and the merely important, the few things that must be done from the many things that might be done. This has great practical benefit. Armed with a clear sense of its strategic priorities, the organization stands ready to make optimal use of its resources across all leadership roles. Clear priorities cut through confusion and lower competition for limited resources, as almost everyone knows what the organization must spend a significant percentage of its time, money, and energy on, and, correspondingly, what it should not invest in. In this sense, the Direction Setter Role informs the Coach, Learner, and Ambassador Roles (see Figure 14.2).

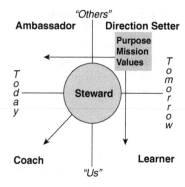

Figure 14.2 Missional integrity.

Third, the framework for widespread participation, ownership, and collaboration is provided. Nearly everyone knows the definition of "success," and is clear on what they must get very good at doing, and on whose behalf they must excel. The simple rule—we exist to keep our promises to the world—is widely embraced, prompting many with little or no formal power to act voluntarily, make tough decisions, take risks, handle threats, and seize opportunities, all without official permission, and, at times, even the knowledge of those with position power. Clear directional imperatives provide the framework for collaborative effort. Shared purpose, mission, core values, and simple rules get everyone on the same page, support a shared decision-making process, and provide a foundation for mutual trust. As a result, the combined talent and insights of many are unleashed to support the organization in keeping its promises to the world.

Fourth, a clear and shared set of directional imperatives releases passion and energy throughout the organization to give its collective best for the few, non-negotiable outcomes worthy of its sacrificial efforts. Fueled by a shared hope, no one quits when things get difficult or take longer than anticipated to accomplish. As French philosopher and Jesuit Priest Tielhard de Chardin (2004) put it, "A great hope held in common" is one of the most powerful forces on Earth (pp. 63–64).

A Word to Leaders

An organization's culture is fundamentally a reflection of the attitudes, behaviors, decisions, and relationships of its Leaders—for better or worse. Like a stone dropped in a still pond, Leaders set in motion a chain reaction of influence throughout the organization, promoting and prompting the attitudes and behaviors they embrace and exhibit, and providing no support for those they do not. They have no choice in the matter. Leaders "cannot not" shape culture. The only question is what kind of culture they will shape. As Direction Setters, Leaders play two critical functions in shaping a New Normal-friendly culture.

First, a Leader's attention is a precious commodity, perhaps the most valuable of organizational resources. What Leaders pay attention to sends the organization a powerful message as to what is central and what is peripheral, what is non-negotiable and what is optional, what must be invested in, and what can go lacking. Consequently, what commands a Leader's attention repeatedly, what he or she is consistently engaged in doing, is a matter of utmost importance. Leaders must decide what gets their attention from among many possible claimants. Bossidy et al. (2002) state, "An organization can execute only if the leader's heart and soul are immersed in the company" (p. 24).

Second, first hand information is the foundation of sound leadership judgment, and, by definition, this cannot be delegated. Toward this end, Leaders stay vitally engaged with the important details—the realities, problems, and opportunities associated with this Role. One way to do this is to ask the kind of questions that display reality and prompt a candid, friendly, and constructive conversation about matters vital to the performance of the organization.

Summary

Leaders and member-leaders serve as architects of organizational culture. The organization's purpose, core values, and mission are the building blocks. These directional imperatives keep the organization on a course to "true North," while providing a strategic framework for the investment of attention, talent, and resources and a criterion for decision-making. When the directional imperatives are clear, widely disseminated, and embraced, they promote widespread ownership, prompt collaboration, sustain momentum, and support the organization in its pursuit of its mission.

CHAPTER 15

The Ambassador Role

Introduction

The New Normal features a proliferation of choice in a fast-moving, hypercompetitive, and ethically demanding operating environment. This combination poses two significant challenges to any organization seeking to keep its promises to the world.

Information Overload

We live in a consumer-entertainment society bombarded by persuasive rhetoric. Buy this. Watch this. Wear this. Go here. We are exposed daily to thousands of such messages, putting us on perpetual high alert. Corporate advertising budgets are testimony to the fact that, in response to this information barrage, most adults have developed sophisticated defenses against being conned, persuaded, or otherwise moved to purchase products or services that do not serve their best interests.

Heightened Expectations

Everyone wants to be respected, treated fairly, and validated as a unique individual. There is nothing new here, but, in the New Normal, this basic human desire has risen to the level of a customer expectation and, correspondingly, to the level of a moral imperative for the organization intending to serve others. As Crawford and Mathews (2001) note, "Human values, not commercial value, have become the contemporary currency of commerce" (p. xx). The values around a transaction, whether a business transaction or the delivery of service from a non-profit organization, are now equally, if not more, important than the value of the product or service itself. Crawford and Mathews (2001) report, "There is a growing gap between the content of a business transaction (the

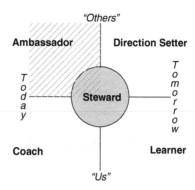

Figure 15.1 Ambassador Role.

value of a product or service) and the context (the values surrounding doing business)" (p. xix). In other words, savings on the dollar value of a product or service is no substitute for respecting the consumer. For instance, most consumers are less concerned with getting the lowest price and more concerned with getting an honest and fair price (Aaker & Joachimsthaler, 2000, pp. 14–16).

Consequently, virtually every interaction and communication between an organization and those it intends to benefit has embedded in it a question of trust: can the "customer" or "consumer"—the "others" the organization intends to serve—trust the organization to act in his or her best interests? Or will the organization act to protect its self-interest, if need be, at the expense of the customer? Organizations that earn the trust of others and keep it will enjoy a significant competitive advantage in the New Normal. Customers will reward the organization that understands them, honors their values, and treats them with fairness and dignity. Organizations that fail to earn trust put themselves at a competitive disadvantage in a moral operating environment where "Context has overtaken content as the primary driver of consumer value" (Crawford & Mathews, 2001 p. 17). The Ambassador plays a critical role in earning and keeping this trust (see Figure 15.1).

The Mandate and Simple Rule

The Direction Setter Role identifies the organization's directional imperatives, including its mission—what it promises to do for a specified group of people. The Ambassador Role delivers on this promise, linking the talent and assets of the organization to the work of bringing concrete benefit to others. If the Direction Setter Role is about identifying whom the organization intends to benefit and exactly how it will benefit them, the Ambassador Role is about shaping the kind of organization that keeps its promises and delivers this benefit day in and day out.

The mandate of the Ambassador Role is to foster an "other-friendly" cultural climate conducive to constructive, beneficial engagement with those identified in the Direction Setter Role. This work seeks to embed one simple rule into the fabric of daily, organizational life: "others matter"—what others think and want is of utmost importance to us; therefore, the entire organization leans in, listens, and learns from those it intends to benefit.

The scope of the Ambassador Role extends beyond those who buy a product or who are directly served by the organization. It includes all "stakeholders"—those with an interest in or who are impacted by any and all actions of the organization. This includes not only its products and services, but also how the products are made and the services distributed. In this sense, the Ambassador Role is concerned with projecting and protecting the reputation and brand of the organization.

What It Is Not

The Ambassador Role is not merely an exercise in public relations, marketing, or image management. It goes well beyond these functions.

The Script: An Overview

Each Role calls for Leaders and member leaders to follow a script—a written set of instructions that serve as behavioral prompts to engage in the formidable task of building a New Normal-friendly organization. The Direction Setter Role sets the script for the Ambassador Role in that it clarifies what the organization must do specifically, for whom specifically—who it must benefit and what it must deliver to them if the organization is live true to its identity and keep its promises. Toward the end of shaping an "other-friendly" culture, the Ambassador focuses the attention and resources of the organization on three script lines, which serve as points of culture-shaping leverage.

Script Line #1: Suit Up and Collaborate

Ambassadors suit up by way of "putting on" the DICE + 1 configuration (Collaboration Quotient, CQ), which is required to collaborate effectively in the culture shaping process. This Role demands more than the occasional effort of a few Leaders or the technical expertise of sales and marketing specialists. Rather, the day-to-day work must be distributed throughout the organization. From the "grass roots" to established Leaders, nearly everyone participates in some way, shape, or form in delivering on the organization's promise to the world.

Script Line #2: Champion the Role

Ambassadors champion engagement with "others"—customers, clients, constituents, anyone the organization intends to benefit—making it a top priority. If the organization is to keep its promises and project and protect its brand, it must get very, very good at staying close to customers. This is a matter of identifying customer "moments of truth"—the opportunity to gain firsthand insight into the quality of an organization's products, service, or people—and listening and learning from the experience of customers in these moments.

Script Line #3: Show Up, Pay Attention, and Ask Good Questions

Leaders and member-leaders show up in the Ambassador Role, communicating through their investment of time and attention that "others matter." Showing up, paying attention, and asking good questions may look different from day to day—meeting directly with customers to better understand their values and needs, identifying trends in the operating environment that impact delivering benefit to customers, regularly evaluating the organization's performance in serving customers, and projecting and protecting the brand. This front-line experience gives those participating in this Role an appreciation for every aspect of organizational life that contributes to developing an other-friendly culture, and provides the framework for rigorous, in-depth, constructive conversations around the organization's performance in bringing benefit to others.

Following the Script: Suit Up and Collaborate

The Ambassador Role demands a sufficiently high level of CQ on the part of all who participate. Block (1993) notes, "Customer service runs deeper than friendliness, listening skills and positive attitude" (p. 20). Beyond these qualities, those who play the Ambassador Role must draw from a generous fund of Courageous Character and Emotional Maturity.

Courageous Character

In the face of ever-escalating customer demands not only for service and quality, but also, more importantly, for trustworthy behavior, the Ambassador Role is, first and foremost, an exercise in courage and love. Trust is the essential lubricant for commerce—no customer will hand over money or consent to be served by an organization not worthy of trust. Customers are either a means to an end (financial profit, meeting internal goals, gaining market share) or served as the end itself—the very reason the organization exists. An organization can operate to serve customers—love them—or it can operate out of selfishness and indifference, using customers only as means to end. It does not take a customer long to recognize the difference and respond accordingly, either placing trust in the organization or rejecting its offerings.

The challenge, to paraphrase Block (1993), is to interact with customers in a manner that is good for the soul, good for the customer, and good for the sustainability of the organization. Aaker and Joachimsthaler (2000) note, "The soul of the brand resides in the soul of the organization" (p. 41). Organizations that focus on serving customers first, and their own internal goals and agendas second, have a decided advantage in the New Normal. Although it is a stretch to say that Google "loves" its customers, it has reaped the benefits of living out one of its top ten principles (Ten Things We Know to be True): "Focus on the user and all else will follow."

Emotional Maturity

It takes a sufficient fund of Emotional Maturity to play the Ambassador Role well. As the name implies, serving as an Ambassador is typically an "away game" played on an unfamiliar field, sometimes before hostile crowds. For instance, Leaders and member-leaders may be called upon to discuss a product recall with the press, answer questions for a skeptical zoning commission, or embrace feedback from a disgruntled customer.

Second, it takes a sufficient fund of Emotional Maturity to stay focused on meeting the needs of others rather than securing one's own comfort and convenience. Listening and learning from customers requires the capacity to absorb high doses of reality, often in the form of customer critiques, complaints, and disappointment. Consequently, those playing the Role must manage their own disappointment and frustration and maintain their positive emotional energy in the face of problems and criticism.

Following the Script: Champion Listening and Learning from Customer "Moments of Truth"

"Moments of Truth" Defined

Swedish management consultant Richard Normann coined the term "moment of truth" in the late 1970s, and formally introduced the idea of a customer-centric value chain, with "moments of truth" as the central, driving feature in his 1983 book *Service Management* (2002). A "moment of truth" is an instance of contact between a customer and organization that provides the customer the opportunity to initially form or change an impression about the organization. As the phrase implies, these are critical and decisive moments of customer clarity that put the organization's brand promise to the test. Moments of truth can make or break an organization, as its brand reputation depends on the sum of these interactions. "These are the moments," writes Scandinavian SAS Airline CEO Jan Carlzon (1989), "when we must prove to our customers that SAS is their best alternative" (p. 3).

Moments of truth happen anywhere, anytime a customer comes in contact with anyone or anything associated with the organization. A 15-second interaction with an airline ticket agent, ordering a meal in a fast-food restaurant, checking into a hotel, or interacting with a greeter at church are moments of truth. Normann (2002) notes, "The logic of the moment of truth holds, even though customers may not have face-to-face contact with the people providing the service" (p. 22). So, making a phone contact or accessing an organization's web site are also moments of truth.

Moments of Truth and the Brand

The word "brand" is derived from the Old Norse *brandr* meaning "to burn" and the Old English *brond*, meaning "a flame, torch, or sword." In the most general sense, a brand is a "special kind of something" bearing a unique mark of ownership. Aaker (2011) states, "A brand has a name reflecting an organization that stands behind the offering" (p. 26). Therefore, to "brand" is the practice of an organization "burning its mark" onto a product or service, calling attention to the fact that it belongs to them and they alone are responsible for its quality and reputation.

Although a brand consists of a collection of physical elements such as a logo, color schemes, and symbols designed to convey a message about a product or service, the substance of a brand exists in the mind of the customer. Perception is reality, and the "brand image" of the organization—what people think, feel, believe, and expect about a product or service—is, for all practical purposes, the reality of the brand, for better or worse. Crawford and Mathews (2001) note that brand is not what the organization says it is. It is what many customers say it is, even over the objections of the organization. In this sense, a brand is not the mark made on a product or service by the organization, but rather, the mark made by the product or service on the customer and a broader group of stakeholders.

This mark is made largely in moments of truth. These experiences might form a positive brand association fostering customer loyalty, as in, "This product lives up to its advertising. These people are respectful and easy to work with. I trust this organization and believe they will look out for my best interests." Or moments of truth may form a negative brand association, with customers lost to the competition, as in, "This product does not live up to its advertising. I seem to be an annoyance to these people. This organization is more interested in selling me something than in serving my best interests." In the final analysis, the customer has all the power, serving as judge and jury and as necessary brand executioner.

In the twenty-first century, moments of truth rarely stay private. Social media provides a global platform for billions to report these moments, for better or worse, to family and friends, and anyone willing to listen. Hundreds of services such as Angies' List, Yelp, Trip Advisor, and Urbanspoon, provide customers the opportunity to record moments of truth and share them with the world—literally. It only takes a few negative moments of truth to sully a brand, whereas a pattern of positive moments of truth can help an organization differentiate itself in a competitive marketplace.

The following four-step process helps Leaders and member-leaders excel in the Ambassador Role, as they protect and project the organization's brand.

Step #1: Identify Moments of Truth. Normann (2002) notes that, anytime a customer engages with a business or organization, he or she participates in a brand-shaping process—a series of moment-of-truth interactions with the products, services, and members of the organization. This process, from the point of view of the customer, defines the quality and trajectory of the customer relationship. Consequently, if an organization wants to know if it is keeping its promises to the world, the only place to begin is by identifying customer moments of truth. This poses three significant challenges. First, the customer is a perpetually moving target, making it difficult to predict and precisely map moments of truth. Second, as moments of truth happen in a wide variety of interactions and venues, some of which are impossible to control (i.e., reading a post on Yelp or interacting with salespersons on the floor of a retail store), they are often difficult to monitor. Third, moments of truth happen in real time, and if the organization gets it wrong, there may be little or no time to make it right. Great damage can be done to brand reputation when customers experience a negative moment of truth, and use social media to critique a product or service to a vast audience almost instantaneously. Organizations must map moments of truth, but even the most sophisticated mapping will leave a "moment of truth" reporting gap.

Step #2: Listening and Learning from Moments of Truth. Once identified, the organization must listen to and learn from customers in moments of truth, taking careful note of both its successes and failures.

Step #3: Shaping Moments of Truth via Organizational Culture. The quality of a customer moment of truth is a reflection of organizational culture, for better or worse. Normann (2002) states:

> On making contact with any really successful service companies, one is aware almost immediately of a special kind of ethos emanating from every employee and infecting the client as well. Infusing an organization with values directly related to the success of the business is an effective (and sometimes the only way) of controlling a decentralized operation which is probably heavily dependent on individual contributions. Many service companies enjoy tens of thousands of client contacts or moments of truth every day, most of them probably involving employees working in the field. There is no other way of achieving high quality in every single contact than by maintaining a pervasive culture and making sure that every employee not only possesses the appropriate skills but is also guided by the appropriate ethos. (p. 56)

An organization's culture not only shapes what happens in its internal day-to-day interactions; it also shapes the quality of countless interactions between employees and customers. The two cannot be separated. Normann (2002) observes, "To be successful, a service company must strive to see that a single set of basic principles pervades the whole organization, from top management, through all levels and right up to the moment of truth" (p. 71). In this sense, a customer moment of truth is a reflection of the quality of the organization's internal moments of truth, which is a function of its culture. Norman (2002) observes, "The internal life of the organization also consists of moments of truth when people and groups from different hierarchical levels and different functional sectors help each other to operate (i.e., provide 'services' for one other) with the ultimate aim of bringing all resources to bear on the customer" (p. 71).

This underscores two inescapable realities. First, it is unreasonable to expect an employee to treat a customer differently than Leaders have treated them. For instance, a ticket agent is less likely to treat a customer with respect if a supervisor disrespects the ticket agent. Second, it is likely an employee will treat a customer as they habitually treat fellow employees in day-to-day organizational life. For instance, a salesperson is more likely to treat a customer with respect if they also treat fellow salespeople with respect.

Step #4: Empower Front-Line Members to Act in Moments of Truth. Carlzon (1989) argues that, if an organization wants to become more customer friendly, it must: (1) flatten the organizational hierarchy; (2) make sure everyone, including front-line employees knows the company's vision; and (3) empower front-line employees to use their best judgment to act on behalf of the customer. Nordstrom's, where customer service is a culture and not a department, has a well-earned reputation for giving front-line employees the right and responsibility to use their best judgment to deal with customer concerns. Former Coca-Cola chief marketing officer Sergio Zyman (2002) notes, "Employees who don't know your strategy or your mission can't possibly advertise your brand effectively. Every single person your customers come in contact with—whether it's a receptionist, a cashier, a driver, a manager, or you—is a walking advertisement" (p. 26).

When employees have the right and responsibility to use their discretion to respond directly and quickly to solve problems and treat customers as individuals, it significantly increases the possibility of a positive moment of truth. Block (1993) notes, "What you lose in control and predictability, you make up in response time and widespread intimacy with the customer" (p. 101).

Following the Script: Show Up, Pay Attention, and Ask Good Questions

Ambassadors connect regularly with those the organization intends to benefit in order to ask questions, listen, and learn first hand how the organization is doing in delivering on its promises. By showing up in this Role, Leaders and member-leaders communicate to customers that they matter, that what they need and value is of utmost importance.

Ambassadors help shape an other-friendly culture by asking questions that matter. These questions are designed to prompt a candid, friendly, and constructive dialog around its progress—or lack thereof—in delivering on its promises to others.

Customers

Who do we intend to benefit? On whose agenda are we—our own or the customer's? Are we listening and learning from them? Do we know what they value, want and need from us? Have we found out from them what we are doing well? Where we need to improve? Do we know why they behave and decide as they do? What is the competition for their loyalty? Why would they want to remain our customer? How might we lose them as loyal customers?

Stakeholders

Who has a genuine interest in our work beyond our immediate customers? How are we impacting them as we deliver benefit to our customers? What do they think about us? Are we listening and learning from them? Are we a good corporate citizen? What impact, for better or worse, do we have on the larger society?

When It Works: Toward an Other-Friendly Culture

When the Ambassador Role is played well, the organization becomes increasingly "other-friendly" and benefits in four ways.

First, listening and learning from customers is given priority in the daily life of the organization. Almost everyone is asking good questions, listening intently, and growing in their understanding of the needs, values, perspectives, decisions, and behaviors of those they intend to benefit. Consequently, nearly everyone in the organization contributes in important ways to protecting and projecting the brand, and delivering on the organization's promises to the world.

Second, the passion of many is unleashed to act as "brand evangelists"—the embodiment of the organization's mission and values, walking commercials for the organization, advocating for what is genuinely worthwhile and attractive about the organization as they go the "extra mile" for the customer. As Starbucks CEO Howard Shultz writes, "[Baristas and store managers] are the true ambassadors of our brand, the real merchants of romance and theater, and as such the primary catalysts for delighting customers" (Schultz & Gordon, p. 77). The spark between the customer and members can transform otherwise wary and skeptical people into true believers in the brand.

Third, a foundation of trust is established as Leaders and member-leaders communicate a set of powerful, "other-friendly messages," as in, "You are important to us. Our very existence is premised on bringing you benefit, and so we care what you think about our products and services. We are here to listen to you and learn from you and we will work hard to keep getting better at keeping our promises to you."

Fourth, a foundation for sustainability is established. No organization can exist for long if it serves its own interests at the expense of customers. When the organization keeps listening to and learning from customers, it gets better and better at delivering on its promises. This strengthens brand integrity and significantly increases the chances for long-term success.

A Word to Leaders

Although no Leader can do all that is necessary to create and sustain an other-friendly organization, Leaders make two contributions to the culture-shaping process.

Leaders Model Other-Friendly Attitudes and Behaviors

Leaders must show they care about customers by showing up on the "front line" to listen and learn. Only here can they get an accurate read on the experience of customers and verify whether the organization is bringing benefit to them. This direct experience is the best antidote to insularity, and provides the foundation for rigorous and realistic conversations about the organization's performance in this Role.

Known for spending more time listening than talking, former Procter and Gamble CEO A. J. Lafley is an unlikely award-winning chief executive. In 2006, he was selected CEO of the year by *Chief Executive Magazine* and identified as one of America's best business leaders by *U. S. News and World Report*. During his tenure as CEO, Lafley's emphasis on listening to customers refocused the company on the customer. Lafley told *Forbes*, "Too much time was being spent inside Procter and Gamble and not enough outside...I am a broken record when it comes to saying, 'We have to focus on the customer'" (Brooker & Schlosser, 2002). Lafley followed his own advice, conducting on-site interviews with consumers, and observing how Procter and Gamble products were used in the home in the hope of discovering unmet and unexpressed consumer needs. As his successor, current CEO Bob McDonald explained, "We don't give lip service to consumer understanding. We immerse ourselves in people's day-to-day lives. We dig deep. We work hard to find the tensions that we can help resolve. From those tensions come insights that lead to big ideas" (Lafley & Martin, 2013, p. 59).

Leaders Provide Member-Leaders Good Reason to Excel in This Role

Leaders infuse the organization with a deep sense of moral purpose, inspiring members to go the extra mile to serve customers. "Give them reasons to believe in their work and that they're part of a larger mission, the theory goes, and they'll in turn personally elevate the experience for each customer—something you can hardly accomplish with a billboard or a 30-second spot" (Kessler, 2012).

Summary

Whether a business or church, a hospital, art institute, or commercial airline, effective organizations serve others. Moreover, others, whether they are patients, parishioners, or passengers, have a core set of values—they want, yes demand, to be validated as individuals, respected, treated fairly, and honestly—no deception, hidden costs, or false promises. Organizations that listen and learn from customers have an opportunity to succeed in the hypercompetitive, ethically demanding New Normal operating environment. Organizations that serve only themselves will find themselves on a fast track to irrelevance or, quite possibly, on the road to extinction.

CHAPTER 16

The Learner Role

Introduction

In times of rapid change, the organization comes face to face with the two iron laws of learning: (1) The faster things change, the faster the value of what the organization presently knows diminishes; and (2) The greater the rate of change, the greater the performance difference between organizations that learn fast and those that do not. This places a premium on learning agility—both for individuals and entire organizations (Appelbaum & Paese, 2011; Eichinger & Lombardo, 2004; Prahalad, 2009). The capacity of the organization to learn, unlearn, and relearn quickly may well mean the difference between sustainable effectiveness and mediocrity, keeping one's promises to the world, and lapsing into irrelevance. The organization that stays put or stands pat is fooling itself, living on borrowed time. When a Leader stops learning, it is time to stop leading. When the entire organization stops learning, it is time to go out of business.

The Mandate and Simple Rule

The mandate of the Learner Role is to foster a "learning-friendly" cultural climate (see Figure 16.1). This work seeks to embed one simple rule into the fabric of daily, organizational life: "keep learning"—we are perpetual learners and take on any learning challenge that makes us more effective in light of our purpose, mission and values. The Learner Role focuses on enlarging the organization's capacity for generative learning—a process of continuous renewal and the generation of new knowledge, new approaches, and new perspectives that increases the organization's ability to address new problems, and survive and thrive in novel and changing circumstances. Generative learning is a New

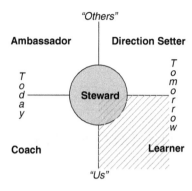

Figure 16.1 Learner role.

Normal imperative, as organizations must develop new ways of thinking, discover new perspectives, and design radically new approaches to address the challenges and opportunities of an uncertain future.

What It Is Not

The Learner Role is not about change for its own sake. It is not about mastering the skills associated with a particular job description. It is not about the transfer of knowledge from the top down. There is a vast difference between job training and developing a learning culture.

The Script: Overview

Each Role calls for Leaders and member-leaders to follow a script—a written set of instructions that serve as behavioral prompts to engage in the formidable task of building a New Normal-friendly organization. Toward the end of shaping a learning-friendly culture, the Learner focuses the attention and resources of the organization on three script lines, which serve as points of culture-shaping leverage.

Script Line #1: Suit Up and Collaborate

Learners suit up by way of "putting on" the DICE + 1 configuration (Collaboration Quotient, CQ), which is required to collaborate effectively in the culture-shaping process. This Role takes more than the occasional effort of a few Leaders or the technical expertise of change management specialists. Rather, it demands the best effort of the entire organization from the grass roots up. Although the proverbial buck stops with established Leaders for initiating and sustaining the learning process, the day-to-day work of learning must be distributed throughout the organization. From the grassroots to top Leaders, nearly everyone is a champion for "learning what we must."

Script Line #2: Champion the Role

Learners champion the process of generative learning in service of the mission. If the organization is to honor its commitment to stay effective and increase the scope of its influence in a dynamic and uncertain world, it is imperative that it get very, very good at collective, generative learning.

Script Line #3: Show Up, Pay Attention, and Ask Good Questions

Leaders and member-leaders show up in the Learner Role, communicating through their investment of time and attention the importance of "learning what we must." "Showing up" may look different from day to day—studying and/or speaking to current trends in the external operating environment, identifying the organization's learning agenda, and regularly evaluating the learning performance of the organization in light of its directional imperatives. This front-line experience gives Learners an appreciation for every aspect of organizational life that contributes to a learning-friendly culture, and provides the framework for rigorous, in-depth, constructive conversations around the imperative of "keep learning."

Following the Script: Suit Up and Collaborate

The Learner Role demands a sufficiently high level of CQ on the part of all who participate. Although we may learn best for ourselves, we rarely learn best by ourselves. Senge (1990) observes, "Team learning is vital because teams, not individuals, are the fundamental learning unit in modern organizations" (p. 10).

Drawing from a rich fund of virtue, Learners model the attitudes and behaviors that fuel collaborative, generative learning.

Dynamic Determination

The continuous renewal of the organization is not possible if Leaders and member-leaders do not deeply care about its purpose, mission, and values. When learning is linked to what we deeply care about, especially fulfilling one's promises to the world, we will overcome almost any obstacle put in our path.

Intellectual Flexibility

Generative learning requires "unlearning" outdated knowledge and breaking ineffective behavior patterns. Staying in the learning process requires humility, and proves difficult for the proud and inflexible.

Courageous Character

Generative learning is fueled by trust. Trust is especially critical in high-risk environments where failure is common, results are slow in coming, and vulnerability is high—an average day in the new Normal (Lau & Liden, 2008). When trust is high, learning is promoted. Members who might otherwise be overcome by a sense of vulnerability come together to share information and engage in candid dialog about performance. They take risks knowing that "good hearted failure" is not punished (Dutton & Heaphy, 2003; Regine & Lewin, 2000). If trust is low, if members do not trust one another's commitment to the common good, if failure is unacceptable, then, the entire organization is less likely to explore, stay open to change, deal with complexity, collaborate, and seize new opportunities. Not without irony, in this low-trust atmosphere, performance in mission-critical tasks is diminished (Burke et al., 2007).

Emotional Maturity

Because generative learning happens outside of one's comfort zone, it is typically an emotionally stressful experience. Comfortable habits must be exchanged for new and better ways of getting important things accomplished. It is painful to have our assumptions questioned and categories rattled, especially if we want to give the impression that we are capable adults. Moreover, Learners have to give themselves and others permission to not have all the answers, to get smarter along the way, to be wrong, to fail, and even to fail openly. It takes emotional strength to stay in the learning process, realizing that not looking good all the time is the price of enlarging one's capacity to stay effective.

Following the Script: Champion Generative Learning

In the New Normal, the learning challenge is clear: If you want to keep your promises, keep learning. The collective practice of generative learning depends on three organization-wide commitments.

First, generative learning depends on a collective commitment to stay effective. The attitudes of Leaders and member-leaders as well as the organization's systems, structures, and procedures—all expressions of culture—must support the learning process.

Second, generative learning depends on a commitment to flexibility. A flexible organization affirms its directional imperatives while remaining open to change in almost everything else. The purpose, mission, and values of the organization serve as organizational bungee cords, giving it considerable range to innovate and change shape, even dramatically now and then, but without compromising its identity or mission; thus, to stay effective while staying itself.

Third, generative learning gives right of way to experimentation at all levels of the organization. Contrary to Old Normal expectations, constructive change and new learning often comes not from sweeping initiatives mandated by a few Leaders, but from the accumulation of many smaller adaptations originating throughout the organization in response to localized challenges and opportunities. In the New Normal, the diffusion of learning, all the way to the edges of the organization, is a necessity. Handy (1995) notes, much of the learning power resides at the edge of the organization. Future-shaping innovations often emerge as a result of the creative actions of those not privileged with formal authority, decision-making prerogatives or access to significant organizational resources. Collins (1999) observes, "History shows us that organizations achieve greatness when people are allowed to do unexpected things—to show initiative and creativity, to step outside the scripted path" (p. 73).

Following the Script: Show Up, Pay Attention, and Ask Good Questions

Learners help shape a learning-friendly culture by asking questions that matter. These questions are designed to prompt a candid, friendly, and constructive dialog around its progress—or lack thereof—in learning what it must.

Overall Organizational Performance

How are we doing in mission-critical areas—the categories of collective performance that deeply matter to us? Where are we winning? Losing? Just getting by? "What have we learned lately about our organization from others—from those who, according to our mission, we intend to benefit?" Those the organization intends to benefit—customers, customers, constituents, etc—are often the greatest source of meaningful knowledge about the organization's performance. Are we collectively applying what we have learned? Is our learning making a difference in keeping our promises to the world? (The Results section will further discuss these questions.)

Organizational Learning Capacity

Are we monitoring changes in the external operating environment? Do we know what it takes to stay effective? Do we presently have what it takes to stay effective? Do we have the people, tools, systems, strategies, and structures to live out our directional imperatives into the indefinite future? Can we articulate the issues involved in poor performance? Can we honestly face up to our failure? Are we capable of learning what we need to learn? Will we do everything in our power to escape from ineffective patterns of behavior?

The Organizational Learning Agenda

In light of our directional imperatives, present performance, and the emerging changes and challenges in the New Normal landscape, what must we learn or "unlearn" to stay effective? What must we get very, very good at? What activities or processes must we improve? What must change if we are to live true to our commitments?

When It Works: Toward a Learning-Friendly Culture

When the Learner Role is played well, the organization becomes an increasingly learning-friendly place, resulting in five benefits to the organization.

First, as the generative learning process is embedded in the organization, it serves as an early warning system, alerting the organization to critical performance issues and emerging opportunities. Hamel (2012) notes, "Deep change is almost always crisis-driven; it's tardy, traumatic and expensive" (p. x). Learning organizations avoid this reactive stance. From top to bottom, center to periphery, the organization is full of people continually scanning the external environment, refreshing their knowledge base, correcting faulty assumptions, and adjusting their cognitive maps to match the realities of their operating context. The diffusion of learning gives the organization a built-in early warning system to spot "game changers" in the external environment—another advantage in the New Normal.

Second, the learning-friendly organization becomes less susceptible to the seduction of past success, as the practice of generative learning keeps it perpetually relevant. Past successes are applauded, but not named sacred and enshrined—remember de Lesseps.

Third, the learning-friendly organization stays "young at heart" and avoids becoming "old." By "young at heart" is meant curious, inquisitive, vigorous, alert to new possibilities, venturesome, open to change, willing to take a risk or two, and with a keen sense that one's best years are ahead. By "old" is meant past its prime and in decline, exhibiting a calcified orthodoxy of attitude and action, rigidly competent, fixed, narrow, and set in one's ways—which may, indeed, be good ways but, nevertheless, betray a decreasing receptivity to learn new things and, with it, the loss of capacity to meet new challenges and opportunities. Learning organizations stay young without being immature and grow up without growing old.

Fourth, the learning friendly organization gets exceptionally good at speed learning—the capacity to make quick adjustments to strategies and practices in response to changes in the external environment. "As stability gives way to change and uncertainty institutions must increase not just efficiency but also the rate at which they learn and innovate, which in turn will boost their rate of performance improvement. 'Scalable efficiency,' in other words, must be replaced by 'scalable learning'" (Hagel et al., 2009, p. 88). The capacity to gain new knowledge quickly, to adapt one's approach, adjust one's perspective, leave behind outdated practices, and explore new possibilities for addressing new problems brings a decided competitive advantage in the twenty-first century.

Fifth, the learning-friendly organization continually renews, deepens, and enlarges its capacity for sustained effectiveness. It grows hardy and robust, able to thrive in harsh circumstances. It faces the facts, even when they are unpleasant, and courageously self-corrects, making whatever change is required to stay effective. It lives productively with the stress and disorientation generated as the old ways of doing things prove ineffective, and new ways of thinking and practice are embraced as part of the learning agenda. It grows in its capacity to face reality, confront deficiencies, and discover what it takes to stay effective. Members are continually re-oriented, re-energized, and realigned around strategies and practices that have been adjusted to meet the demands of effectiveness in the operating environment. The organization gets better and better at the things that really matter most—a decided advantage in the New Normal.

A Word to Leaders

No Leader can guarantee that members will actively participate in the learning process. However, they can, through their attitudes and actions, serve as catalysts, encouraging and prompting generative learning, and weaving mission-critical learning into everyday organizational life.

Here is how they can do so.

First, Leaders leverage the dynamism of the external environment to prompt generative learning. New Normal organizations exist in what has been termed "the edge of chaos" (Osborn et al., 2002). Contrary to Old Normal expectations, Leaders do not eliminate uncertainty. Rather, one of the primary contributions of a Leader is to monitor changes in the external environment and highlight what needs to be learned, changed, or adapted to in the life of the organization in order to remain effective. This means that Leaders may, at times, disrupt existing patterns of collective behavior to pave the way for more effective approaches to dealing with emerging challenges and opportunities.

Second, Leaders stay solid and help members do the same. Change is perpetual and escalating, and the learning challenges associated with it daunting and anxiety producing. Old, counterproductive habits must be jettisoned, often before new ones are learned, with no guarantee of success. Contrary to Old Normal expectations, Leaders do not provide all the right answers. Rather, they provide the emotional support the organization needs to stay in the learning process, even when the answers are being pursued.

Third, Leaders stay comfortable with leading while learning. Although a Leader may not be the expert on any particular item in the learning agenda, they are expert learners, learning quickly from anyone, any place, and at any time. They are the first to face the discomfort of the change they espouse; the first to break old habits and lay aside outdated practices. Perhaps most importantly, Leaders normalize "not knowing." They readily admit that they do not have all the answers and will have to figure it out just like everyone else. When a Leader adopts this learning stance, the message is powerful: Those who have to be right and want to be effective are seldom either. We can look a bit foolish now but smarter later, or we can try to look smart now, and look foolish later—and fail, in the process.

Fourth, Leaders guard and support the learning process. Leaders make sure that good ideas get a legitimate hearing regardless of their source and despite their potentially disruptive implications. Bartz (2009) noted that one of the chief responsibilities of senior leaders is to "foster a culture of openness to fresh thinking—the greatest energy an organization can have" (p. 128). Affirming that learning is not restricted to the hierarchy, Leaders make accurate and relevant information available throughout the organization. They encourage experimentation and listen to those at the edges of the organizational life—the home of a considerable portion of the organization's ingenuity.

Summary

Peters (1988) observed, "The world has not just 'turned upside down.' It is turning every which way at an accelerating pace...Today, loving change, tumult, even chaos is a prerequisite for survival, let alone success" (pp. 55–56). The last two decades have proven him correct and then some. What does it mean to "love change?" At a minimum, it means to keep learning. In a world of rapid, discontinuous change, the rate of learning in an organization must at least match the rate of change in the external world. In this sense, a passion for learning is more important than what an individual or organization currently knows.

CHAPTER 17

The Coach Role

Introduction

By what metric can an organization measure its capacity to keep its promises to the world? The answer: the quality of its efforts to identify, develop, and deploy more leaders. Hesselbein (1996) states:

> The three major challenges CEO's will face have little to do with managing the enterprise's tangible assets and everything to do with monitoring the quality of: leadership, the work force, and relationships... The leader for today and the future will be focused on how to be-how to develop quality, character, mind-set, values, principles, and courage. The 'how to be' leader knows that people are the organization's greatest asset and in word, behavior, and relationships she or he demonstrates this powerful philosophy. (pp. 121–122)

In the New Normal, sustainability and leadership development are synonymous, as the organization's future is inextricably connected to its capacity to generate more leaders.

The Mandate and Simple Rule

The mandate of the Coach Role is to foster a "leader-friendly" cultural climate (see Figure 17.1). This Role seeks to embed one simple rule into the fabric of daily, organizational life: "more leaders." Coaches value the leadership potential of all members, and seize any and all opportunities to identity, develop, and deploy members in mission-critical work.

The Coach and the Direction Setter Roles are vitally connected. The Direction Setter Role provides the strategic context in which the Coach Role is played. The Direction Setter clarifies the identity, mission,

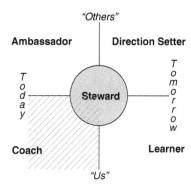

Figure 17.1 Coach role.

and values of the organization. The Coach clarifies the qualifications for serving and leading in light of these directional imperatives, and focuses the resources of the organization on identifying, developing, and deploying members who meet these requirements.

What It Is Not

The Coach Role is not a "cookie-cutter" approach to mold new Leaders or member-leaders into the image of established Leaders. It is not a job-training program to increase the technical skills of members for present job descriptions.

The Script

Each Role calls for Leaders and member-leaders to follow a script—a written set of instructions that serve as behavioral prompts to engage in the formidable task of building a New Normal-friendly organization. Toward the end of shaping a leader-friendly culture, the Coach focuses the attention and resources of the organization on three script lines, which serve as points of culture-shaping leverage.

Script Line #1: Suit Up and Collaborate

Coaches suit up by way of "putting on" the DICE + 1 configuration (Collaboration Quotient, CQ), which is required to collaborate effectively in the culture-shaping process. This Role takes more than the occasional effort of a few Leaders. It requires more than the technical expertise of Human Resource specialists. Rather, as Kouzes and Posner

(1996) state, "Leadership is everyone's business" (p. 108). From the grassroots to established L̲eaders, nearly everyone is a champion for the emergence of new L̲eaders and member-leaders.

Script Line #2: Champion the Role

Coaches champion the leadership-development pipeline process. If the organization is to honor its commitment to stay effective and increase the scope of its influence, it is imperative that it get very, very good at identifying, developing, and deploying more leaders.

Script Line #3: Show Up, Pay Attention, and Ask Good Questions

L̲eaders and member-leaders show up in the Coach Role, communicating through their investment of time and attention the critical importance of "more leaders." "Showing up" may look different from day to day— identifying emerging L̲eaders, meeting with new leaders to discuss job performance, addressing the organization's future leadership needs, and regularly evaluating the performance of the organization in developing more leaders. This front-line experience gives Coaches an appreciation for every aspect of organizational life that contributes to a leadership-friendly culture, and provides the framework for rigorous, in-depth, constructive conversations around the imperative of "more leaders."

Following the Script: Suit up and Collaborate

The Coach Role demands a sufficiently high level of CQ on the part of all who participate. This Role asks L̲eaders to avoid the temptation to hoard leadership prerogatives and, instead, take pains to avoid stifling the agency and creativity of others. Established L̲eaders do not create followers. They create more L̲eaders and member-leaders. Their aim is not "more power for me" but "more leaders for us." De Pree (1989) observed, "The signs of outstanding leadership appear primarily among the followers. Are the followers reaching their potential? Are they learning? Serving? Do they achieve the required results? Do they change with grace? Manage conflict?" (p. 12).

Following the Script: Champion Missional Development and the Pipeline Process

Missional development is the practice of developing people as they are deployed to contribute to the welfare and progress of the organization.

New Leaders and member-leaders are best developed in the context of doing mission-critical work—the best way to get ready to lead in the future is to do important leadership work today. The development of people and progress in the mission work in sync—both happen simultaneously, with each reinforcing the other.

Developing more new Leaders and member-leaders and sustained effectiveness in the mission are seamlessly interwoven, with each feeding from the success of the other. The organization can expand its work only to the degree that new Leaders and member-leaders are identified, developed, and deployed. More capable people means increased capacity to do the mission, and increased capacity to do the mission means more leadership work and, thus, more opportunity to identify, develop, and deploy new Leaders and member-leaders. As individuals develop, the organization benefits. Furthermore, as the organization makes progress, it, in turn, invests resources in becoming a richer developmental environment. In light of this "both-and," leadership-friendly organizations see no inherent tension, let alone contradiction, between a commitment to: (1) Effectively address today's challenges and opportunities; and (2) Get the next generation ready to address tomorrow's opportunities and challenges.

The Requirement of Generativity

The Coach role calls on established Leaders to leverage their formal authority and personal assets to provide a generous flow of resources to support the emergence of new Leaders and member-leaders. As Heifetz et al. note, "Leaders don't so much gather followers as they generate more leaders. The measure of an effective leader is not the number of followers, but the quality of the leaders they help emerge. It is an illusion to expect that an executive team on its own will find the best way into the future. So you must use leadership to generate more leadership deep in the organization" (2009, p. 68).

The disposition to serve as a catalyst for the development of the next generation and to abandon one's ego to the talent and contribution of others is called generativity The adjective "generative" is related to the noun "generation" as in "the next generation," and the verb "generate" as in "to produce or bring into being." Generativity refers to the attitudes and behaviors that help the next generation come into their own and successfully meet the challenges and opportunities set before them. Generativity involves the creative blending of both intimacy and a healthy power motivation (McAdams, 1993). In the act of generativity, individuals both create something of value and willingly give it up on behalf of others, surrendering control over that which they themselves have produced. McAdams (1989) notes, "Generativity challenges us to be both powerful and intimate, expansive and surrendering at the same time. In motivational terms, generativity draws on our desire to be strong and our desire to be close to others, mandating that we integrate and reconcile power and intimacy motivation" (p. 163).

Generative Leaders know that the organization is only one generation from extinction, or worse, irrelevance. This healthy sense of organizational mortality, coupled with the significance of the organization's mission, spurs them on to invest in younger people, to generously share and pass on anything of value—wisdom, experience, practical help, material resources—needed to succeed. The torch must be handed off. The DNA of the organization must be passed on to a "mission-capable" next generation.

Accordingly, generative Leaders provide a hospitable environment for those Gardner (1995) calls "the pathfinders"—creative, "out of the box" emerging leaders who "break the mold," see new visions, find new solutions to new problems, and identify new pathways to advance the mission of the organization. (Pathfinders are not to be confused with narcissistic charismatic individuals.) Pathfinders hold special promise to eclipse the accomplishments of the present generation. Knowing that the acid test of leadership is quality of one's legacy, generative Leaders embrace their resourcefulness and initiative in the hope of leaving behind an organization that will be good, perhaps exceptional, or even great without them.

Working the Leadership Pipeline Process

If the organization wants to increase its capacity to keep delivering on its promises to the world, it must get very, very good at (1) identifying, (2) developing, and (3) deploying the next generation of Leaders and member-leaders. New Normal organizations sweat this process big time and full time, weaving leadership development into the fabric of everyday organizational life.

Identifying. Leadership-friendly organizations do not talk around the edges with "round words" and abstract phrases—we want "good people," or "motivated people" or people with "good values." Rather, they have a keen sense of what "good" looks like by way of specific, demonstrable attitudes, and behaviors. In addition to manifesting sufficient CQ, emerging Leaders and member-leaders must embody the purpose, mission, and values of the organization in demonstrable ways.

Developing and deploying. Leadership-friendly organizations believe that vast, untapped potential resides in many throughout the organization, regardless of position, and that these individuals stand ready and willing to test and stretch their leadership capacities, especially when presented with genuine opportunities to contribute. Moreover, leadership-friendly organizations believe that the organization is systematically weakened, and its capacity for keeping its promises to the world is seriously compromised when no such opportunities are presented and leadership is limited to an elite few. Fueled by these convictions, leadership-friendly organizations develop and deploy as many members as can be identified.

In a leader-friendly organization, development and deployment happen simultaneously. As Figure 17.2 depicts, a leader-friendly culture thrives along a 45-degree angle that represents a covenant of growth between members and the organization. As individuals grow and develop the organization prospers, and as the organization prospers, so does the individual. Keeping the development process tracking more or less along the 45-degree angle—there is room for short-term deviation—requires the intentional effort of Leaders, member-leaders, and the entire organization.

Too steep. If the developmental angle is too steep (Figure 17.2), the organization will develop a transactional culture, and become a "more bricks less straw" kind of place. Members may sense they are "worker bees," a mere means to an end, that tasks are more important than

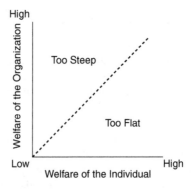

Figure 17.2 Missional development.

people. The not-so-subtle message: "Expect to be used but not developed." In extreme cases, the message is "You are expendable. We won't hesitate to sacrifice you on the altar of progress." Although worker bees get a lot done, they do not make it into the next season. This diminishes the sustainability of the organization as few, if any, will volunteer for leadership opportunities if they know that are expendable—a mere cog in the wheel of the organizational progress.

Too flat. If the developmental angle is too flat (Figure 17.2) the organization will develop a *laissez-faire* culture. There may be a lack of focus, a pervasive sense that there is no critical work to accomplish. Members may drift into complacency or mediocrity, using their time and talent to accomplish their personal agenda—taking home a paycheck or using the present job as a career launching pad—with no thought to the welfare and progress of the organization.

Following the Script: Show Up, Pay Attention, and Ask Good Questions

Coaches help shape a leadership-friendly culture by asking questions that matter. These questions are designed to prompt a candid, friendly, and constructive dialog around its progress—or lack thereof—in generating more leaders.

Organizational Culture

Are we a leadership-friendly place? Does our culture enhance the resourcefulness and initiative of the next generation of leaders? Do we expect established Leaders to invest in emerging leaders? Given our directional imperatives, do we know what "good" looks like by way of a new Leader or member-leader? Do we have enough of the right kind of Leaders and member-leaders to keep our promises to the world today and into the indefinite future? Do we take the identification, development and deployment of new leaders seriously? Do we really work at it? Track it? Evaluate it?

Established Leaders

Are established Leaders inviting the next generation to participate in mission-critical work? Are they "chasing the strength" of emerging leaders? Are established Leaders generative people and, thus, able to champion the emergence of the next generation of Leaders and member-leaders? Are they serving as a catalyst to release the talent of others? Are they spending sufficient time and energy in the leadership pipeline process? Are they modeling the mission and core values of the organization? Are they invested in the emergence and success of the next generation?

Emerging Leaders

Are we a hospitable place for emerging member-leaders? Does everyone get a chance to shine? Are we connecting emerging member-leaders with missional opportunities? Are they themselves generative people and, thus, capable of developing more new leaders? Who are these men and women? Can we name them?

When It Works: Toward a Leadership-Friendly Culture

When the Coach Role is played well, the organization becomes an increasingly leadership-friendly place typified by the following.

First, "more of the right kind of Leaders and member-leaders" becomes a core commitment and core competency of the organization, a valued end worthy of the organization's best, collective effort. The organization generously invests its time, attention, and resources in the pipeline process, which becomes a collective pursuit and daily routine; something the organization does exceptionally well.

Second, the organization achieves a rare mix of high performance and developmental soundness. Leadership prerogatives are generously distributed, creating ample space for many to explore their untapped potential. The organization exudes a warm and generous affect, coupled with a passion for results. Although achieving goals is critically important, the organization does not sacrifice the welfare of its members on the altar of accomplishment. It tempers drive and initiative with a concern for the individual. It values progress and people, morale and mission, relationships and results.

Third, the organization becomes "talent-friendly." Drucker (1993) anticipated the idea of a talent-friendly organization over six decades ago in his groundbreaking book, *The Concept of the Corporation*. "Any organization has to be organized so as to bring out the talents and capacities within the organization; to encourage men (and women) to take the initiative, give them a chance to show what they can do, and a scope within which to grow" (p. 28). Organizational structures, policies, and procedures support, rather than oppose, unleashing the talent of many to accomplish important leadership work. As a result, the "bench strength" or "leadership bandwidth" of the organization increases and, with it, its capacity to sustain its performance and expand its influence.

A Word to Leaders

Leaders best serve the organization when they use their formal authority and personal assets (charisma and competence) to serve as a catalyst to release the talent of members. They accomplish this is in three ways.

First, Leaders act in a generative manner, developing and unleashing, rather than ignoring or controlling, the next generation. They make an intentional effort to avoid stifling the agency and creativity of member-leaders. Although their presence may, indeed, loom large, they do not cast a shadow.

Second, Leaders do not overvalue what they can do or undervalue what emerging Leaders or member-leaders can contribute. Drucker noted:

> Successful leaders don't start out asking, "What do I want to do?" They ask, "What needs to be done?" Then they ask, "Of those things that would make a difference, which are right for me?" They don't tackle things they aren't good at. They make sure other necessities get done, but not by them. Successful leaders make sure that they succeed! They are not afraid of strength in others. Andrew Carnegie wanted to put on his gravestone, "Here lies a man who attracted better people into his service than he was himself." (Karlgaard, 2004)

Third, Leaders do not hand out orders. They distribute responsibility. If all Leaders do is to give orders, all the organization will end up with are order-takers. Those with creative insight will remain silent or be driven from the organization. Sharing responsibility requires sharing information. As Heifetz et al. note, "To distribute leadership responsibility more broadly, you need to mobilize everyone to generate solutions by increasing the information flow that allows people across the organization to make independent decisions and share the lessons they learn form innovative efforts" (2009, p. 68).

Imagine the difference between Leaders who hoard power and prerogatives and those who distribute leadership opportunity throughout the organization; between those who diminish the contribution of others and those who attract talented people and give them opportunity to contribute at their highest level of ability; between those who use position and power to showcase their superior intelligence and those with the courage to admit they do not know it all; between those who make all the decisions and those who create the space for dialog and even debate. The second idea of trusting the insight and talent of others and distributing leadership prerogatives throughout the organization differentiates the New Normal Leader from the Old Normal Leader.

Summary

Establishing a leadership-friendly culture is, perhaps, the highest and most valuable act of New Normal leadership. The work of identifying, developing, and deploying new Leaders and member-leaders is not an afterthought. It requires forethought. It is not a peripheral concern. It is a central focus. It is not elective. It is essential. It is not a luxury. It is a vital necessity.

CHAPTER 18

The Steward Role

Introduction

Meeting the obligations of each Role presents the organization with three challenges. First, no rulebook exists to guide the organization in distributing its attention and resources between each Role. The status of the organization's internal life, as well as the shifting demands of the external environment, often requires a disproportionate emphasis on some Roles over the others, at least for a time. For instance, strategic clarity (Direction Setter) may take precedence for a time over change initiatives (Learner), or change initiatives over the development of more leaders (Coach).

Second, there is an inherent tension embedded in the Roles. For instance, the Direction Setter calls on the organization to stay true to its directional imperatives, whereas the Learner calls the organization to adapt to meet the shifting demands of the external operating environment. Third, shaping a New Normal-friendly organization requires widespread participation, ownership, and collaboration. Consequently, the distribution of authority and power must be negotiated.

These challenges highlight the need for a summative, "macro-Role"—a Role that integrates the culture-shaping work of each of the four leadership Roles, manages the inherent tensions between the Roles, and serves as a catalyst for collaboration between Leaders and member-leaders in the work of building a New Normal-friendly organization. This is the focus of the Steward Role (see Figure 18.1).

A Steward Defined

A steward holds something of value in sacred trust for others by providing watchful, wise, and forward-looking care. In ancient times, stewards were placed in charge of large households or estates with the mandate to attend to the financial and material interests of the owner. In this sense, a

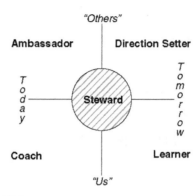

Figure 18.1 Steward Role.

steward is entrusted with the welfare and progress of something not their own—an organization, nation, or, in the case of environmental stewardship, the Earth.

The care and oversight exercised by the Steward is active and forward looking. They plan ahead, investing resources wisely, exercising a sense of proportion and perspective, balancing short- and long-term interests, and exhibiting the situational savvy to employ the right means to secure the right ends.

A Fitting Metaphor for the New Normal

The idea of a steward as one who holds a sacred trust evokes images of moral authority—selfless service, faithfulness, humility, and moral responsibility. Block notes (1993) stewardship is "the willingness to be accountable for the well-being of the larger organization by operating in service, rather than control, of those around us" (p. xx). The Steward is a fitting image for those who rise above self-interest to exercise diligent care over the assets and daily affairs of the organization. Whether a CEO, board member, or "rank and file" member, those who place organizational assets, such as positional authority, human and financial capital, as well as personal assets like competence and charisma, in the service of the larger good of the organization and those it serves, act as good stewards.

The Mandate

The mandate of the Steward Role is to help shape a New Normal-friendly culture by: (1) wisely managing the organization's investment of attention and talent, and other resources in service of each Role;

(2) wisely managing the tensions inherent between the Roles; and (3) maximizing the talent and insight of Leaders and member-leaders by building collaborative partnerships and distributing power and authority throughout the organization to address the obligations each Role.

What It Is Not

The Steward Role is not about raising capital, identifying operating efficiencies, or managing budgets, as important as these activities are.

The Script

Each Role calls for Leaders and member leaders to follow a script—a written set of instructions that serve as behavioral prompts to engage in the formidable task of building a New Normal-friendly organization. Toward this end, the Steward focuses the attention and resources of the organization on three script lines, which serve as points of culture-shaping leverage.

Script Line #1: Suit Up and Collaborate

Stewards suit up by way of "putting on" the DICE + 1 configuration (Collaborative Quotient, CQ), which is required to collaborate effectively in the culture-shaping process. Stewards recognize that the demands of success in the New Normal are beyond the capabilities of any one person. Accordingly, this Role takes more than the occasional effort of a few Leaders. Rather, the Steward Role extends to member-leaders, including those without formal authority, as they decide how to best invest their time, attention, and resources to serve the welfare and progress of the organization.

Script Line #2: Champion the Practice of "Both-And" to Secure the Welfare and Progress of the Whole Organization over Time

Stewards wisely manage the inherent "both-and" tensions in the mix of the four leadership Roles, and translate these tensions into opportunities to shape and sustain a New Normal-friendly organization.

Script Line #3: Show Up, Pay Attention, and Ask Questions

The Steward shows up in all four Roles, making sound decisions on the investment of their time, attention, and resources based on the necessities of the moment and opportunities of the future.

Following the Script: Suit up and Collaborate

The primary obligation of a Steward is to relate, decide, and act with the moral insight to recognize the common good, and sufficient moral strength to rise above self-interest; to put the power and resources at their disposal in service of the welfare and progress of the organization. Stewards draw from the DICE configuration of virtue and manifest a high CQ.

Dynamic Determination

The Steward Role is an exercise of faith in that it views resources— one's attention, time, talent, and all that is at one's beck and call—as a sacred trust to serve a larger interest, rather than the means for personal gain.

Intellectual Flexibility

The Steward discerns what the organization needs at any given time and, thus, what Role should be emphasized, and to what degree. There are no prepackaged responses based on formal rules, no manual to consult that informs Leaders and member-leaders when they should place emphasis on a particular Role, and how much of the organization's limited resources should to be invested to secure valued ends associated with each Role. This juggling act places a premium on the application of Intellectual Flexibility.

Courageous Character

The Steward Role is an exercise in courage in that it calls upon individuals to risk comfort and security and personal interests in favor of the good of the larger organization and those it serves. The Steward Role is an exercise of love in that it serves the interests of others above one's own.

Emotional Maturity

The Steward Role is an exercise in self-control in that it calls upon individuals to withstand the temptation to hoard power, expand their prerogatives, and use their assets to seek control, security, and personal pleasure.

Following the Script: Champion "Both–And"

New Normal organizations must perform on the "both–and edge," holding the concerns of each Role in perpetual, creative tension. The Steward manages four inherent tensions: (1) Today–tomorrow tensions; (2) us–others tensions; (3) continuity and change tensions; and (4) centralized and distributive tensions.

Today–Tomorrow Tensions

The Direction Setter and Learner Roles place emphasis on the "tomorrow" of the organization—what it must continue to do well and learn into the indefinite future if it is to stay true to itself and stay effective in a dynamic operating environment. The Ambassador and Coach Role place emphasis on a set of "today" outcomes—identifying, developing, and deploying more leaders, and bringing benefit to those it serves. Employing prudent oversight, Stewards effectively manage this dual focus, accomplishing important things today—there is no holiday from short-term success—and doing this in such a manner that the organization stays effective tomorrow and the next day.

Stewards appreciate the connection between short-term performance and sustained progress—sustainable effectiveness is impossible apart from many, successive, short-term successes. Important things must get accomplished today, but in a manner that enhances and does not diminish the organization's capacity to keep getting results into the indefinite future. Heifetz et al. (2009) observe, "Executives today face two competing demands. They must execute in order to meet today's challenges. Moreover, they must adapt what and how things get done in order to thrive in tomorrow's world. They must develop "next practices" while excelling at today's "best practices" (p. 65). Late Chicago newspaper columnist Sidney Harris put it well: "An idealist believes the short term doesn't count. A cynic believes the long run doesn't matter. A realist believes that what's done or left undone in the short run determines the long run." Stewards exercise realism, knowing that today's outcomes are the raw material of tomorrow's success (see Figure 18.2).

Us–Others Tensions

The Direction Setter and Ambassador Roles place emphasis on "others"—those the organization intends to benefit. The Coach and

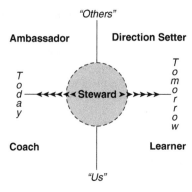

Figure 18.2 Today–tomorrow tensions.

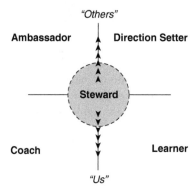

Figure 18.3 Us–others tensions.

Learner Roles place emphasis on "us"—the internal capacity of the organization as determined by the quality and number of new Leaders and member-leaders, as well as the content and quality of its learning. Stewards appreciate the vital connection between the internal health of the organization and its capacity for sustained effectiveness in the external world. They understand the "inside-out" nature of sustained performance—high performance over time is a function of the quality of the organization's internal life. Accordingly, Stewards attend to the "both–and" as they prompt new learning, develop the next generation of leaders, and translate these assets—new leaders and new learning—into sustained high performance in delivering benefit to others (see Figure 18.3).

Continuity–Change Tensions

The Direction Setter identifies the non-negotiable directional imperatives of the organization—its purpose, mission, and core values. The Learner prompts constructive change and adaptation in order to stay effective over time in light of the directional imperatives. This generates a polarity tension that must be wisely managed. This tension goes by a variety of names: continuity versus change, discipline versus creativity, focus versus flexibility, and stability versus agility.

Whatever the name, the tension is similar: some things are core to the identity of the organization and must remain stable, unchanging, and non-negotiable. These essentials must be widely embraced, regularly emphasized, focused on, held dear, and not deviated from if the organization is to operate with integrity and put forth a sustained, coherent, collective effort in delivering on its promises. Conversely, if the organization wants to keep delivering on its promises in a changing world, it must give itself permission to adjust. Kanter (2008) observes, "To compete effectively, large corporations must respond quickly and creatively to opportunities wherever they arise, and yet have those dispersed activities add up to a unified purpose and accomplishments" (p. 44).

Stewards manage this "both–and" tension, ensuring that the organization provides for its growth and renewal while staying true to itself. Stewards distinguish between what Heifetz et al. (2009) call the "essential from the expendable" (p. 65). They defend the essential at all costs, while making sure everything else—strategies and tactics, structures and systems—is open to review and revision. They employ the directional imperatives as an organizational bungee cord, the unbreakable but flexible tie that binds, that which allows the organization to stay effective while remaining itself. This provides the organization ample opportunity to adjust and change shape, even dramatically, but without compromising its identity or losing its way. The result is an organization that is focused and consistent in doing the necessary things well, but without becoming narrow and rigid (see Figure 18.4).

Centralized–Distributed Tensions

Perhaps the greatest challenge of the Steward Role is to constructively manage the centralizing and distributive forces in organizational life. Centripetal forces refer to the organization's centralizing tendencies. These forces bring the disparate parts of the organization together, and

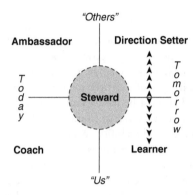

Figure 18.4 Continuity–change tensions.

move each person or function toward its unifying center. Centrifugal forces refer to the distributive tendencies of the organization. These forces separate the various, diverse individuals or functional parts of an organization, moving the organization away from its unifying center. Organizations are under constant bombardment from these competing forces and are susceptible to the destructive impact of both tendencies if left unchecked.

The centralized–distributive tension is not embedded in the competing demands of the Roles, but in two opposing necessities: (1) The compelling need for Leaders to insure the integrity and effectiveness of the organization around its directional imperatives and to do what only they can do as Leaders to add value to the organization; and (2) The equally compelling need for broad participation and ownership among "front-line" member-leaders in the leadership work. McCraw (2001) observed, "In the running of a company of whatever size, the hardest thing to manage is usually this: the delicate balance between the necessity for centralized control and the equally strong need for employees to have enough autonomy to make maximum contributions to the company and derive satisfaction from their work. To put it another way, the problem is exactly where within the company to lodge the power to make different kinds of decisions" (p. 1).

The Principle of Subsidiarity and the Distribution of Leadership

Gardner (1995) notes, "Dispersing power is an endless task: it never stays dispersed for long. In authoritarian systems, of course, it never gets dispersed at all" (p. xv). Making sure power and decision-making prerogatives reside with those closest to the action is called the principle of *subsidiarity*. Subsidiarity is the idea that a central authority should perform only those tasks that cannot be performed effectively at a local level. Those closest to the task, problem, or opportunity are typically in the best position to decide and act because they are the most likely to know firsthand the realities of the situation and directly experience the ramifications of their decisions and actions. This principle opposes the centralizing impulse found in most societies and organizations as ineffective and ultimately dehumanizing in that it keeps "ordinary" citizens or organization members in a perpetual state of dependence on a distant, powerful few.

In an organizational context, subsidiarity holds that nothing should be done by the more powerful, centralized part of the organization that can be done just as well by less formally powerful parts. Or conversely, centralized authority should take on only the work that exceeds the capacities of individuals or smaller groups acting independently of the central authority. Thus, top Leadership does what only it can do in those areas that fall within its exclusive competence. For business organizations, this may include providing for the flow of information throughout the organization and making long-range strategic decisions on the investment of capital and research and development efforts. Accordingly, Leaders take care not to usurp the prerogatives or undermine the initiative of member-leaders closest to the action.

Managing This Tension through Simple Rules

Stewards employ the simple rules associated with each Role to manage this tension (we exist to keep our promises to the world, others matter, keep learning, and more leaders). Without consensus around the simple rules, the organization is at the mercy of centripetal forces, easy prey for factions and splits around competing agendas and personalities. However, the collective embrace and application of the simple rules makes possible widespread and powerfully effective actions by member-leaders as they respond constructively to the complex and dynamic realities and novel opportunities set before them. Kanter (2008) notes, "People versed in universal standards are often most innovative when they apply those standards to local situations" (p. 48).

The power of simple rules resides in their function as an internal guidance system, prompting member-leaders to act in support of the organization's purpose, mission, and core values without being told. Simple rules generate "spontaneous coherence" as they guide the choices and actions of diverse or otherwise disconnected individuals or teams to work independently, but not at cross-purposes. The simple rules serve as an invisible hand, an informal but exceptionally powerful influence over the daily life of the organization, guiding and aligning the scattered and independent actions of member-leaders without input from central, formal authority. The simple rules prompt member-leaders with little or no formal power to act voluntarily, make tough decisions, take risks, handle threats, and seize opportunities all without official permission and, at times, even the knowledge of those with formal power.

Toward this end, Stewards with positional authority do not hoard the hard currency of leadership prerogatives in the form of envisioning a better future, setting strategic goals, taking the initiative to bring about constructive change, and accessing organizational resources, especially information. Instead, Leaders foster an ethic of ownership, serving as a catalyst for widespread participation and collaboration (described further in chapter 21). This means distributing leadership prerogatives—resources, especially important information, as well as accountability for critical outcomes—throughout the organization. Furthermore, it means inviting member-leaders into constructive conversations around strategic opportunities and how to best invest the resources of the organization, what Adler et al. (2011) calls participative centralization. "It's participative because the collaborative enterprise seeks to mobilize everyone's knowledge; it's centralized because that knowledge must be coordinated so that it can be applied at scale" (p. 100). This structure is "simultaneously innovative and efficient, agile and scalable...By marrying a sense of purpose to a robust operating structure, these collaborative organizations are harnessing knowledge workers' creativity in a flexible—but also highly manageable—fashion" (p. 97).

This is no "soft" approach to organizational life. It is exceptionally rigorous. Everyone assumes accountability for outcomes and answers for how they use resources to secure valued ends. Everyone has the opportunity and obligation to contribute, to get important work done, to help create an organization they care about and that will deliver on its promises to the world today and in decades to come. As full partners in the success of the organization, member-leaders hear all the news, not just the positive and encouraging news, but also the sober realities that touch on the welfare and progress of the organization. Everyone is given a voice to discuss what the organization should look like and how it should work, as well as the responsibility to make it work.

Summary

Polarity tensions cannot be resolved—nor should they be. Collins and Porras (2004) note:

> A visionary company doesn't seek to balance between short-term and long-term. It seeks to do very well in the short term and very well in the long term . . . it doesn't simply balance between a tightly held core ideology and stimulating vigorous change and movement; it does both to an extreme . . . Irrational? Perhaps. Rare? Yes. Difficult? Absolutely. But as F. Scott Fitzgerald pointed out, "The test of a first-rate intelligence is the ability to hold two opposed ideas in the mind at the same time and still retain the ability to function." This is exactly what the visionary companies are able to do. (pp. 44–45)

Stewards productively manage these tensions, refusing to allow one aspect of organizational life to dominate the other, knowing that, if this happens, the effectiveness and sustainability of the organization is placed at risk. Without both ends of the polarity in play (either–or) the organization has the benefit of neither. However, when both ends of the polarity are held in constructive tension (both–and), the organization has something special, something significantly better than either end of the polarity exercised independent of the other.

Following the Script: Show up, Pay Attention, and Ask Good Questions

Stewards help shape a New Normal-friendly culture by asking questions that matter. These questions are designed to prompt a candid, friendly, and constructive conversation around its performance in each Role. In addition to discussing the questions previously identified for each Role, the following questions are specific to the Steward Role.

Us–Others Tensions

Does our internal strength match our external commitments—are we doing sufficiently well in the Coach and Learner Roles such that we are strong enough to sustain our performance in bringing benefit to others?

Today–Tomorrow Tensions

Are we sacrificing the future on the altar of the present? Are we preserving the past at the expense of future effectiveness? Does our short-term success contribute to our sustainable performance? Or is our short-term success draining us of resources and energy?

Continuity–Change Tensions

What is essential and non-negotiable? Are we staying true to these? Are we quick to change in negotiable areas to improve our effectiveness?

Centralized–Distributed Tensions

How are we doing in sharing the leadership work? Are Leaders doing what only they can do? Do member-leaders own the leadership work?

When It Works: Toward a New Normal-Friendly Culture

Many organizations are constitutionally unfit to meet the exacting demands of a New Normal operating environment. Some lack clear strategic direction or betray an inward focus. Others cannot—or will not—learn. Moreover, perhaps most damaging, many organizations rely primarily on the assets of one or a few exceptional Leaders and relegate the contribution of member-leaders to the strict confines of a functional job description.

When the Steward Role is played well, it prevents these from happening by building two capabilities into the organization.

Focused Flexibility

New Normal-friendly organizations manifest a rare "both–and" combination of focus and flexibility, discipline and creativity, and stability and agility. The organization is both principled and responsive. Effective twenty-first-century organizations are built on a solid foundation of core values and a clear mission, with an adaptive overlay of continuous learning—a rock-solid foundation with an ever-changing structure on top. The Direction Setter and Learner Roles complement, rather than detract, from the other. The directional imperatives are clearly understood, widely embraced, and tenaciously practiced—the discipline part (Direction Setter Role). However, the organization simultaneously manifests flexibility in living out these non-negotiable commitments—the creative and adaptable part (Learner Role). In this "both–and" frame, discipline amplifies creativity rather than diminishes it. Furthermore, creativity is exercised not for its own sake, but for the welfare and progress of the organization.

Widespread Participation, Ownership, and Collaboration

The Steward Role addresses an aspect of organizational life that is, perhaps, the most difficult to change and most important to New Normal success—the distribution of power and leadership prerogatives. Although the unique obligations of Leaders are taken seriously, the counterproductive Old Normal themes of control and unilateralism are rejected. In New Normal-friendly organizations, every member-leader, no matter his or her place on the organizational chart, has a stake in the effective performance of the organization. The authority to act is decentralized so that those closest to the problems and opportunities can execute and innovate within the context of directional clarity and supported by the simple rules.

A Word to Leaders

The idea of stewardship does not nullify the formal authority of Leaders or suggest they abdicate power. Power is a fact of organizational life. The issue is how Leaders utilize it. Leaders can employ power to contribute to the welfare and progress of the organization or to weaken it. They can abuse power in the service of self-interest, or rise above self-interest and infuse the organization with moral strength to serve the greater good.

As Stewards, Leaders operate out of a deep sense of gratitude and accountability, recognizing that the organization, in itself, creates the very possibility of possessing power. They believe that the formal authority they possess is not a birthright, not a means of control, and, certainly, not a means for the expansion of self-interest. As Stewards, they are deeply aware that the resources of the organization are not their own; that every resource at their disposal, including formal authority, is a loan of trust given them to use judiciously and constructively to ensure the welfare and progress of the organization and benefit those it serves.

Summary

The metaphor of the Steward provides an organizing framework, a powerful, synthesizing vision of leadership as the work of shaping an organization capable of thriving in the New Normal—a humane and productive organization. This metaphor is a reminder that the practice of New Normal leadership is driven by a deeply ethical and communitarian vision of organizational life. Building a New Normal-friendly organization is a shared moral project, requiring the contribution not only of a powerful few at the top of the organization, but also by many member-leaders distributed throughout the organization, each intent on creating an organization worth inhabiting, as well as one uniquely qualified to thrive in the twenty-first century.

SECTION V

The 4R Model: Responsibilities

The act of leading—leadership as a verb—includes a short list of practices that cut across both Old and New Normal narratives. Both narratives call for Leaders to establish and communicate a particular direction for the organization. Both emphasize the collective processes that achieve the valued outcomes associated with this direction. Specifically, both Old Normal and New Normal narratives call upon Leaders to practice the following: (1) cast vision, (2) develop strategies, (3) get members to do the vision and participate in the strategies, and (4) help members continue in difficult times.

The New Normal Difference

The New Normal version of each leadership practice differs significantly from the Old Normal version. Specifically, New Normal leadership practices are a collaborative effort, requiring Leaders and member-leaders to draw from the DICE + 1 virtue configuration (Relationships) to effectively implement each practice.

If effective leadership is framed as virtue-driven influence, it is best to think of the work of leading less as focused "in" or "on" a particular person or persons, and more as embedded in the interactions between and among Leaders and member-leaders. Leadership emerges from the interactions of many as they relate, decide, and respond to the realities set before them and seek to keep their promises to the world. Leading is something many do together, not something a few special people do on behalf of the many who, due to their status as "ordinary" members, are obliged only to respond and follow.

The direct influence of a Leader is mediated by a complex set of relational networks, some of which extend to the fringe of the organization, far beyond the control of those with formal authority. Although it may be humbling, at times exasperating and perhaps troubling to Leaders, it is, nevertheless, true that the welfare and progress of the organization depends on the cumulative, day-to-day efforts of "ordinary" members who work well beyond their direct influence.

Consequently, leading in the New Normal demands not just a few Leaders at the top of the organization casting a compelling vision or making brilliant strategic decisions. A hierarchy of powerful Leaders giving orders to compliant followers may get tasks done efficiently and accomplish short-term goals, but it will not sustain progress in a complex and unpredictable operating environment. Progress is sustained only as long as many members connected by a shared sense of the future and working in collaboration act in the service of the directional imperatives of the organization.

This section discusses the Responsibilities of leading—what Leaders and member-leaders do together to advance the organization's mission and secure its long-term welfare and progress.

CHAPTER 19

Vision Casting

Introduction

At its most fundamental level, leadership is about energy—generating it, channeling it, releasing it, and sustaining it. Leading in the New Normal is about dispensing a particular kind of energy—the energy of a virtue-driven, collective effort in service of a noble cause. Vision Casting focuses on generating momentum. Strategy Making focuses on creating momentum-bearing structures, pathways to the future which insure that the energy generated by the vision is effectively employed. Aligning focuses on releasing momentum in and through members such that many are vitally engaged in closing the gap between the vision and reality. Encouraging is focused on sustaining momentum amid difficulties, delays, and discouragement. It all starts with vision.

The Practice

The term vision is derived from the Latin *video*, from the root word *videre*, meaning "to see." Whether in Old or New Normal contexts, the work of leading begins when a person or group sees a state of affairs, an alternative future, that does not yet exist, and which, in substantive ways, is better than the present. Of necessity, this state of affairs is in conflict with the present status quo. The vision signals an ethical imperative in that it imagines a better state of affairs than the present—a "there" that is superior to "here," and, thus, must be pursued. MacIntyre (1984) stated, "There is no present which is not informed by some image of some future and an image of the future which always presents itself in the form of a *telos*—or a variety of ends or goals—toward which we are moving or failing to move in the present" (pp. 215–216).

Vision critiques the gap between the world-as-it now-is and the world-as-it-must one-day-become. Things must change and, as they do, the world will be a better place. This critique is a value judgment—the present, the "here and now," is, in fundamentally important ways, inadequate, even "wrong." The world, or at least the corner of it in which the organization operates, must be transformed in accordance with its directional imperatives.

Furthermore, a clearly articulated vision gives the organization guidance on two critical questions: (1) What must stay the same in terms of its deep identity, operating philosophy, values, and enduring commitments; and (2) What future, among many alternative futures, is the organization obliged to pursue. Collins and Porras (1996) state, "Vision provides guidance about what core to preserve and what future to stimulate progress toward" (p. 66).

Definition

Vision Casting is the process of identifying and articulating a new and better version of the world. Vision Casting involves: (1) crafting an intellectually credible and emotionally engaging picture of a better future in line with the organization's directional imperatives; (2) communicating this picture in a variety of venues, both inside and outside the organization; and (3) continually revising this picture based on the realities and opportunities faced by the organization.

In the context of the 4R Model, vision is a picture of an ideal future that embodies the directional imperatives of the organization as determined in the Direction Setter Role—the purpose, mission, and core values of the organization. The work done in the Direction Setter Role provides the context, framework, and "raw material" for Vision Casting, with the directional imperatives shaping the vision, setting its trajectory, and defining its boundaries.

Although the terms purpose, mission, and vision are often used interchangeably, the 4R Model differentiates between each term. Purpose is the organization's general direction, its North Star, its reason for existing. Mission is the answer to the question, "What, specifically, will we do for whom?" Vision is the cumulative expression of the directional imperatives communicated in an intellectually credible and emotionally compelling manner. It is the completion of the sentence, "I see a day when." The primary contribution of the Direction Setter Role is to provide strategic clarity. The primary contribution of Vision Casting is the generation of energy and momentum in the service of directional imperatives. This is a substantive, not semantic, difference. Individuals and organizations need both clarity and energy. One cannot substitute for the other.

The Old Normal Version

The Old Normal assumption—born of the myth of charisma and technical–managerial competence—is that visionaries and grand strategist are the real Leaders. Everyone else is a "follower" responsible to carry out the details. The work of Vision Casting is the product of the creative insight of a few special Leaders who anticipate the future and identify grand possibilities for the organization. As one author put it, "I have found that 'executive vision' or the ability to view scenarios in terms of extended planning horizons, is an integral part of the upper management psyche. Some top executives, for example, are capable of planning in 20 year time spans" (Jacques, 1985, p. 8). The assumption is that an elite few are endowed from birth—this is not a learned skill—with the ability to anticipate the future and communicate it as, more or less, a finished product.

A New Normal Twist: Vision Casting Is a Collaborative Practice Supported by Sensemaking

Although there is nothing inherently wrong with the Old Normal approach to Vision Casting, the New Normal version of the practice places a new layer of demands and expectations on Leaders and member-leaders as well. Specifically, the New Normal version of Vision Casting is an exercise in collaborative engagement featuring the collective exercise of sensemaking.

Twist #1: Effective New Normal Vision Casting Is a Collaborative Practice

Burns (2003) and Kuhn (2012), among others, have observed that vision is the creative product of collective, constructive discontent—a process of "creative abrasion" that serves as a catalyst for imagining new possibilities for the organization in the context of its problems or dilemmas. Something is not working; there is gap between the "is and ought," prompting a growing sense of dissatisfaction, confusion, or irritation.

In the dynamic operating environment of the New Normal, it takes the creative insight of many to make sense of the interplay between the shifting realities of today and the emerging possibilities of tomorrow. Although many effective New Normal Leaders do, indeed, see future possibilities clearly, they also appreciate the fact that "ordinary" members often see through a lens just as powerful and imaginative. Consequently, the work of Vision Casting is less about the creative insight of one or a few Leaders, and more about a collaborative process calling on the entire organization to make sense of today and envision a better tomorrow. Heifetz observes:

> Imagine the differences in behavior between leaders who operate with the idea that "leadership means influencing the organization to follow the leader's vision" and those who operate with the idea that "leadership means influencing the organization to face its problems and live into it opportunities." That second idea—mobilizing people to tackle tough challenges—is what defines the new job of the leader. (Taylor, 2003)

Twist #2: Effective New Normal Vision Casting Depends on the "Next Practice" of Sense Making

Deep change necessitates commensurate deep dissatisfaction with the status quo, and this, in turn, demands an accurate appraisal of present realities—the entire organization must get on the same "reality page." The organization must collectively identify what, specifically, is so terribly wrong with the present that it must leave it behind to embark on a journey to an unknown future. The answer is found in the juxtaposition of a vision of what could be, superimposed over a sober assessment of what is. As these two fields of sight are aligned, it provides the organization a new interpretive framework to assess the present state of affairs. What was a confusing jumble of circumstances is now brought into sharp focus as an unacceptable situation alive with possibilities and ripe for change. This shared reality is the starting point for the journey to the future.

Doing the Work of *Vision Casting*

Vision Casting is the ongoing work (it is a process, not an event) of shaping and sharing an intellectually satisfying and emotionally compelling narrative about the organization, highlighting its directional imperatives. The present, in all of its inherent confusion, ambiguity, and difficulty, and the future, in all of its opportunity and possibility, is translated into a simple and powerful set of words and ideas, goals and mental images that define the next chapter of the organization's story.

The following process provides a framework for this collective leadership work.

Step 1: A Better Future Is Out There for the Taking

Almost everyone in the organization is asking a few fundamentally important questions: "Are our best years ahead of us or behind us?" "Is there a next chapter?" The answer is "yes." A better future is not only possible, it is right around the corner, and we can see it emerging, even now. The aim of this step is to infuse the organization with a hopeful picture of its preferred future that reflects the organization's deepest values and highest aspirations—the organization at its best making its corner of the world a better place. Naïve hopes, vague generalities, or subjective abstractions in the mind of a few Leaders will not suffice. Rather, a clear and compelling picture must be painted—a picture that is full of promise, possibilities, and opportunities.

Step 2: Getting on the Same Reality Page

The aim of this step is to get the organization on the same "reality page," to awaken members to the deficiencies and unacceptable realities of the present chapter of organizational life. A vision for a better future is attractive to the degree that the present is intolerable. The organization must be dissatisfied with the present situation if it is to embrace the change promoted by the vision—significant change necessitates deep dissatisfaction with the status quo. The need is for a hard dose of reality, bleak and stark though it may be—the present is incongruous with the directional imperatives of the organization. Consequently, we cannot go on like this anymore.

This is not about manufacturing a crisis, although crisis is often an important facilitating condition for the embrace of a transforming vision (Conger & Kanungo, 1987; 1994). Rather, it is about making a credible case that the status quo is more dangerous than launching into an unknown future; that the difficulties inherent in the journey to the future—and there will be many—pale in comparison to the difficulties of staying put.

Step 3: There Is a Way Forward

This aim of this step is to identify the next steps forward—what the organization can and must do today to turn the page and begin its next chapter. This step is an affirmation that there are concrete alternatives to the status quo, a credible path out of the unacceptable present, that a better future is ours to claim and begin working toward. The next chapter begins today, here and now, and here is how.

This step relies on the work done in the previous two steps. Now the argument for taking constructive action can be made with urgency, credibility, and conviction. Fatalism is countered, friendship with the status quo is challenged, and hope is given a constituency. What was yesterday an intolerable situation beset with hard facts and immovable obstacles is now alive with possibilities and ripe for change. When this step is done well, it sets the stage for the work of Strategy Making (see chapter 20).

Step 4: Getting the Right People Moving in the Right Direction

The aim of this step is to communicate the story line of the next chapter in clear and compelling words and images that can be readily understood and embraced by many as feasible and practical. The case must be made that the preferred future is not merely one of many possible futures. It is our future—the kind of future demanded by our purpose, mission, and values. The vision is not merely an abstract mix of good ideas, but an invitation to share in creating an organization and a world that members deeply care about and are willing to work toward. When this step is done well, it sets the stage for the work of Aligning.

Step 5: Let Us Start Now

Hopeful people see the possibilities for a better future, and what they see fills them with positive energy to begin the journey. The aim of this step is to put hope to work by identifying opportunities to act on the vision—a difference can be made, and here is how, together, we can begin making it. It is time to turn the page to a new chapter, so let us begin writing the first lines together, today. When this step is done well, it also sets the stage for the work of Aligning.

When Vision Casting Works

Energy and Momentum Is Generated

Vision that is well communicated generates energy and momentum. Vision jump-starts the future. Like a magnifying glass focusing the sunlight, vision generates energy sufficient to break the power of the status quo. As a compelling picture of a preferred future is communicated, every corner of organizational life in infused with energy and momentum.

Discretionary Effort Is Unleashed

Vision infuses the organization with hope and courage, moral purpose, a good and compelling reason to continue the journey, the "why" that prompts many to go the "extra mile" in difficult times. "If we discern a plot to our lives, we are more likely to take ourselves and our lives seriously. If nothing is connected, nothing matters" (Taylor, 2001, p. 2). When people see themselves as participants in a shared story, they are reminded that their choices matter, that they are not alone, and that the possibilities of the future requires their best effort today.

Collaborative Action Is Initiated and Sustained

When many see the future clearly and feel it deeply, and give a discretionary effort, it provides the basis for collaborative action, unleashing the collective talent and creativity of the organization.

Shared Trust Is Cultivated

As discretionary effort becomes the norm, it lays the foundation for shared trust. A clear vision, widely embraced, prompts the organization to pay attention to what is critically important, and to order its collective life around these vital necessities. The vision gives members a baseline to discriminate among the good, better, and best of daily options for investing limited time and energy, providing the framework to make the small, but significant, daily contributions required for turning the vision into reality. This evokes a shared sense of responsibility and mutual accountability that, in turn, fosters trust between and among members to do what the vision requires, to play their part as a character in the story, and trusting that others will do the same.

A Word to Leaders

Leaders Go First as Necessary

Vision Casting is an exercise in inviting others bound up in an all-too-real present to work toward a future that does not yet exist. Members may need prompting to question cherished assumptions or help in identifying the gap between "what is" and "what could be." This often requires Leaders to speak and act first. Burns (2003) states, "The key distinctive role of leadership at the outset is that leaders take the initiative. They address their creative insights to potential followers, seize their attention, spark further action. The first act is decisive because it breaks up a static situation and establishes a relationship. It is, in every sense, a creative act" (p. 172).

Leaders Call for a Collaborative Effort

Going first does not mean going alone. Leaders serve as catalysts for widespread participation, calling on member-leaders to bring their talent and insight, energy and experience, to the work of Vision Casting. They best serve the organization by leveraging its collective assets of those who will be called upon to implement the vision. Henton et al. (2004) call this new kind of Leader a "visionary pragmatist." Visionary pragmatists "see the value in working in more collaborative ways to solve complex problems based on fundamental principles and shared values" (pp. 233–234).

4R Model Connections

Relationships

Vision Casting is not a "workshop skill" learned in a half-day seminar, although there are technical skills associated with this practice such as presentation skills and setting priorities. Rather, it is a collaborative process dependent on attitudes and behaviors found in the DICE + 1 configuration.

Dynamic Determination

Vision Casting draws on the faith and hope found in Dynamic Determination. Informed by faith, Leaders and member-leaders infuse the organization with a transcendent perspective, giving it the ability see beyond the confinements and confusion of the present, and strengthening many to collaborate and give a discretionary effort on the journey to the future. Informed by hope, Leaders and member-leaders live constructively in the tension between the painful realities of an unacceptable today, and the anticipation of a better tomorrow. They make the credible case that the best days of the organization are still ahead, that there is a better future worth sacrificing for—one that is worthy of its best collective effort, even its enduring sacrifice.

Intellectual Flexibility
Vision Casting draws upon the perceptive capacity of Leaders and member-leaders to envision a better future for the organization beyond the boundaries of its past experience and the confinement of its present reality; to make sense of the complex and shifting landscape—the problems and possibilities, opportunities and obstacles faced by the organization; to stay alert to new beginnings and opportunities on the horizon and to discern the way forward.

Courageous Character
The fundamental, driving force of New Normal leadership is a moral vision secured by means consistent with this vision—virtuous ends accomplished by virtuous means employed by virtuous people (Bass & Steidlmeier, 1999). As agents of moral change, Leaders and member-leaders must personally embody the moral quality of the change they envision and pursue (Burns, 2003).

Emotional Maturity
Vision Casting is a relational and emotional process. There may be good reasons for members to take issue with the vision including a differing hierarchy of values, divergent priorities, incompatible assumptions about the present, and competing visions of the future. Even if there is general agreement on these concerns, the vision calls flesh and blood people with their own hopes and fears, aspirations and anxieties—including those casting the vision—to face hard realities and move forward in the face of difficulty.

Roles and Organizational Culture

Organizational culture enhances or inhibits Vision Casting—culture always wins. If collaborative engagement is valued (Steward) and simple rules are embedded in daily organization life (we exist to keep our promises to the world, we need more leaders, we learn what we must, and what others think and want is of utmost importance to us), it enhances Vision Casting. If the organization is insular, lacks directional clarity, ignores the simple rules, and leadership prerogatives are not widely distributed, even the most compelling vision will likely go lacking for support.

Summary

In the work of Vision Casting, Leaders and member-leaders invite the organization to make sense of the present and envision a better future. The vision sets before the organization a worthy but difficult journey, and generates the energy and momentum to begin. When Vision Casting is done well, it lays the foundation for the work of Strategy Making and Aligning.

CHAPTER 20

Strategy Making

Introduction

The most powerful vision is merely a good idea until it is translated into a series of actionable steps that make a real-world difference. Warren Bennis notes, "For action without vision is stumbling in the dark, and vision without action is poverty-stricken poetry" (Nanus, 1992, p. xv.) Dreaming must be joined with doing, ideas with implementation, envisioning with executing—all in the context of relentless change and fierce competition. Determining the next, best steps and providing the collective framework to take them is the work of Strategy Making.

The Practice

The term "strategy" is derived from the Greek *strategos,* meaning "a general." The general who understands battle conditions more clearly, adjusts to shifting conditions more readily, seizes opportunities more boldly, and outthinks his opponents improves his chances of victory. Borrowing from military imagery, strategy is the art and science of maneuvering people and resources into the most advantageous position in light of a competitive threat, whether the threat is from an opponent, a rival organization, or simply the fact that "reality is stacking the deck" against achieving the vision.

Strategy Making Defined

Strategy Making is the disciplined search for the best ways to accomplish the vision. It is "the process by which ends are related to means, intentions to capabilities, objectives to resources" (Gaddis, 2005, p. viii). Strategy Making is the work of designing a conceptual framework, a series of next best steps, a first level of detail that captures the energy and momentum generated by the vision, and wisely utilizes the assets of the organization to achieve the vision.

Strategy as a Conceptual Framework

A strategy is a conceptual framework, a way of thinking about seizing the opportunity for advancement toward one's objectives. Mintzberg (1994a) notes:

> No one has ever touched a strategy. Strategies, in other words, do not exist as tangible entities. They are abstract concepts, in the minds of people. And the best of them seem to be gestalt in nature, tightly integrated, whether intended strategies as synthesized patterns of preferences prior to the taking of actions or realized strategies as synthesized patterns already formed among actions. (p. 240)

A strategy is "The preferred if ever-evolving framework by which companies understand what is happening to them and how they should react" (Kiechel, 2010, p. xi). Although you cannot pick up a strategy and touch it, nevertheless, it powerfully shapes how the organization invests its recourses and conducts its collective, daily life in service of its vision.

Strategy as a Sustainable Competitive Advantage

A strategy is a catchall framework for understanding "all-the-organization-must-do" to stay effective in a fast changing and hyper-competitive environment. According to Porter (1998a), strategy is about achieving a "sustainable competitive advantage" over business rivals. Porter frames strategy as the choice to be different from competitors that is aimed at creating a product or service of greater value to the customer or a comparable value at lower cost (Porter, 1998b). The organization must then work in a disciplined manner to achieve "fit"—an alignment of all organizational activities and assets with this choice. Lafley and Martin (2013) state, "Strategy is an integrated set of choices that uniquely positions the firm in its industry so as to create a sustainable advantage and superior value relative to the competition" (p. 3). Simply put, strategy is a coherent and disciplined approach to winning over time.

Strategy Serves Vision

Strategy serves vision in three ways.

First, strategy serves as a bridge from "here to there," linking the organization's vision with present realities by providing a series of "next best steps" forward. It provides feet to vision's wings—the framework in which the organization accomplishes its dreams.

Second, strategy provides an overarching framework for the disciplined release of resources, the combination and sequence by which the organization most effectively invests its resources—the attention of Leaders and member-leaders, its unique assets, talent, energy, and finances—to accomplish its vision.

Third, strategy provides the framework through which the vision is progressively accomplished through a pattern of collective effort. A strategy translates the organization's vision into coherent, collective "action sequences" that make it possible for many members to act daily in the service of the vision.

The Old Normal Version

The Old Normal narrative assumes that strategic insight is embedded in the organizational hierarchy—a few Leaders and strategic planning experts being the smartest and best-informed people in the organization. The narrative assumes that the route to the future is relatively straightforward and linear—the shortest distance between two points is a straight line. Old Normal Leaders design strategies based on an assessment of present realities and needs, and make decisions on how to invest organizational resources to get from point A to point B in a fast and efficient manner. The strategy is presented to the organization as, more or less, a finished product—a polished work of genius. Members are expected to execute the strategy. If they are competent and work hard, all will be well—strategic goals will be accomplished and measurable progress is assured—typically, in the short term. If strategies do not work, the problem resides with the shortcoming of members, not the strategy.

A New Normal Twist: Strategy Making as an Emergent, Collaborative Practice

The Old Normal version of Strategy Making puts the organization at a competitive disadvantage in the New Normal. Hamel warns, "In most companies, strategy making and resource allocation are centralized, a fact that seriously undermines resilience" (2012, p. 187). The New Normal version of Strategy Making places a new layer of demands and expectations on Leaders. Strategy Making is not an act of genius by a few. It is not about plotting a straight course from "here to there"—straight routes are rare in the wilderness. Rather, it is a learning process engaged in by many throughout the organization. It is a collaborative and participatory endeavor, where an idea or insight is judged by its merit, not the authority level of its source, and many are given the opportunity to contribute.

Twist #1: Effective New Normal Strategy Making Is More a Messy Process Than a Tidy, Centrally Planned Event

It is a fiction born of the myths of charisma and technical–managerial competence that strategies are formulated, Mozart-like, as an instantaneous event in the mind of an exceptional Leader. Strategies do not roll off the assembly line ready for organization-wide implementation. They do not emerge from quarterly planning meetings as fully detailed plans of action. The idea of one or a few Leaders operating as strategic gurus developing "silver-bullet, can't miss strategies" is incongruous with a rapidly changing and complex world where information travels at the speed of light and problems and opportunities come and go just as quickly; where the logic of events, rather than the intuition of one or a few individuals, drives strategic effectiveness.

Effective strategies typically emerge over time as part of a messy, nonlinear process embedded in complex interpersonal and organizational dynamics. Mintzberg calls this emergent strategy (1987, 1994a, 1994b). Emergent strategies bubble up to the surface of organizational life one action and one decision at a time, to converge in a set of consistent and effective strategic behaviors. Although the first stages of the emergent strategy are often ill defined, the new action pattern gradually gains specificity and definition as the organization learns in real-world contexts and makes necessary adjustments (Mintzberg, 1989; Quinn, 1980).

Twist #2: Effective New Normal Strategy Making Is a Collective Learning Process

Seeing through the clutter of options and opportunities and finding the most efficient and effective pathway to the future is, of necessity, a collective learning process implemented at every level of the organization. It is more about the combined wisdom of the organization than the brilliance of a few Leaders. Consequently, access to strategically important information, and the opportunity to participate in the choice, evaluation, and revision of strategies must be widely distributed throughout the organization.

Twist #3: Effective New Normal Strategy Making Manages the Tension Between Focus and Flexibility

The emergent nature of Strategy Making poses a challenge in managing the tension between strategic focus and operational flexibility. On one hand, strategies work only as the organization works at them. Once the strategy, for all its emergent imperfection, is decided upon, it must be rigorously executed, and this requires high levels of dedication and focus.

Furthermore, although the organization must stay sufficiently focused, it must also exercise sufficient flexibility to respond quickly and constructively to performance feedback, as well as shifts in the internal and external environment signaling new strategic realities. Occasionally, a strategy may be instantaneously effective. However, it is far more likely that it will return from its forays in the external operating environment somewhat the worse for wear and in need of refinement, revision, and, occasionally, outright replacement.

Doing the Work of Strategy Making

What differentiates an effective strategy—one that works in the real world, from a "paper strategy"—one that looks good in concept, but never delivers real-world performance? The answer resides not only in the content of the strategy itself, but also in the process used to design, evaluate, and refine the strategy. The following is a robust framework for Strategy Making, a practical way to create a strategy worth the effort required to execute it.

Step 1. Revisiting the Future

The Strategy-Making process begins with revisiting the vision and directional imperatives of the organization. In this step, the organization asks if it is thinking properly about the future and its possibilities. Lafley and Martin (2013) call it the organization's "winning aspiration."

Step 2. Facing the Present

Strategy Making asks the organization to see the world anew, in all its possibilities (Step 1) whereas also conducting a rigorous analysis of the world and the organization as it now, in actuality, is. The SWOT analysis, developed by Kenneth Andrews in the 1960s, is a tried and true way to evaluate the organization's Strengths and Weaknesses, and rigorously assess the external operating environment in terms of emerging Opportunities and Threats. This calls the organization to take a cold, hard look at the present state of affairs within the organization and its immediate operating environment.

The SWOT analysis has a 3-fold function. First, it identifies the organization's competitive strengths and weaknesses—does the organization possess the skills, structures, systems, and staff to accomplish its strategic objectives in a competitive environment? Strengths identify the unique and enduring value the organization has to offer the world. A strength must be rare—if it is available to any competitor, it will not confer a sustainable advantage. It must be difficult to imitate—if not based on unique assets, competitors will duplicate them. It must be non-substitutable and, thus, of durable value—not carbon paper and typewriters in an electronic age. Weaknesses identify the organization's competitive liabilities—a lack of talent or resources, or areas of underperformance that put the organization at a competitive disadvantage.

Second, the SWOT analysis assesses threats and opportunities in the external operating environment. A threat is a competitor, demographic trend, or set of customers that may nullify the effects of the organization's strategy. Porter's (1998b) Five Forces Driving Industry categorize the competitive threats faced by any organization: (1) The threat of new entrants; (2) Rivalry among existing firms; (3) The threat of substitute products or services; (4) The bargaining power of buyers; and (5) The bargaining power of suppliers. Opportunities refer to favorable economic or demographic trends in the competitive climate for the expansion of products or services—wind at the back of the organization's strategies.

Third, the SWOT analysis generates a picture of the organization's strategic situation by matching its strengths with opportunity, and guarding against the intersection of its weakness and threats. Rumelt (2011) states, "The most basic idea of strategy is the application of strength against weakness. Or, if you prefer, strength applied to the most promising opportunity" (p. 9). This step calls Leaders and member leaders to create a narrative around the facts identified in the first two steps, to develop a "feel for the situation"—an intuitive sense on how the future might play out in light of the facts. The challenge is similar to competing in chess, where disciplined observation and analytical skill is joined with intuitive insight. Chess Grand Masters see beyond the facts, the present location of the chess pieces, to the meaning and implications of the facts, how the game might play out in the next five, ten, 50 or more moves. The Germans call this *positionsgefuhl*, meaning an instinct for position, an intuitive sense of the future implications of the facts.

Similarly, the organization must get a read on contours and trajectory of the strategic landscape. The facts must have their say. However, facts are not stable, discrete, isolated objects that can be lined up one after the other and placed under a microscope for analysis. Rather, facts are embedded in a larger, dynamic flow of circumstances and events; still frames in the motion picture of life; part of an emerging mosaic embedded in a larger, complex, and ever-changing strategic situation. This analytical–intuitive challenge demands a process of give and take around strategic alternatives, consideration of alternative perspectives, and weighing the pros and cons of various responses to opportunities and threats. Although the process can be messy, it fosters a conversation that engages members, as well as produces better decisions around strategic alternatives. The SWOT framework is a helpful framewoprk for this conversation (see Figure 20.1).

STRENGTHS	WEAKNESSES
validated competitive assets	validated competitive liabilities
OPPORTUNITIES	**THREATS**
favorable trends/new products and services, etc.	Porter's Five Forces

Figure 20.1   SWOT analysis framework.

Step 3. Investing Assets

The organization must come to agreement on how to best invest organizational assets—leadership attention, the talent of members, financial assets, product and service offerings, and so on—in light of the first two steps. Strategy is about leverage. Richard Rumelt (2011) states, "Good strategy works by focusing energy and resources on one, or a very few, pivotal objectives whose accomplishment will lead to a cascade of favorable outcomes" (p. 53). This choice must find expression in an investment in something particular and concrete, hard-edged and tangible. For example, the strategy may call for an investment in leveraging difficult-to-imitate behaviors, applying unique organizational capabilities, or implementing processes with superior efficiency—all aimed at translating these organizational assets into something of unique and enduring value for those it intends to serve.

Step 4. Staying in a Learning Stance

It is easy to draw up a brilliant touchdown play on the chalkboard. However, then the defense takes the field, with their own brilliant response. In similar fashion, it is easy for an organization to draw up an unbeatable plan, one sure to take it to the "next level." However, the real-world intervenes. Adjustments must be made. Effective strategies must be robust, able to survive and thrive in a harsh operating environment populated by smart and agile competitors. The strategic agenda of the organization must adapt to fluid, unpredictable, and often confusing circumstances, out of which crises appear without warning, and unanticipated opportunities arise. Consequently, the organization must adopt the stance of a humble learner and remain vigilant with respect to shifts in the internal and external environment that necessitate reframing, revising, and, at times, replacing strategies.

Summary

The Strategy-Making process provides a framework for the organization to engage in a collective, candid, and constructive conversation about its opportunities and obstacles, its assets and liabilities, to read the strategic situation, taking into account the full range of internal and external factors relevant to sustaining the progress of the organization in fulfilling its vision.

When Strategy-Making Works

Momentum Is Constructively Channeled

When the Strategy-Making process works, momentum-bearing structures are created that establish a coherent framework for collective action.

Priorities Get Clarified

When the Strategy-Making process works, members get clarity around a critical question: "How can I best utilize my time and talent to contribute to our vision?" Strategies provides the answer in the form of a framework for members to discriminate among the good, better, and best of daily options for making a contribution to the progress of the organization.

The Foundation for Sustained Effectiveness is Established

When the Strategy-Making process works, it alerts the organization to factors in the external environment that are critical to its success, keeps it in touch with its capabilities, and increases the chances it will be resilient in failure.

A Word to Leaders

The fact that the Strategy-Making process is a collaborative endeavor requiring the participation of many does not mean that Leaders abdicate involvement or remain passive in the process. Leaders contribute to the Strategy Making in three ways.

Leaders Make Choices That Reflect the Identity of the Organization

There is no getting around it. Even the most collaborative Leaders must make hard choices, often assuming sole responsibility for decisions that impact the strategic direction of the organization. Montgomery (2012) notes, "It is the leader—the strategist as meaning maker—who must make the vital choices that determine a company's very identity, who says, 'This is our purpose, not that. This is who we will be. This is why our customers and clients will prefer a world with us rather than without us'."

Leaders Stay in Touch with the Progress of Strategies

Hertz CEO Mark Frissora notes:

> It is critical that leaders spend a lot of time where the work actually gets done—that they get into the guts of the business and see what happens there. The further down the chain you go, the easier it is to see how your strategy might not work the way you'd intended. You might even discover that the strategy itself is backwards. You always walk away with a new insight or a new opportunity. (Frissora and Kirkland, 2013)

Charismatic Leaders, and strategic geniuses may quickly lose interest with the details of execution, deeming the process boring or beneath them, and best left to others of lesser standing in the organization. However, when it comes to making sure strategies actually work, there is no substitute for the firsthand experience of senior Leaders.

Leaders Call for Collaborative Effort

Although the strategic intuition of Leaders is indispensable, effective strategies do not necessarily originate with one or a few Leaders. Good strategies often come from unexpected places at surprising times. They can originate from the grass roots or even outer fringes of the organization. Moreover, bad strategies can come from the top, especially when Leaders have little working knowledge or experience with respect to what it takes to execute the strategy. The strategic intuition of the few must be merged with the wisdom and experience of the many who will be called on to execute the strategy.

Leaders meet this challenge by creating the framework for maximum participation—a space for collective, candid, friendly, and rigorous conversations about the strengths and weaknesses, opportunities and threats faced by the organization. Procter and Gamble invites employees to dialog with senior Leaders at strategy review sessions. Lafley and Martin (2013) state, "The goal was to create a culture of inquiry that would surface productive tensions to inform smarter choices. The explicit goal was to create strategists at all levels of the organization" (p. 138). Motivated by the belief that the company will not improve if change is driven from the top, Ritz-Carlton engages its 47,000 employees in an annual SWOT exercise. This inclusive practice reflects Ritz Carlton Service Value 9, which states, "I am involved in the planning of the work that affects me" (Michelli, 2008, p. 142). Employee engagement in the planning process is viewed as integral to the company's competitive advantage (Michelli, 2008, pp. 142–144).

When Leaders protect this "collaborative space," it sends a powerful message to the organization: "This is uncharted territory. None of us has been here before, but we are confident that together we will find our way forward." Imagine the difference between Leaders who operate on the assumption that only an elite few should participate in Strategy Making, and those who believe they best serve the organization as they leverage the insight and experience of many. The second idea of mobilizing members to share in the leadership work differentiates the New Normal Leader from the Old Normal Leader.

The 4R Model Connection

Relationships

Strategy Making is not a "workshop skill" learned in a half-day seminar, although there are technical skills associated with this practice like planning, decision-making, and problem-solving. Rather, it is a collaborative process dependent on attitudes and behaviors found in the DICE + 1 configuration.

Dynamic Determination
Strategy Making calls for Leaders and member-leaders to stay productively engaged in the process, even when it is difficult and without immediate results. Wilberforce—no stranger to enduring in difficulty—noted that great endeavors "Aim at great ends by the gradual operation of well adjusted means, supported by a courage which no danger can intimidate, and a quiet constancy which no hardship can exhaust" (1982, p. 28).

Intellectual Flexibility
Strategy Making is an exercise in wisdom and humility. Wharton Business School professor Michael Useem observes:

> Because the world is now more complicated and more uncertain, I think that on top of always having a great vision there will be a premium on thinking strategically and on being able to come back from setbacks, and maybe above all, on being very good at reading the increasingly ambiguous and uncertain universe we operate in. (Javetski, 2012)

Dogmatism, untested assumptions, and obsolete perspectives are not allowed. Leaders and member-leaders must display proper sensitivity to context and identify novel connections and patterns that signal emerging opportunities and threats. They must integrate and apply new information, listen intently to others, explore new perspectives, make distinctions among good, better, and best ways forward, and, perhaps most importantly, change one's mind as new information is available, and make the adjustments to the organization's course of action.

Courageous Character
The Strategy-Making process depends on a collaborative effort, and this will not happen if trust goes lacking.

Emotional Maturity
In the New Normal wilderness, great ideas often come to nothing. Sound strategies fail. Moreover, reasonable people often differ on the next best steps to take. This calls on those engaged in the process to stay hopeful and solid in the face of adversity and confusion.

Roles and Organizational Culture

Organizational culture enhances or inhibits Strategy Making—culture always wins. If collaborative engagement is valued (Steward), and the simple rule, "keep learning," is embedded in daily organization life, Strategy Making is given right of way. If this simple rule is ignored and the organization does not take a learning stance, if leadership prerogatives are not widely distributed, even brilliant strategies will go lacking for support.

Summary

Strategy Making is the process of creating a framework for vision-informed action while coping with the hypercompetition, volatility, complexity, uncertainty, and ambiguity of the New Normal operating environment. When the Strategy-Making process is done well, it lays the foundation for the work of Aligning, which translates the conceptual work done in Strategy Making into collective, real-world action.

CHAPTER 21

Aligning

Introduction

In the work of Vision Casting, energy and momentum is generated. In the work of Strategy Making, a "momentum-bearing" framework for taking collective action on the vision is established. However, so far, nothing has actually happened. It is time to release momentum and engage the organization in executing the vision. This is the work of Aligning.

The Practice

The work of Aligning is premised on the fact that, in any organization, there exist multiple disconnects between what its vision and strategies demand, and patterns of daily organizational life. Aligning is the work of addressing these disconnects in order to make the strategies work and "get something done." According to Kotter (1990), alignment is "A condition in which a relevant group of people share a common understanding of a vision and set of strategies, accept the validity of that direction, and are willing to work toward making it a reality" (p. 60). Collins (1999) uses the term "mechanisms with teeth" and "concrete mechanisms" to describe the day-to-day engagement of the organization's talent and energy to do the strategies.

Bossidy et al. (2002) refer to this process as execution. The word "execute" is from the Latin for "follow up or pursue," with the idea of producing, accomplishing, or completing something in accordance with an aspiration or design blueprint, such that it has practical, real-world effect. Therefore, an artist executes a statue, a musician executes a piece of music, and a lawyer executes a contract. In similar fashion, organizations execute strategies.

Although not negating the power of vision and strategy, the primary issue in organizational effectiveness is, typically, not a lack of vision or workable strategies, but a lack of execution. In the 1980s, Walter Kiechel (1984) of *Fortune* magazine polled consultants who claimed that less than 10 percent of strategies are successfully implemented. Tom Peters referred to that figure as "wildly inflated." A 1987 study of the performance of top executives of US companies explored the principal reasons why some of their decisions led to failure. Two crucial failure factors were identified: the personality of the CEO, and the ability of the CEO to translate simple ideas into workable strategies. In other words, CEOs failed not for a lack of ideas, but because they did not execute the ones they already had (Lamb, 1987).

Swedish business executive Percy Barnevik (1994) noted, "In my experience as the leader of a 'global' company, I have found that execution, not strategy per se, is primarily what differentiates the winners from the losers, whether they operate on a global or a local scale...When you study a thriving company, you're bound to find execution as the key to its success." Barnevik continues, "When I am asked how I split my time between strategy formulation and execution, I answer 10% and 90% respectively...I would argue, in fact, that the common thread among successful companies is their leaders' combination of vision, leadership, communication and execution" (pp. xi–xii).

Bossidy et al. (2002) make the case that effective leadership is less about imagination and more about execution. Bradley and Dawson (2013) warn, "A strategy is unfinished until you've been able to roll back the future into tangible, proximate goals, until you can communicate it very clearly to convey the real magic of what has to change for people, and until resources have been shifted." Until the organization understands what it needs to do differently because of the strategy, and begins to do it, the strategy has not taken hold. Aligning is the process of giving traction to the strategy, of getting results where there formerly were none, by leveraging the attention and talent of members who formerly were not producing these results.

The Old Normal Version

According to the Old Normal narrative, the work of Aligning calls on Leaders to formulate winning strategies, and issue directives, establish goals, and assign members to job descriptions in order to implement the strategy. Top Leaders build an unassailable case for their "can't miss" strategy, and sell it to everyone—or demand everyone comply and get to work. This is problematic. Poor execution downstream is typically symptomatic of inadequate involvement upstream. Those called upon to execute the strategy must be engaged in the Strategy-Making process—weighing in early on fosters buy-in later on. When the plan is handed down to those who have had no input in it, it produces only the appearance of compliance, and is likely to generate more than a fair share of foot dragging. The doers of the plan are less likely to take the initiative to make adjustments and improvements on the plan (Bass, 1970). In this regard, the Old Normal approach to Strategy Making and Aligning has a final serious drawback, as it fails to lay the groundwork for the widespread commitment and ownership required to execute the strategy.

A New Normal Twist: Aligning as a Collaborative Practice

Where does strategy end and execution begin? Montgomery observes: "There isn't a clear answer—and that's as it should be. What could be more desirable than a well-conceived strategy that flows without a ripple into execution?" (Montgomery, 2012). This seamless flow from strategy to execution is the aim of the New Normal practice of Aligning.

The New Normal version of Aligning places a new layer of demands and expectations on Leaders and member-leaders. Specifically, Aligning is a highly relational, collaborative process, giving it a distinctive New Normal flavor.

Twist #1: Effective New Normal Aligning Is More Relational Than Technical

Aligning is more than a technical process of matching people and job descriptions. This is important, but quite different from inviting members to work together in creating a new future. Aligning is not about exercising control or bringing order. Rather, it is a highly relational endeavor aimed at eliciting an affective commitment from members such that they identify with and participate in moving the organization toward the realization of its vision. It is about getting members to join from the heart for the long haul, getting the right people moving collectively in the right direction for the right reasons.

Twist #2: Effective New Normal Aligning Is About Increasing the Number of "Owners" and Decreasing the Number of "Renters"

The Old Normal narrative views members primarily as "renters"—those lacking a deep sense of psychological ownership, and whose contribution to the organization is limited to their job description. Renters are typically motivated by transactional, *quid pro quo* (this for that), shorter term interests. As such, they operate under a "low ceiling of self-interest." Their performance is prompted by external rewards—retaining one's job, increasing compensation, or securing promotion. Whatever the motivation, "renters" stay engaged only as long as they perceive their interests are served, and that they are appropriately reciprocated for their work. It is a rare renter who gives a discretionary effort to upgrade property belonging to others and which they only temporarily occupy.

The aim of Aligning is not to generate "renter buy in" for decisions that Leaders have already made, but to create an "owner class" of members, a distributed network of individuals throughout the organization that think and act like owners, regardless of their place in the organization. Aligning invites members into a leadership "zone of operation" to deal with difficult and challenging issues, to give their best thinking and a fully engaged effort to support the welfare and progress of the organization. In this "ownership space," no member is invisible, a mere commodity, or cog in the wheel. Rather, each knows that his or her insight and effort counts.

The Ownership Difference

An Argentine study followed 1,800 squatter families who, in 1981, occupied a one-square-mile piece of what they assumed was public land on the fringes of the capital, Buenos Aires, that had once served as a garbage dump (Moffett, 2005). The San Francisco Solano study, conducted by two Argentine universities and Harvard Business School compared households established on identical lots, occupied by blue-collar workers with comparable wages. Through a quirk of the legal system, roughly one half of the households gained title to their property, whereas the other half did not. Over the course of two decades, the title-holders (the owners) surpassed those who did not gain title in a host of key social indicators, including quality of house construction, educational achievements, and teenage pregnancy rates.

Twenty-five years later, the results indicate the power of ownership to stimulate effort and motivate people to high levels of performance. Although the households that gained title did not earn more money than those without the title, they did exhibit a more entrepreneurial mindset and rejected the fatalism and fear of being tossed off their land that defined the poor of the region. As one of the authors of the study observed, "You give people titles and they start to feel they belong to society." Owners put additions on their homes. Renters did not.

Architects affiliated with the study concluded that homes on titled lots had sturdier walls, sounder roofs, were more spacious, and had better sidewalks. Owners, although they did not make more money than non-owners, did spend their money differently, choosing to invest in the property and the education of their children. They were emotionally invested in their futures and believed that hard work would pay off for them and their extended families.

What Owners Believe
The renter mentality is contrasted with the attitudes and behaviors of owners. Ownership is not a set of formal obligations associated with one's position in the organization. Rather, it is a set of beliefs about one's work that overflows into concrete actions. Owners subscribe to seven beliefs. First, owners believe they that they are "equity partners" in shaping the future of the organization. The organization houses their dreams and embodies their values. Like a homeowner building up "sweat equity," owners invest their time and talent in the welfare and progress of the organization, believing that they benefit as the organization prospers.

Second, owners believe they have a measure of control over their circumstances and choices. Psychologist and Nobel Prize winner Daniel Kahneman conducted hundreds of experiments to gauge the factors that motivate people to make particular choices in uncertain situations. Before the 1973 Superbowl, Kahneman conducted a football lottery—the tickets were football cards featuring a famous football player. Each ticket cost a dollar and the grand prize was $50. The participants were placed in two groups: a "choice" and "no choice" group. The "choice" group was given the opportunity to personally select a football card from a box of 227 cards. A matching card was placed in a container from which the winning card would be selected. The other half were assigned to the "no choice" group and given the card selected by the previous person and, thus, assigned the card randomly. Before drawing the winning card, the researchers offered to purchase back the tickets from the participants. The question they wanted to answer was whether they would they have to pay those in the "choice" group more than those in the "no choice" group. The lottery was pure chance, and each participant had the same chance of winning, regardless of his or her group. However, the participants did not act in a purely rational manner. The researchers had to pay, on average, over four times more to those who personally selected a card—the "choice group" sold their card for $8.67, whereas the "no choice" group sold it for $1.96. The takeaway: Because people are intrinsically motivated to control or master their environments, when they choose for themselves, when they are involved in the decision, especially in uncertain situations, they are far more likely to be invested in the outcome than when they believe they have no choice and, thus, are out of control of their circumstances (Kahneman et al., 1982, pp. 236–238).

Third, owners believe the extra mile is their mile. Owners give a sacrificial effort and persevere in difficulty for reasons less tangible, but more powerful, than salary, rewards, or prestige—a sense of obligation takes us only so far. The voluntary sacrifice of owners is embedded in the principle of "self-concordance"—the extent to which one's goals are authentic in that they accurately represent one's personal loyalties, interests, and values. Inauthentic goals are goals over which the person does not claim ownership despite having either created them or having "signed on" to them at the request or demand of others.

Goal self-concordance is a good predictor of enduring effort and is correlated with higher goal attainment (Sheldon, 2002; Sheldon & Kasser, 1998). The content of our striving—whether our goals are intrinsically or extrinsically motivated—makes a difference in the quality of our effort and well-being (Deci & Ryan, 1985). Intrinsic motivation, the kind of motivation that generates endurance, includes one's personal interests, valued outcomes, or enjoyment of the process—what researchers call "autonomous strivings." External motivations, the kind of motivation that is less likely to produce endurance, includes the expectations of others, guilt, or shame-driven actions. The sacrificial effort of an owner reflects one of the most powerful internal motivations, "intimacy-related striving" (Emmons, 1999). Where there is intimacy, there is energy and, where there is energy, there is the capacity to persevere in difficulty.

Fourth, owners believe they can make a meaningful difference and lasting contribution to the organization, that the difference is theirs to make, and that their actions, no matter how seemingly insignificant, are consequential.

Fifth, owners believe they have the power and right, even obligation, to decide and act without asking permission from Leaders to do so, as long as it serves the directional imperatives of the organization. They take the initiative, contributing to the welfare and progress of the organization—both within and beyond one's job description.

Sixth, owners believe they are responsible for the consequences of their actions. Knowing that ownership does not mean immunity from

RENTERS	OWNERS
Short term	Long term
Renters move on	Owners stay
Complacent	Engaged
Apathy	Intimacy
Indifference	Caring
Maintaining at best	Improve at least
Spending one's time	Investing one's whole person
Safety	Risk

Figure 21.1 Renters and owners.

disappointment, risk, or failure, owners assume responsibility for sustaining their morale and improving their performance.

Seventh, owners believe that the organization is served best as they collaborate with other owners. Ownership is not autonomy. It does not mean the freedom to pursue one's personal agenda, do what one wants, and get all that one asks for. Rather, owners believe they share a common future with other owners, and so serve the organization best as they work with other owners (Figure 21.1).

Twist #3: Effective Aligning Fosters Collaboration Not Control

Aligning calls for Leaders and member-leaders to re-examine their assumptions and expectations around the distribution of authority, power, and influence in the organization—what it means to lead and follow, and who participates in making important decisions and doing critical leadership work. In the New Normal, sustained success is not dependent on the efforts of a few star players doing all the important leadership work. Rather, it depends on many working together to accomplish that which is beyond the capabilities of even the most gifted, energetic, and intelligent Leader. This means that every leadership practice (Vision Casting, Strategy Making, Aligning, and Encouraging) is a collaborative endeavor.

Moreover, although centralized authority is typically necessary, it is limited in its ability to impact the outcome of the thousands of "moments of truth" on the front line of mission-critical activity (see Ambassador Role). Problem-solving and decision-making powers localized at the top of the organization are incapable of addressing rapidly unfolding situations. The need is for member-leaders (1) with a firsthand understanding of the situation, (2) who share the directional imperatives and simple rules of the organization, and (3) who are ready to act in a manner that meets the leadership need of the moment.

Effective leadership, then, is less about the influence of a Leader over followers and more about the cumulative interactions between and among members who influence one another through relationships, the exchange of information, learning, decision-making, and mission-critical interactions. This means that the organization must address essential questions about what Leaders ought to control, what they ought to "give away" and to what degree members should share in doing important leadership work.

"Strategic Compression" and the New Normal Operating Environment

In the New Normal, the question of who controls what is less a decision made by a few top Leaders, and more an acknowledgment that strategic influence is already widely distributed throughout the organization. The concept of strategic compression refers to the fact that, due to the widespread availability of information and access to social media, nearly every organization member, even those doing the most mundane work, is capable of having a significant impact on the welfare and progress of the organization. Like it or not, Leaders cannot fully control and restrict access to strategic influence.

The term "strategic compression" was coined in a military context. It is defined by the Small Wars Council (2009) as "the overlapping or merging of the three levels of war: strategic, operational, and tactical." Strategic compression occurs when these levels of activity are compressed into a single event or circumstance. A much-discussed case is that of Army Lt. Colonel Christopher Hughes who commanded a battalion of the 101st Airborne Division during the 2003 invasion of Iraq. As his troops advanced on the Grand Mosque of Ali in the city of Najaf, Hughes sensed a surge in hostility from the civilian residents. Knowing that a misstep could escalate into a firefight, Hughes gave an unusual order. He told his troops to "take a knee" and point their weapons at the ground, hoping that this gesture of respect would diffuse the dangerous situation and convince the people of Najaf that they meant no harm to them or the mosque. Articles in *Time* and *Newsweek* as well as a radio address by President Bush noted the profound strategic implications of this act in terms of how the Iraqi War would be fought in months to follow.

Closely related to strategic compression is the concept of the "strategic corporal." Individual soldiers like Hughes—although he was a lieutenant colonel—have the opportunity, through tactical actions, to impact the strategic operating environment. The power to shape strategic realities is amplified through what is known as the "CNN effect"— ordinary people armed with smart phones now operate like unofficial reporters and can take any local incident global in a matter of minutes by uploading it on You Tube or submitting it to CNN or any number of news outlets. The 2011 "Arab Spring" uprisings in Egypt and other parts of the Middle East are testimony to the growing influence of "citizen-reporters."

The implications for Leaders and organizations are profound. Every employee is a "citizen reporter," a candidate to go viral with any message of their choosing, at any time of their choosing, through a readily available assortment of social media. The decisions and actions of member-leaders with little or no formal authority—the organizational equivalent of a strategic corporal—can have dramatic, widespread consequences. Consequently, Leaders may need to reframe what it means to lead and follow, and make a significant shift in how authority and power are dispersed throughout the organization.

Doing the Work of Aligning

Aligning is the work of releasing momentum throughout the organization by creating a network of owners committed to executing the organization's vision and strategies. Aligning, thus, aims to evoke an owner's response from every member at every level of the organization. The practical challenge is to reverse the impulse to rent, to assume a spectator stance, a mindset of "let others worry about it," to stay on the sidelines and play it safe, and let the Leaders and technical experts do the work.

Turning renters into owners requires a collaborative effort around a four-step process.

Step 1: Revisit the Future

Aligning connects the values and aspirations of members to the vital interests of the organization. This begins with directing the attention of members "back upstream," to the vision. In this step, the directional imperatives are clarified—this is who we are, what really matters, and why—and members are given the opportunity to sign on or re-enlist from the heart. Aligning is more about invitation than compulsion. It is not about persuading members to buy in to a strategic direction or set of values that have little or no resonance with their own. When it comes time to act as an owner—or not—members do not make a pros–cons list or consult a job description. Rather, they make a "gut" call based on what they value and are passionate about, what they know is right, good, and necessary.

Step #2: Revisit Strategies

Aligning gives members a conceptual grasp of how the vision flows into workable strategies, and how—in concrete and practical ways—they can participate in turning the vision into a reality.

Step #3: Connect Members with Opportunities for Ownership and Execution

Aligning cultivates a sense of agency—the confidence that as long as one's attitudes and behaviors are consistent with the directional imperatives of the organization, as long as one is serving the vision, any member at any level of the organization is free, yes even obligated, to decide and act in the service of the welfare and progress of the organization. Accordingly, members are invited, regardless of rank or position, to think and act as an owner, to participate in strategies not merely to fulfill the requirements of a job description, but to contribute their time and effort to engage with the organization's most pressing problems and promising opportunities.

When Aligning Works

Widespread ownership has four benefits.

Extra-Mile Effort Is Increased

When Aligning works, it serves as a catalyst for widespread owner's effort. It draws out of members what cannot be coerced, demanded, or otherwise bought (Figure 21.2). When members believe their contribution transcends their job description, when they believe they belong and that they are playing an indispensable role in something worthy of their best effort, they give what can only be voluntarily given—a fully engaged, "extra mile" effort.

CAN BUY	CAN'T BUY
A day's energy	Enduring enthusiasm
Motion (hand)	Motivation (heart)
Activity	Engagement
Performance	Passion
Involvement	Investment
Duty	Sacrifice
Participation	Partnership

Figure 21.2 Things you can and can't buy.

Momentum Is Released

Ownership and momentum are synonymous. When Aligning works, the collective passion, energy, and talent of the organization is released to accomplish the strategies and bring the vision to reality. Aligning calls on Leaders and member-leaders to serve as catalysts for "organizational citizenship behavior." These behaviors include altruism (demonstrating care for fellow members and those the organizations serves), conscientiousness (following through on critical goals without being asked or supervised), sportsmanship (tolerating less than ideal circumstances without complaining), courtesy (showing respect for others), and civic virtue (participating in and being concerned about the larger organization beyond one's particular role). These behaviors are voluntary and discretionary—not merely a requirement of a job description. They cannot be cajoled or demanded. Members must be intrinsically motivated to deliver on them (Podsakoff et al., 2000). Owners act as what Bass (1985) calls "high involvement individuals" who perform beyond expectations, and voluntarily contribute beyond the technical requirements of a job description.

Missional Integrity Is Enhanced

When Aligning works, the right things get done well by many over time—a shared strategic framework provides for integrated and coordinated action in keeping the organization's promises to the world. Day-to-day organizational life—from the "small things" to the critical tasks and processes—serve the directional imperatives of the organization.

The Leadership Workload Is Shared

When Aligning works, the leadership workload is shared. The talent and insight of members at all levels of organizational life is awakened to participate in the organization's most important and difficult challenges.

A Word to Leaders

The distribution of leadership prerogatives does not mean creating a chaotic organization or tolerating ineffectiveness. Certain aspects of organizational life must be appropriately controlled—setting the budget at the highest levels, making the final call on grand strategy, and making long-term capital investments. New Normal-friendly organizations need order, structure, and consistency, but in the right doses and in the right places.

Whereas some control is needed in any organization, too much control will foster complacency and compliance, stifle the initiative of members, and undermine ownership. The challenge is to lead in such a manner that the talent and energy of members is released and not restricted. This requires Leaders to affirm in attitude and action that strong leadership at the top of the organization does not preclude widespread participation in the work of leading among member-leaders.

Leaders walk this fine line by doing three things.

Leaders Go First

What Leaders say and do is the most powerful Aligning mechanism. They must act like owners, willing to go the extra mile, sacrifice, and do whatever is necessary to serve the best interests of the organization. Leaders can ask nothing of others they have not already modeled.

Leaders Call for a Collaborative Effort

Going first does not mean going alone. Leaders serve as catalysts for widespread participation, inviting member-leaders to bring their talent and insight, energy and experience to the work of Aligning. Accordingly, Leaders use their organizational assets, formal authority and other resources, and personal assets, charisma and/or technical-managerial competence, as catalysts for ownership and collaboration. Leaders fan the flame of ownership by providing opportunities for members to participate in the work of Vision Casting, Strategy Making, Aligning, and

Encouraging. They involve members in the feedback and evaluation process (Results) as well as the work of shaping a New Normal-friendly culture (Roles).

Summary

Imagine the difference between Leaders who operate on the assumption that only an elite few should participate in the leadership work, and those that build an organization of owners ready to take on the most difficult leadership work; between Leaders who try to get "buy-in" on decisions they have already made, and those who call on many to weigh in early; between an organization where only a few do all the important leadership work, and one where all have the right and responsibility to decide and act to serve the welfare and progress of the organization. The second idea of mobilizing members to act as owners differentiates the New Normal Leader from the Old Normal Leader.

4R Model Connection

Relationships

Aligning is not a "workshop skill" learned in a half-day seminar, although there are technical skills associated with this practice like hiring, staffing, building effective teams, organizing, and delegation. Rather, it is a collaborative process dependent on attitudes and behaviors found in the DICE + 1 configuration.

Courageous Character

Aligning is an exercise in trust. A trust-gap develops when Leaders and member-leaders profess one thing and practice another. Whether it is a cool cynicism or flagrant disrespect, when trust is undermined, members disengage, flying under the radar for the purpose of self-protection. Consequently, those doing the Aligning must be deemed trustworthy and credible, especially when they ask a sacrificial effort of others.

Emotional Maturity

Creating an organization of owners is, decidedly, not about creating a safe environment, if by "safe" is meant risk free. Taking on leadership work typically comes with an emotional price tag, as there are days when being a renter is more convenient and less taxing. Sharing in the work of addressing the organization's most pressing problems and intractable dilemmas is the heavy lifting on the way to the future—the price of progress in the wilderness. Consequently, those doing the Aligning work must draw from sufficient reserves of Emotional Maturity.

Roles and Organizational Culture

Organizational culture enhances or inhibits Aligning—culture always wins. If collaborative engagement is valued (Steward), and the simple rule—"more leaders"—is embedded in daily organization life, it enhances the practice of Aligning. However, if this simple rule is ignored and leadership prerogatives are not widely distributed, the vision and strategies will likely go lacking for support.

Summary

The collaborative struggle for constructive change begins with the work of Aligning. Aligning aims to proliferate a "property owning" class of members at all levels of the organization. In the work of Aligning, momentum is released throughout the organization by engaging members not as renters around a task, but as owners around the vision.

CHAPTER 22

Encouraging

Introduction

The wilderness journey takes its toll. The way to the future is longer and more difficult than most imagine. Adversity and disappointment are the order of the day. Progress is not inevitable. Every step is contested as stubborn problems and intractable dilemmas bar the way. Leaders and member-leaders battle frustration, setbacks, and, at times, one another. Too often, there is too little to show for too much effort. Moreover, things get worse. At the first signs of difficulty or delay, the naysayers roll into high gear. Morale suffers. Some grow weary and lose heart, forgetting why they began the journey. The momentum-killers, fatigue and cynicism, erode the will to continue. Many complain. Some despair. Pessimism spreads. Quitting—surrender to the status quo—becomes an attractive option. However, the journey must continue. Encouraging is the leadership work of strengthening one another to continue the journey to the future.

The Practice

Motivating (or Encouraging as I call the New Normal practice) is the work of supporting and sustaining personal and organization momentum, especially in difficult circumstances. The leadership challenge is to impart hope, instill a spirit of optimistic resolution, and infuse individuals, teams, and entire organizations with the strength to continue in the face of difficulty. In the work of Encouraging, Leaders convince others—and, sometimes, themselves—that they can and must continue the journey. This typically takes the form of "inspirational motivation," when Leaders communicate positive messages about the organization intended to enhance its resolve and increasing the probability that it will successfully cope with difficulties and persist in its efforts.

The Old Normal Version

In the Old Normal narrative, the Leader keeps everyone moving forward. Sometimes, this takes the form of the adrenalin rush of a big event or response to a crisis. Other times, it may take the form of rallying around a common goal, common enemy, or shared concern. Often, it comes as a downburst of inspiration from a charismatic Leader—akin to a Knut Rockne half-time talk to a team on the verge of losing the big game. Whatever the form, the Leader leverages external forces—personality power, the pressure of events, the threat of failure, or a mix of incentives, such that those lagging in enthusiasm or who lack the will to continue keep moving forward—at least in the short term.

The Old Normal approach to motivating makes two major assumptions. First, most people do not have the internal strength to sustain their effort in the face of difficulty—people are inherently weak and/or lack a deep commitment to continue the journey when the going gets tough. Second, people persevere only when their effort yields an immediate and favorable result or tangible reward. They keep score on a built in, "is it worth it" meter. When they perceive the work as something they enjoy or in their best interests to continue, they stay engaged. If not, they slow down or quit.

These assumptions are grounded in classic behaviorism, which assumes that all biological life is programmed to seek pleasure and reward, and avoid pain and punishment. The Old Normal version of motivation supposes that people act much like laboratory rats—they can be counted on to quit when a threshold of frustration or pain is reached. When things get sufficiently difficult, most people slow down and eventually disengage. Consequently, only a burst of energy supplied by an external source—inspiration provided by a Leader, thoughtful incentives (carrots and sticks), or a combination of the two—will sustain individual and collective effort in the face of difficulty.

Theory X and Theory Y

McGregor (1960) identified two sets of assumptions about human nature (Theory X and Theory Y) and explained how each shaped the attitude of leaders toward followers, especially with respect to the work of motivating. McGregor found that most leaders (he uses the terms "manager" and "leader" interchangeably) believed that most followers (in his case, employees of modern business organizations) are lazy, uninterested in pursuing excellence, undependable, cannot be trusted to make good decisions, and, if left to themselves, are incapable of high performance. They have an inherent dislike of work, shirk responsibility, and will quit at the first sign of difficulty. If they do perform well, it is only when they are motivated by a system of workplace "threats and bribes." Therefore, employees must be controlled and, as necessary, coerced if the employer is to get a "day's pay for a day's work."

McGregor called these dark assumptions about human nature, and the leadership practices that flowed from them—Theory X. Theory X represents the "carrot and stick" approach to motivation. Those who deviate from performance criteria set by the Leader are motivated best by punishment in the form of any number of "sticks"—a reprimand, disciplinary action, loss of position, loss of promotion, loss of money, loss of job, etc. Those who do their tasks well are rewarded by any number of "carrots"—accolades, promotions, increased pay, etc. Organizations embracing the "carrot and stick" approach create job descriptions and structure work to insure a maximum level of accountability and management control. Old Normal Leaders and organization, to varying degrees, operate in the context of Theory X assumptions.

A New Normal Twist: Encouraging as a Collaborative Practice of Rekindling Ownership

The Old Normal narrative assumes a journey that, although difficult and uphill, is, nevertheless, relatively straightforward, with mile markers posted along the way to validate progress. The New Normal narrative assumes a journey akin to a marathon through a confusing wilderness—there is no mile markers or distant peak to calibrate progress. The journey is typically longer than first imagined. The most compelling vision and brilliant strategies may take years to produce results—the future does not arrive at the beck and call of the Leader, no matter how gifted or competent. The journey is likely to generate significant frustration and disappointment, even fear and anxiety. It is a good bet that the resolve of some, perhaps many, even those aligned and owning the vision and strategies, will dissolve well short of the Promise Land. We need strength, both individually and collectively, to sustain the wilderness journey. The New Normal work of Encouraging supplies this strength.

Twist #1: Effective New Normal Encouraging Taps into Intrinsic Rather Than External Factors

McGregor's research established a new way of thinking about employee motivation that he called Theory Y. Theory Y countered Theory X on nine important assumptions: (1) It is with our nature, not against it, to give an honest day's effort to serve the organization; (2) Most people want the work experience to count for something beyond the work itself, and want to know that what we do contributes to something greater than the task itself; (3) Most people are self-motivated and self-regulating and, consequently, require not control but the necessary resources to accomplish the work; (4) Most people can, in light of explicitly stated organizational direction, direct their own behavior and modify it to work toward the accomplishment of shared goals and outcomes; (5) Most employees (followers) like to work with others (peers and leaders) in mutual partnerships; (6) Most people aspire to excellence, and, therefore, personal performance is not primarily based on the fear of punishment or the desire for reward, but rather, on the innate desire to live up to one's own standards of a job well done; (7) Most people want to have input on important decisions and are smart enough to make good decisions when given the opportunity; (8) Most people are eager to grow, learn, and develop the personal capacities, skills, and abilities to contribute maximally to the organization and its broader goals; and (9) Most people are willing to assume ownership and responsibility for important goals and will work in a trustworthy and dependable manner to accomplish goals that are both important to them and the organization (see McGregor, 1960, pp. 47–48).

Pink (2009), drawing on the research of Ryan and Deci, provides an updated version of McGregor's work, arguing that what motivates us is not carrots and sticks, but autonomy, mastery, and purpose (Ryan & Deci, 2000; Deci & Ryan, 1985, 2000, 2008). Sinek (2011) argues that people decide to keep giving a sacrificial effort because of a compelling "why"—what they believe to their core, what they personally own, or a higher purpose for which they are willing to sacrifice if necessary.

The work of Encouraging taps into Theory Y assumptions and practices. Passion born of noble purpose—one's "why"—is the primary motivating force, as opposed to external factors that drive Theory X motivating practices. Given this distinction, a different term for this leadership practice is merited—Encouraging. As the structure of the word suggests, to en-courage is to impart courage. The term courage is derived from the Middle English and Old French *corage* and the Latin *cor* meaning heart. Courage is strength from one's heart to endure hardship, to stand strong, and keep moving forward in spite of the dangers and difficulties.

Encouraging is the work of infusing others with courage and confidence, hope and optimistic resolution, especially in negative or trying circumstances, days when there is no good reason to continue and plenty of reason to quit—an average day in the New Normal where progress is hard-won and setbacks, discouragement, and failure are plentiful. Encouraging aims to embolden, hearten, spur on, stimulate, and strengthen others to keep moving forward in the face of difficulty, to finish what they have voluntarily begun. This sustained momentum is not prompted by external factors typically associated with motivating—an inspiring talk or "must win" crisis situation. This kind of motivation lasts only as long as the external factors are in play—a brief burst of energy and enthusiasm may get us moving again, but not for long. Inspirational talks wear off and crises come and go. Encouraging, however, releases a virtuous strength more substantive and lasting than a burst of adrenalin.

Twist #2: Effective New Normal Encouraging Aims to Rekindle Ownership

Individuals we call "highly motivated" are, typically, ordinary men and women acting like owners. Those we call "unmotivated" are, typically, those acting like renters. Renters continue only in favorable circumstances. Owners keep going in pursuit of what they value, no matter the circumstances. For owners, quitting is not an option.

Encouraging aims to rekindle a deep sense of ownership—the abiding sense of responsibility for one's progress and perseverance cultivated in the work of Aligning. Encouraging is the invitation to keep acting as an owner in the face of difficulties and delays, to keep giving an owner's effort when the going is unusually tough and renting or selling is an attractive option. An owner goes the extra mile because it is their mile; because obstacles and delays encountered along the way interfere with the fulfillment of what is in their heart.

Twist #3: Effective New Normal Encouraging is the Work of Many, Not a Few

Encouraging is the work of any and every member, no matter where they reside on the organizational chart. Leaders and member-leaders remind anyone who is discouraged—yes, even, at times, other Leaders and member-leaders—what it means to live and work in the company of owners. They remind fellow travelers on the journey why they began in the first place, what they deeply care about, and why it is worth continuing. In this kind of organization, no one is so deprived of support, so isolated, hopeless or powerless that he or she has no option but to quit in the face of difficulty.

Doing the Work of Encouraging

The work of Encouraging aims at sustaining personal and collective momentum so that individuals, teams, and entire organizations keep moving in the right direction through the hard times and headwinds. Encouraging, as the grammar suggests, is a never-ending process, not an event. It is a rare day when no one needs Encouraging.

Step #1: Renewing Hope and Courage by Remembering the Future

The choice to continue in the face of difficulty requires a personal ratification of the directional imperatives and vision of the organization. In the work of Encouraging, Leaders and member-leaders invite those who are experiences difficulties or discouragement to travel "back upstream" to remember the future, reminding them why they began the journey, and reconnecting them with opportunities to work toward a better tomorrow.

Step #2: Renewing Hope and Courage by Providing Personalized Care

The aim of Encouraging is to come alongside of others amid difficulty and help them keep moving in the right direction. This demands close relational proximity. Those doing the Encouraging must enter the emotional space of others to understand firsthand their challenges and difficulties, to listen such that they understand that they are understood. It must register that they are cared for, that they matter, that they are not alone on the journey. Caring and continuing are inseparable. We are more likely to continue in the pursuit of what we care about when we know others care about us. This means taking the time to listen, understand, and provide practical, individualized help when needed.

This calls for a personal touch, with inputs chosen according to the needs of the individual in the context of his or her unique struggles and challenges. Personalized care, by definition, comes in a variety of packages. Depending on the circumstances, the work of Encouraging ranges from the "soft" input of consoling in loss, comforting in difficulty, to the "neutral" input of informing advising, and reminding, to the "hard" input of cautioning and correcting. One size does not fit all. Whatever form it takes, Encouraging addresses the requirements of the moment, providing what others need to keep moving in the right direction in the face of difficulty.

When Encouraging Works

Hope and Courage Are Rekindled

When Encouraging works, hope is renewed—our best days are yet ahead. Courage is rekindled—we find the strength to venture another step on the journey to the future. Moreover, confidence is restored—we know we are making a difference, and the sacrifice is worth it.

Momentum Is Sustained

When Encouraging works, forward motion is sustained as the organization remembers and reconnects with its vision. Hope is rekindled and the energy provided to sustain the owners "extra-mile" effort in the tough times and hard places.

A Word to Leaders

Leaders Go First as Necessary

In the wilderness, Encouraging is a full-time job, a daily necessity. Those wavering and hesitant must be supported and helped to stay the course and take the next difficult step. Leaders must often go first. At a minimum, this means practicing self-encouragement. For, if the Leader is to encourage others, they must first encourage themselves. This means monitoring one's own morale, as well as the morale of other Leaders and member-leaders and, when it is low, to come alongside and remind them of the reason for the journey—the vision—and give them the individualized care they need to stay the course.

Leaders Call for a Collaborative Effort

Going first does not mean going alone. Leaders serve as catalysts for widespread participation, calling on member-leaders to bring their talent and insight, energy and experience to the work of Encouraging. Going solo is a dangerous practice in the wilderness, where isolation is the enemy of endurance. Although Leaders directly encourage others, much of the Encouraging work is the responsibility of member-leaders and not just an elite few.

Imagine the difference between Leaders who operate on assumption that only a few should participate in this leadership work, and those who invite member-leaders to share in the work of attending to the morale of others. The second idea of mobilizing members to join in the work of Encouraging differentiates the New Normal Leader from the Old Normal Leader.

4R Model Connections

Relationships

Encouraging is not a "workshop skill" learned in a half-day seminar, although of course there are technical skills associated with this practice like listening, negotiating, and understanding others. Rather, it is a collaborative process dependent on attitudes and behaviors found in the DICE + 1 configuration.

Dynamic Determination

Leaders and member-leaders must maintain a deep sense of higher purpose if they want to help others stay the course. Faith, hope, and courage are essential amid the delays and disappointments of daily life.

Intellectual Flexibility

The work of Encouraging places emphasis on individualized care—timely and appropriate input based on an accurate assessment of the needs of others. The challenge is to accurately identify the factors that contribute to the discouragement or difficulty encountered by others—to properly assesses the "motivational state" of individuals or the organization. In a fast-changing operating environment, those doing the Encouraging must identify the social and emotional currents and cross-currents that shape the daily life of the organization and be ready with a wide repertoire of responses. This requires being tuned in to "what," "how," and "why" people feel, think, and act as they do. Of course, there may be as many motivational states as there are people, requiring the wisdom and discernment found in Intellectual Flexibility.

Courageous Character

Encouraging requires saying the right thing at the right time. However, the right words have to be spoken by the right person—a credible person who genuinely cares for others and who is modeling the perseverance they ask of others. It takes someone who has endured or is enduring in the face of difficulty to help others to do the same. What Leaders and member-leaders do in the tough times, not what they say in the good times, is foundational to the work of Encouraging. When the chips are down, when progress does not come easily, and when sacrifice is the order of the day, then, those who are discouraged and tempted to quit evaluate whether the journey is worth it by what Leaders and member-leaders actually do. If they perceive a "say–do gap," it will fuel cynicism and resentment. However, if Leaders and member-leaders persevere in difficulty, many will take courage in their example.

Emotional Maturity
Those doing the work of Encouraging are just as vulnerable to discouragement as those who need their help. If Leaders and member-leaders expect to bring hope and encouragement, they cannot succumb to discouragement and anxiety even as others around them do. They cannot drown in self-pity or pessimism. Neither can they be unrealistically optimistic. They have to stay solid. They must honestly acknowledge difficult circumstances, and maintain a measure of emotional objectivity and a realistic optimism. This takes a sufficient reserve of Emotional Maturity.

Roles and Organizational Culture

Organizational culture enhances or inhibits Encouraging—culture always wins. If collaborative engagement is valued (Steward), and the simple rules are embedded in daily organization life, it enhances the practice of Encouraging. If the way forward is unclear, if the organization is insular, if it fails to keep learning, and leadership prerogatives are not widely distributed, the work of Encouraging will likely be diminished.

Summary

The difference between Encouraging and motivating is substantive, not semantic. Motivating capitalizes on the adrenaline rush of an inspiring message or urgent situation. Getting others to respond to a crisis is one thing—anyone can enlist others to throw a bucket of water on a fire. Getting someone to sustain their contribution in difficult times is quite another. In the work of Encouraging, Leaders and member-leaders sustain momentum by reminding others what they care about, and demonstrating they are cared for.

SECTION VI

The 4R Model: Results

The wilderness journey demands radical honesty about one's performance, and a keen awareness of the operating environment—the flow of circumstances, the possibilities present to the organization, and the threats ahead. This section explores the connection between performance feedback and sustained effectiveness in the New Normal.

CHAPTER 23

Results

Introduction

In the New Normal operating environment, paying attention to performance is more important than ever. Roger McNamee states, "The late '90s were all about people who looked good in the spotlight. I call it the CNBC CEO. Now it's about people who get things done. The question isn't, What's your vision for the future? The question is, What are you doing today? You still need a vision, but that is no substitute for a realistic plan" (LaBarre, 2003). The founding editors of *Fast Company* observe, "To win in the New Normal calls for fresh thinking and for smart adaptation, for a focus on relentless execution and on solid performance" (Founding Editors, 2003). However, no organization drifts into solid performance. Leaders, member-leaders, and the entire organization need a way to continually assess and improve performance. The Results component of the 4R Model addresses this need, highlighting the critical contribution of performance feedback to sustained effectiveness in a landscape of harsh realities, changing rules, and high expectations.

The Practice

Results are the unmistakable footprint of effective leadership. How to get important things accomplished is not a mystery. GE CEO Jeff Immelt (2004) notes, "There is no real magic to being a good leader. But at the end of every week, you have to spend your time around the things that are really important: setting priorities, measuring outcomes, and rewarding them." Effective organizations stay in touch with the realities of the marketplace, set strategic goals in line with the mission, vision, and values of the organization, monitor progress in crucial areas of activity, and make adjustments as necessary.

The Old Normal Version

The Old Normal narrative highlights short-term performance with primary emphasis on the activity of one or a few Leaders who bear final responsibility for outcomes. "Good Leaders" take charge and draw on an assortment of assets including formal authority, formidable intelligence, an exceptional mix of competencies, and a strong personality to provide for the welfare and progress of the organization. According to the narrative, these gifted few possess sufficient insight and technical expertise to solve difficult problems, overcome obstacles, accomplish goals, and take the organization to the "next level." Old Normal Leaders are paid to be uplifting, resolutely optimistic about the future, and to rally the troops—pessimists need not apply. Highlighting unpleasant realities is deemed bad leadership practice and avoided like the plague. Instead, Old Normal Leaders uphold the party line that things are good and getting better. They infuse the organization with optimism and positive self-regard with respect to its capability and performance, if need be, in the face of evidence to the contrary. Of course, if nothing changes for the better, Leaders can blame others. If this does not work, they may lose their job to a new leader who can deliver more, sooner.

A New Normal Twist: Results as a Collaborative Process

With respect to monitoring, evaluating, and improving performance, the New Normal organization differs from its Old Normal counterpart in two ways, each of which places a new layer of expectations on Leaders and member-leaders.

Twist #1: Monitoring Performance Is a Collaborative Effort

The Old Normal narrative assumes that one or a few Leaders know most and best and, consequently, should make all the important performance-related decisions. Although Leaders typically bear final accountability for evaluating and improving performance, they cannot do it alone. In a New Normal operating environment, no Leader possesses the breadth of perspective or insight to unilaterally address performance issues. Consequently, monitoring and evaluating organizational outcomes is not something a few Leaders do for the entire organization, but rather something the entire organization must do for itself. Like Roles and Responsibilities, the New Normal narrative sees the work of Results as a collaborative effort, a collective act of stewardship requiring the participation of Leaders as well as member-leaders.

Twist #2: Sustained New Normal Effectiveness Is the Product of Organizational Culture

The Old Normal narrative features strong, confident Leaders who deliver valued outcomes on schedule. However, the New Normal narrative does not view performance as a linear process with inputs leading directly and inevitably to valued outcomes. Sustained effectiveness is not the direct consequence of a Leader's decisions and actions—although these are of course important. Rather, primary emphasis is placed on organizational culture as the key factor in sustained performance. Sustained effectiveness flows from the inside out, reflecting the internal health of the totality of organizational life—personal and collective attitudes and behaviors, as well as the systems, structures, and processes that shape daily organizational life.

The Results Process

In the New Normal, uninterrupted progress is rare. The best organizations move forward in fits and starts. Bursts of enthusiasm, creativity, and new growth are often followed by stretches of mediocrity, squandered resources, and wasted opportunities. Hard-won ground is lost, and important lessons are often forgotten.

Every organization underperforms. The fundamental issue is how it responds. Effective organizations take a disciplined approach to evaluating progress by embedding candid, friendly, and constructive conversations around its performance in the daily fabric of organizational life. These conversations address five questions: (1) What, exactly, do we want to happen? (2) What is actually happening? (3) Why is it happening (or not) to the degree it is happening (or not)? (4) What should we do to improve performance given what is happening and why? and (5) how should we now think and act differently in light of our answers to the first four questions?

The Results process provides a framework for Leaders and member-leaders to address these questions.

Step #1: Define and Clarify Critical Performance Categories

The challenge of this step is to determine what difference the organization intends to make in the world, and what internal factors sustain its performance and thus merit its attention. "Outcome categories" are typically grounded in the organization's directional imperatives—what success or effectiveness looks like in light of the organization's purpose, mission, and values; what deeply matters to the organization, what counts, and, thus, must be counted.

Choosing what to measure is of fundamental importance for three reasons. First, "Every organization has a culture, and that culture—for better or worse—is largely determined by what its leaders have chosen to measure and to reinforce with incentives. This is why the choice of measurement is so important; measures eventually determine the behavior of personnel and the culture of the organization" (Labovitz and Rosansky, 1997, p. 156).

Second, identifying result categories is an exercise in organizational integrity, clearly identifying what the organization must do often and exceptionally well if it is to stay true to itself and make good on its promises to the world. For business organizations, the hard numbers of the marketplace and the position of the organization relative to its competition make sense as a good starting point. For non-profits, critical performance outcomes typically reflect the degree to which its mission is being fulfilled and its promises kept. Whether a business or non-profit, often, the most important things are not things, and not everything that counts is easily counted. For instance, qualitative concerns related to sustained performance may be critical performance categories. Morale, candor, and trust levels, the credibility of the organization's Leaders and brand, or the health and robustness of its innovation pipeline, to name a few, are intangible outcomes vitally connected to the sustained performance.

Third, the competitive pressures of the New Normal require organizations to be creative about what they pay attention to, especially around learning and talent acquisition. Hagel et al. (2009) recommend, "Companies must therefore design and then track operational metrics showing how well they participate in knowledge flows. For example, they might want to identify relevant geographic clusters of talent around the world and assess their access to that talent. In addition, they might want to track the number of institutions with which they collaborate to improve performance" (p. 88).

Investments and Expenditures
If the organization's critical performance categories are not clearly delineated, it will lack the basis on which to distinguish investments from expenditures, valued outcomes from temporary, superficial outputs. In the broad sense, to invest is to make use of what one already has, with careful thought given to what might be gained by way of future advantages or benefits: to judiciously concentrate and commit resources with a view to earning a future return. An investment is never a self-contained event. Rather, it sets in motion a chain reaction of cumulative return that creates value and secures an increased asset base. With respect to organizations, to invest means to employ resources—money

and the time, attention and talent of Leaders and member-leaders—in a manner that yields valued outcomes and increases the capacity of the organization to sustain its welfare and progress.

In contrast, to expend something is to pay it out, consume it, exhaust it, wear it out, and use it up, and, therefore, to squander and waste a resource. Expenditures are the spending of resources with little or no thought given to a future return. Spending is a self-contained event, bringing no benefit or reward. When we say a person is spent, we mean they are drained of energy and of no future consequence—finished. When a resource is spent, it is gone forever. With respect to organizations, to expend means to employ resources without reference to valued outcomes or sustainable performance, and so to consume the resource with nothing to show for it save superficial, temporary outputs. Expenditures waste precious resources and eventually diminish the capacity of the organization to sustain its performance.

The proliferation of expenditures—the diversion of resources to activities other than those critical to the organization's sustained effectiveness in light of its mission—is most dangerous. No organization can afford to waste the time and attention of its Leaders and member-leaders, or its financial resources, on activities that yield, at best, only temporary outputs. This is more than a matter of efficiency. It is a matter of integrity, as expenditures diminish the capacity of the organization to keep its promises to the world.

Step #2: Review: Measuring—Paying Attention—To What Is Happening in Key Performance Categories

This step calls on Leaders and member-leaders to "count what counts," to take a hard look at organizational performance in the categories identified in the first step. The challenge is for Leaders and member-leaders to get on the same "reality page" by generating a flow of timely and accurate information that enables the organization to take a hard look at what it is actually accomplishing in critical performance categories.

With reference to quantitative or "hard" categories (how much or how fast), this is a relatively straightforward process. However, often, the most important performance categories are the most difficult to measure. Qualitative or "soft" categories such as the health of organizational culture, collective morale, or the level of trust in the organization and its brand are vitally important but notoriously difficult to measure with precision. Perhaps, it is best to describe Leaders and member-leaders as "paying attention" to these crucial but hard-to-measure categories. Here, precision is less important than establishing a baseline on which performance trends can be regularly evaluated. For instance, is the trust level between Leaders and member-leaders "low," "medium," or "high?" Or, perhaps more importantly, what is the trend line? Is trust increasing or decreasing?

Whatever measurement techniques are employed, the aim of this step is to produce a flow of timely and reliable information to determine if the organization is making the kind of difference it intends to make in the world (external measures) and, just as importantly, if its efforts are sustainable (internal measures).

Step #3: Reflect: Interpreting What Is Happening

The challenge of the third step is to determine why the organization is getting the outcomes it is getting. This step explores the connection between organizational culture and sustained effectiveness. This calls for a Roles audit, as an organization's culture mediates its performance, either enhancing or diminishing progress.

Direction Setter

Do we manifest missional integrity? Are we crystal clear about our directional imperatives? Do we have a clear and unambiguous sense of what the organization is supposed to do for whom—our mission? Are Leaders and member-leaders acting accordingly? For better or worse, how is this impacting our performance?

Ambassador

Are we "other-friendly?" Are we delivering on our promises to others? Are we projecting and protecting our brand? What would others say about us? Are we keeping up with competitors? For better or worse, how is this impacting our performance?

Coach

Are we "leader-friendly?" Are we identifying, developing, and deploying more member-leaders? Is the leadership pipeline working? Do we have enough of the right kind of Leaders and member-leaders to keep delivering on our promises to the world? For better or worse, how is this impacting our performance?

Learner

Are we "learning-friendly?" Are we learning, unlearning, and relearning in the service of our directional imperatives? Are we growing in our capacity to keep our promises to the world, especially in light of changing circumstances in the external environment? For better or worse, how is this impacting our performance?

Steward

Are we good stewards of our resources? Are we sacrificing short-term gain for long term sustainability? Are we focusing an appropriate percentage of our resources on "others" as opposed to "us?" For better or worse, how is this impacting our performance?

Step #4: Revisit and Revise: Learning and Improving

The fourth step calls the organization to put the insights gained in Step 3 to constructive use to improve performance. In this step, Leaders and member-leaders ask one another, "What factors enhance or diminish our progress?" "Given what we know about the relationship between our performance and our culture, our progress and our capabilities, what can we do about it—now?"

This step calls for a Responsibilities audit. The follow questions surface reality, expose weakness, and send the organization back to the drawing board to evaluate assumptions, correct problems, and take constructive steps to improve performance.

Vision Casting

Is our vision animating the daily life of the organization? Given our performance, does the vision need to be modified or clarified?

Strategy Making

Are our strategies working? If so, why are they working well and how might they be improved or further resourced? If not, how should they be adjusted or replaced? Are our goals bigger than our capacity to execute around them?

Aligning

Are we an organization of "renters" or "owners?" Are we executing? Does each member-leader know what he or she should do next, and how this fits with the larger vision and mission of the organization?

Encouraging

How is our momentum and morale? Are there "momentum-breaking" issues that must be addressed—cynicism, lack of trust, chronic discouragement? Are there important milestones to celebrate?

Step # 5: Reengage

This step asks, "Given what we now know, now what?" Performance feedback is, typically, not enough. The organization can always ignore it, dismiss it as irrelevant, blame underperformance on others or bad luck. This step calls the organization to embrace the feedback, and actually do something to improve its performance. Armed with fresh insight around performance issues, as well as recommendations for adjustments and changes, the organization is now in a better position to sustain its progress.

Summary

In the New Normal, change is the rule, and there is no set of rules that govern effectiveness in times of change, save one: success is transitory. Organizations do not improve by magic. Excellence is not an accident. The critical question is whether the organization has put a process in place to listen, learn, and get better at what matters most. This calls for regular, candid, friendly, and constructive conversations from top to bottom and across the organization. The Results process provides the framework for these conversations.

A Word to Leaders

Leaders Go First as Necessary

Leaders cannot demand growth or legislate new learning by making authoritative pronouncements. However, they can champion the Results process as a way to "get on the same reality page," and lean into the organization's most pressing and difficult issues. De Pree (1989) states, "The first task of a leader is to define reality. Leaders tell it like it is, and show what it can become" (p. 11).

Leaders Call for a Collaborative Effort

Going first does not mean going alone. Leaders serve as catalysts for widespread participation in the conversation around performance, inviting member-leaders to bring their talent and insight, energy and experience to the critical work of identifying how to get better at what matters most.

Beware of Leader Ailments

The Results process protects the organization from three, Leader "ailments" that prevent those in charge from getting honest and timely performance feedback, and creates the conditions for poor, at times disastrous, decision-making.

Information Filtering
The filter principle states that the higher a Leader goes in an organization, the more insulated he or she becomes from honest performance feedback. (This is less likely to happen at lower levels of the organization where member-leaders have direct access to the consequences of their decisions and actions.) Top Leaders often assume that, if their decisions or performance is in some way deficient, someone will tell them the unvarnished truth. This is unlikely for two reasons.

First, perpetually in a transmit mode, many Leaders listen poorly, learn slowly, and do not readily embrace input or advice. Second, it is not uncommon for member-leaders to withhold, adjust, or spin information for fear that the messenger bearing bad news might be shot. It is understandable if member-leaders do not consider the risk worth taking. Although counterintuitive, the higher up they are in the organization, the harder Leaders have to work to get candid performance feedback.

Reality Editing
While information filtering protects the Leaders from hearing bad news, reality editing refers to the Leader's counterproductive response to the bad news once they hear it. T. S. Eliot (1980) observed in *Four Quartets*, "Human kind Cannot bear very much reality" (p. 118). Leaders may edit bad news to perpetrate the illusion that things are not so bad, that problems can be engineered away, and that there is a painless way forward. Or, more ominously, due to deficits in Emotional Maturity, some Leaders may need to protect their public image as a powerful, all-wise person in charge of events and immune from error. Fearing failure more than they love progress, they maintain they are always right even in the face of clear evidence to the contrary. However, Leaders who would rather be right than effective are neither. They can insist on always being right, at least in their own minds, or they can strive to become increasingly effective in the real world. But they cannot have it both ways.

The Cycle of Escalating Commitment
Historian Barbara Tuchman (1985) describes human history as the "unfolding of miscalculation." Perhaps, the most common version of organizational miscalculation is called "doubling down," or the cycle of escalating commitment. Block (1993) calls it "hope through repackaging" (p. xv). Past triumphs are enshrined as inviolable laws of cause and

effect. Tried and true ways of doing things are declared sacrosanct. As particular strategies worked yesterday, it is assumed they must work today. Operating from this logic, Leaders recommit to an ineffective strategy in the vain hope that it will eventually be vindicated. More resources are released to support the failed practice, and members are urged to work harder to support it. Remember de Lesseps.

The Performance Advantages of the Results Process

Once embedded in the daily life of the organization, the Results process delivers five New Normal performance advantages.

Performance Advantage #1: Strengthening and Renewal

As the organization is brought face to with its most difficult problems, new learning is prompted—fresh insights often come packaged in unpleasant realities. Experimentation and active listening is encouraged, engaging even those at the peripheries of the organization—the home of a considerable portion of the organization's ingenuity and innovative drive. The organization takes stock of its assumptions, reassesses its directional imperatives, reaffirms or reorders priorities and goals, reconfigures resources, and cultivates a heightened sense of responsibility to those it intends to serve. Latent energies are revitalized, enthusiasm rekindled, and strength renewed to sustain the journey to the future.

Performance Advantage #2: Speed Learning

In the New Normal, the ability to recognize and quickly adjust to a changing operating environment is a necessity for survival, let alone flourishing. "The more the business environment changes . . . the faster the value of what you know at any point in time diminishes. In this world, success hinges on the ability to participate in a growing array of knowledge flows in order to rapidly refresh your knowledge stocks" (Hagel et al., 2009, p. 87). As the Results process is embedded in daily organizational life, it serves as an early warning system alerting the organization to critical performance issues and emerging opportunities, prompting Leaders and member-leaders to learn what it must fast. When things are not working, attitudes and behaviors contributing to underperformance must be addressed immediately. When things are going well, the organization cannot relax—the external operating environment will change sooner than later, placing new performance demands on the organization.

Performance Advantage #3: Hopeful Realism

As the Results process is embedded in the organization, it fortifies Leaders and member-leaders with a rich blend of hope and realism— necessities in an imperfect world occupied by imperfect people, where failure is ever-present, and consistent improvement is a requirement for survival. By way of realism, the Result process prompts the organization to honestly face the troubling disparity between its aspirations and real-world performance, but without resorting to self-condemnation or blaming others. The process reminds the organization that failure and ineffectiveness is part of the human condition and a central theme in the New Normal narrative. By way of hope, the Result process reminds the organization that failure is never final, that weak does not mean worthless, that improvement is possible, and that Leaders and member-leaders do not have to be perfect to stay effective—just wise, humble, and teachable.

This mix of hope and realism allows the organization to pursue excellence and tolerate imperfection, to take healthy pride in progress and full responsibility for failure, to have high aims without succumbing to grandiosity, and to celebrate success without tolerating pride or complacency. Hopeful realism is an enormously valuable personal and collective asset, as it enlarges the capacity of individuals and entire organizations to face troubling realities, deal constructively with stubborn obstacles, and come back tomorrow for more.

Performance Advantage #4: Protection from Top Leader Ailments

As the Results process is embedded in the organization, it counteracts information filtering by fostering the unobstructed flow of timely and accurate information, even the bad news, throughout the organization. This healthy information circulation system exposes every corner and every level of the organization, including top Leaders, to high doses of reality, keeps feedback loops open, and provides for candid and constructive dialog around key performance issues. The Results process protects against reality editing, as key performance information is accessible to the entire organization, making it more difficult for Leaders to spin the facts out of self-interest or self-protection. Moreover, the Results process protects against the cycle of escalating commitment, as it calls on everyone—Leaders and member-leaders alike—to honestly face fundamental performance issues, learn fast, and make wise adjustments, even to strategies supported by top Leaders.

Performance Advantage #5: Sustainable Progress via a New Normal-Friendly Culture

As the Results process is embedded in the daily life of the organization, it provides it with what is perhaps its greatest advantage—the regular opportunity to evaluate, shape, and renew its culture. The Results process shapes culture in two ways. First, the Results process explicitly links the organization's collective performance to its culture, for better or worse, prompting the organization to participate in regular, candid conversations about this complex relationship. The Results process evaluates the totality of organizational life, the attitudes and behaviors, systems, structures, and processes, assumptions and intentions that shape organizational culture and, thus, contribute to the performance of the organization over time.

Second, the Results process serves as a catalyst for the development and exercise of the virtues that drive and sustain a New Normal-friendly culture. Specifically, the Results process calls forth the DICE + 1 configuration of virtue from Leaders and member-leaders, while simultaneously serving as a catalyst for growth in these same virtues. This is the topic of chapter 24.

Summary

New Normal organizations find themselves awash in accelerating change, hypercompetition, and sky-high expectations. Progress is not assured, and no gain is safely secured. There are no silver bullets. Complacency is the kiss of death. Enter the Results process. The Results process disciplines the organization to wisely invest its assets, take action to achieve desired outcomes, and make the necessary adjustments to successfully navigate the future. It asks the organization to constructively respond to things as they are, not as they wish them to be, or mistakenly perceive them to be. In this regard, the Result process functions as a safety net for the organization in anticipation of its inevitable human frailty and blind spots, especially those of its Leaders. As Leaders and member-leaders discuss, reflect, self-assess, and self-correct, the organization gets better and better at what matters most—keeping its promises to the world.

CHAPTER 24

Results and Relationships: Back to the Core

Introduction

The New Normal wilderness cannot be tamed. However, it can be productively engaged. This requires the personal and collective expression of virtue. This is sobering news, but also good news. Leaders and member-leaders do not have to be powerfully charismatic or hypercompetent to make a sustainable difference. Although the New Normal operating environment is demanding, it does not demand perfection from individuals or organizations—just the willingness to maintain a humble, learner stance and collaborate along the way.

The "right stuff" is not reserved for an elite few. The personal assets that sustain an effective Results process are accessible to "ordinary" individuals. Everyone is capable of facing the demands of reality, honestly evaluating one's progress and performance and, with the help of others, getting better at the things that matter most. In this sense, it is inaccurate to think of virtue as only personal, moral goodness disassociated from real-world effectiveness. Virtue is the capacity, both individually and collectively, to deal constructively with real-world performance demands.

Results Depend on Relationships

Every organization has a mission set before it—a promise to the world to deliver a particular benefit to a specified group. Progress and performance in this mission is hindered by a variety of obstacles, both within the organization and from the external operating environment. It takes virtue to overcome these obstacles. Organizations full of perfect people working in easy circumstances do not need virtue. However, the exercise of virtue is a vital necessity for organizations full of people susceptible to fear, discouragement, and self-interest, trying to succeed in a harsh environment. The virtues embedded in the DICE + 1 configuration are the cognitive, moral, and emotional qualities that guide and support the organization as its attempts to sustain its performance and fulfill its mission in the face of these difficulties (see Figure 24.1).

Staying productively engaged in the Results process both demands the exercise of virtue (Relationships) and, simultaneously, provides a rich context for the development of virtue.

Dynamic Determination

The Results process prompts Leaders and member-leaders to passionately embrace its directional imperatives, to care enough about keeping its promises to the world to face troubling performance information and make difficult decisions about its investment of precious resources. This demands the exercise of faith and hope found in Dynamic Determination. In contrast to faith in a larger noble purpose and hope that the organization's best days are ahead of it, apathy, cynicism, and selfishness will undermine the Results process.

Intellectual Flexibility

The Results process calls on the organization to translate performance feedback into new learning and constructive action—a byproduct of the

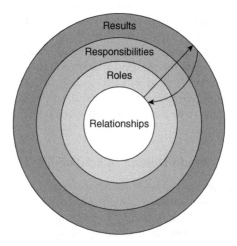

Figure 24.1 Relationships and results.

prudence and humility found in Intellectual Flexibility. Constructive insights, new learning, and practical wisdom do not naturally flow from the raw data or even firsthand experience—experience is beneficial only when the right lessons are taken to heart. In fact, some experiences may be "mis-educative," fostering counterproductive ways of interacting with the world. The Results process calls on the organization to exercise individual and collective Intellectual Flexibility in order to translate data and experience into real-time, real-world performance improvements.

Courageous Character

The rigorous dialog and candid self-assessment prompted by the Results process both demands and develops the individual and collective expression of Courageous Character. The Results process takes the organization on a collective journey toward "deep integrity"—an accurate picture of the demands of success matched up against the capacity of the organization to meet these demands. The troubling disparity—between performance demands and the organization's real-time capabilities, between aspirations and actual performance, good intentions and the capacity to deliver—is brought to the light of day. If the organization is to translate this hard-to-hear feedback into constructive action, it must embody and practice what Heifetz et al. (2009) call a "culture of courageous conversations" (p. 67).

Emotional Maturity

The Results process prompts the organization to learn about itself, its deep dispositions, capabilities, and performance and to translate this self-knowledge into constructive action. This requires the personal and collective capacity to operate with realism, take personal responsibility for decisions and actions, and bounce back after failure—a byproduct of Emotional Maturity.

Collaborative Quotient

The Result process is the collaborative search for the truth about the organizations capacities and performance—nothing more, but nothing less. This search both demands and develops in the organization a deep sense of interdependence and mutual accountability, binding Leaders, member-leaders, and the entire organization together in a collective struggle for sustained effectiveness.

Summary

The seeds of organizational progress and renewal reside in the capacity of Leaders and member-leaders to listen and learn, embrace the truth about personal and collective performance, and do whatever is necessary to keep the organization's promises to the world. This demands sufficient cognitive, moral, and emotional strength to handle heavy doses of the New Normal operating environment.

Counterintuitive and troubling though it may be, predictability, certainty, harmony, and equilibrium does not promote growth in individuals and organizations. In the New Normal, there are rich possibilities, as well as a competitive advantage, for individuals and organizations that keep growing and learning.

Gardner (1995) sums up the learning and leadership challenge.

> For men and women who have accepted the reality of change, the need for endless learning and trying is a way of living, a way of thinking, a way of being awake and ready. Life isn't a train ride where you choose your destination, pay your fare and settle back for a nap. It's a cycle ride over uncertain terrain, with you in the driver's seat, constantly correcting your balance and determining the direction of progress. It's difficult, sometimes profoundly painful. But it's better than napping through life. (p. xii)

The Results process, fueled by the personal and collective virtue of Leaders and member-leaders, keeps the organization awake and alert on the journey through the uncertain terrain of the New Normal.

References

Aaker, D. A. (2011). *Brand relevance*. San Francisco, CA: Jossey-Bass.

Aaker, D. A. & Joachimsthaler, E. (2000). *Brand leadership*. New York: Free Press.

Adler, P., Heckscher, C., & Prusak, L. (2011). Building a collaborative enterprise. *Harvard Business Review, 89*(7/8), 94–101.

Ainslie, G. (2001). *Breakdown of will*. Cambridge, England: Cambridge University Press.

Allport, G. W. (1921). Personality and character. *Psychological Bulletin, 18*, 441–455.

———. (1927). Concepts of trait and personality. *Psychological Bulletin, 24*, 284–293.

Anscombe, G. E. M. (1958). Modern moral philosophy. *The Journal of the Royal Institute of Philosophy, 33*(124), 1–19.

Appelbaum, L. & Paese, M. (2011). What senior leaders do: The nine roles of strategic leadership. *DDI Whitepaper*, 1–9. Retrieved on June 23, 2013 from http://www.principals.in/uploads/pdf/leadership/ddi_WhatSeniorLeaders DoTheNineRoles_wp.pdf

Aristotle. (2006). On rhetoric: A theory of civic discourse (2nd Edition). (trans. G. A. Kennedy). New York: Oxford University Press.

Barnevik, P. (1994). *Global strategies: Insights from the world's leading thinkers*. Boston, MA: Harvard Business School Press.

Bar-On, R. (2002). *EQI BarOn emotional quotient inventory*. New York: Multi-Health Systems.

Barton, D., Grant, A., & Horn, M. (2012, June). Leading in the 21st century. *McKinsey Quarterly*. Retrieved on January 7, 2014 from http://www.mckinsey .com/insights/leading_in_the_21st_century/leading_in_the_21st_century

Bass, B. M. (1970). When planning for others. *Journal of Applied Behavioral Science, 6*(2), 151–171.

———. (1985). *Leadership and performance beyond expectations*. New York: Free Press.

Bass, B. M. & Steidlmeier, P. (1999). Ethics, character and authentic transformational leadership. *Leadership Quarterly, 10*(2), 181–217.

Bartz, Carol. (2009, November 21). Leadership in the information age. *The Economist: The World in 2010*, 128.

Baumeister, R. F. (1991). *Meanings of life*. New York: Guilford Press.

Baumeister, R. F. & Exline, J. J. (2000). Self-control, morality, and human strength. *Journal of Social and Clinical Psychology, 19*, 29–42.

Belmonte, K. (2002). *Hero for humanity*. Colorado Springs, CO: NavPress.

Bennis, W. G. & Thomas, R. J. (2002). Crucibles of leadership. *Harvard Business Review, 80*(9/10), 39–45.

Bligh, M. C. & Kohles, J. C. (2009). The enduring allure of charisma: How Barak Obama won the historic 2008 presidential election. *The Leadership Quarterly, 20*, 483–492.

Block, P. (1993). *Stewardship: Choosing service over self-interest*. San Francisco, CA: Berrett-Koehler.

Block, G. & Drucker, M. (1992). *Rescuers: Portraits of moral courage in the Holocaust*. New York: T. V. Books.

Boatright, J. R. (2000). *Ethics and the conduct of business*. Upper Saddle River, NJ: Prentice Hall.

Boorstin, D. J. (1985). *The discoverers*. New York: Random House.

Bossidy, L., Charan, R., & Burke, C. (2002). *Execution: The discipline of getting things done*. New York: Crown Business.

Bown, S. R. (2012). *The last Viking*. Boston, MA: Da Capo Press.

Boyatzis, R. E. (1982). *The competent managers: A model for effective performance*. New York: Wiley-Interscience.

Boyatzis, R., Goleman, D., & Rhee, K. (2000). Clustering competence in emotional intelligence: Insights from the emotional competence inventory (ECI). In R. Bar-On & J. D. A. Parker (Eds.), *Handbook of emotional intelligence* (pp. 343–362). San Francisco, CA: Jossey-Bass.

Bradley, C. & Dawson, A. (2013). The art of strategy. *McKinsey Quarterly*. October. Retrieved on January 6, 2014 from http://www.mckinsey.com/insights/strategy/the_art_of_strategy

Brooker, K. & Schlosser, J. (2002, September 16). The Un-CEO: A. G. Lafley doesn't overpromise. He doesn't believe in the vision thing. All he's done is turn around P&G in 27 months. *Fortune*, 88. Retrieved on November 14, 2014 from http://archive.fortune.com/magazines/fortune/fortune_archive/2002/09/16/328576/index.htm

Buchwald, A. (Writer). (2006, November 2). Art Buchwald celebrates his life. [Profile on CNN Newsroom]. Atlanta, GA: CNN.

Burke, C. S., Sims, D. E., Lazarra, E. H., & Salas, E. (2007). Trust in leadership: A multilevel review and integration. *The Leadership Quarterly, 18*, 606–632.

Burns, J. M. (1978). *Leadership*. New York: Harper.

———. (2003). *Transforming leadership*. New York: Grove Press.

Carlzon, J. (1989). *Moments of truth*. New York: HarperBusiness.

Carson, C. (1995). Martin Luther King Jr.: Charismatic leadership in mass struggle. In J. Thomas Wren (Ed.), *Leaders companion* (pp. 318–324). New York: The Free Press.

Chandler, C. (2012, September). Leading in the 21st century: An interview with Chanda Kochhar. *McKinsey Quarterly*. Retrieved on January 5, 2014 from http://

www.mckinsey.com/insights/leading_in_the_21st_century/an_interview_with_chanda_kochhar

Christensen, C. (1997, 2013). *The innovator's dilemma.* Boston, MA: Harvard Business School Press.

Cloud, H. (2006). *Integrity: The courage to meet the demands of reality.* New York: Harper.

Collins, J. (1999). Turning goals into results: The power of catalytic mechanisms. *Harvard Business Review, 77*(4), 70–82.

———. (2001). *Good to great.* New York: Harper Collins.

———. (2005). *Good to great and the social sectors.* New York: HarperCollins.

Collins, J. C. & Porras, J. I. (1996). Building your company's vision. *Harvard Business Review,* 74(5), 65–77.

———. (2004). *Built to last.* New York: HarperBusiness.

Compte-Sponville, A. (2001). *A small treatise on the great virtues.* New York: Metropolitan Books.

Conger, J. A. & Kanungo, R. N. (1987, October 1). Toward a behavioral theory of charismatic leadership in organizational settings. *Academy of Management Review, 12*(4), 637–647.

———. (1994). Charismatic leadership in organizations: Perceived behavioral attributes and their measurement. *Journal of Organizational Behavior, 15*(5), 439–452.

Coutu, D. L. (2002, May). How resilience works. *Harvard Business Review, 80*(5), 46–55.

Covey, S. M. R. (2006). *The speed of trust.* New York: Free Press.

Crawford, F. & Mathews, R. (2001). *The myth of excellence.* New York: Three Rivers Press.

de Chardin, T. (2004). *The future of man.* New York: Image Books.

Deci, E. L. & Ryan, R. M. (1985). *Intrinsic motivation and self-determination in human behavior.* New York: Plenum.

———. (2000). The 'what' and 'why' of goal pursuits: Human needs and the self-determination of behavior. *Psychological Inquiry, 11*(4), 227–268.

———. (2008). Facilitating optimal motivation and psychological well being across life's domains. *Canadian Psychology, 49*(1), 14–23.

De Pree, M. (1989). *Leadership is an art.* New York: Dell.

Drath, W. H. & Paulus, C. J. (1994). *Making common sense: Leadership as meaning making in a community of practice.* Greensboro, NC: Center for Creative Leadership.

Drucker, P. (1992). *The age of discontinuity.* New York: Harper & Row.

———. (1993). *The concept of the corporation.* Piscataway, NJ: Transaction Publishers.

Dutton, J. & Heaphy, E. (2003). The power of high-quality connections. In K. Cameron, J. Dutton, & R. Quinn (Eds.), *Positive organizational scholarship* (pp. 263–278). San Francisco, CA: Berrett-Koehler.

Eichinger, R. W. & Lombardo, M. M. (2004). Learning agility as a prime indicator of potential. *Human Resource Planning, 27*(4), 12–15.

Eliot, T. S. (1980). *T. S. Eliot: The complete plays and poems, 1909–1950*. New York: Harcourt Brace & Company.

Eliot, G. (2003). *Middlemarch*. New York: Penguin Classics.

Emmons, R. A. (1999). *The psychology of ultimate concerns*. New York: Guilford Press.

Engelbrecht, A. S. (2002). The effect of organisational leadership on value congruence and effectiveness: An integrated model. *South African Journal of Economic & Management Sciences, 5*(3), 589–606.

Engelbrecht, A., Van Aswegen, A., & Theron, C. (2005). The effect of ethical values on leadership and ethical climate in organisations. *South African Journal of Business Management, 36*(2), 19–26.

Fernandez-Araoz, C. (2014). 21st Century Talent Spotting. *Harvard Business Review, 92*(9), 46–56.

Foote, P. (2003). *Natural goodness*. New York: Oxford University Press.

Founding Editors (2003, May). Welcome to the new normal. *Fast Company Magazine*, 70. www.fastcompany.com/46592/welcome-newnormal

Frankfurt, H. G. (1998). *Necessity, volition, and love*. New York: Cambridge University Press.

Frankl, V. E. (1959). *Man's search for meaning*. Canton, NY: Beacon Press.

Friedman, T. L. (1995). *From Beirut to Jerusalem*. New York: Anchor Books.

Frissora, M. & Kirkland, R. (2013, November). Leading in the 21st century: An interview with Hertz CEO Mark Frissora. *McKinsey Quarterly*. Retrieved on January 3, 2014 from http://www.mckinsey.com/insights/strategy/leading_in_the_21st_century_an_interview_with_hertz_ceo_mark_frissora

Fromm, E. (1965). *Escape from freedom*. New York: Henry Holt & Company.

Frost, R. (1995). *Frost: Collected poems, prose & plays*. New York: Literary Classics of the United States.

Gaddis, J. L. (2005). *Strategies of containment*. New York: Oxford University Press.

Gardner, J. W. (1995). *Self renewal*. New York: W. W. Norton & Company.

Gergen, D. (2001). *Eyewitness to power*. New York: Simon & Schuster.

Gioia, D. A. & Thomas, J. B. (1996). Institutional identity, image, and issue interpretation: Sensemaking during strategic change in academia. *Administrative Science Quarterly, 41*, 370–403.

Glad, B. & Blanton, R. (1997). F. W. de Klerk and Nelson Mandela: A study in cooperative transformational leadership. *Presidential Studies Quarterly, 27*(3), 565–590.

Goleman, D. (1995). *Emotional intelligence*. New York: Bantam.

———. (1998). *Working with emotional intelligence*. New York: Bantam Books.

Greenleaf, R. K. (1977). *Servant leadership: A journey into the nature of legitimate power and greatness*. New York: Paulist Press.

Grint, K. (2010). *Leadership: A very short introduction*. Oxford, England: Oxford University Press.

Guinness, O. (1998). *The call*. Nashville, TN: Thomas Nelson.

Hagel, J., Brown, J. S., & Davison, L. (2009, July–August). The big shift: Measuring the forces of change. *Harvard Business Review, 87*(7/8), 86–89.

Halstead, T. (2003, January). The American paradox. *Atlantic Monthly, 291*(1), 123–125.

Hamel, G. (2007). *The future of management.* Boston, MA: Harvard Business School Press.

———. (2012). *What matters now.* San Francisco, CA: Jossey-Bass.

Handy, C. (1995). Managing the dream. In S. Chawla & J. Renesch (Eds.), *Learning organizations: Developing cultures for tomorrow's workplace* (pp. 44–55). Portland, OR: Productivity Press.

Heifetz, R. A. (1994). *Leadership without easy answers.* Cambridge, MA: Belknap Press.

Heifetz, R. A. & Laurie, D. L. (2001, December). The work of leadership. *Harvard Business Review, 79*(11), 131–140.

Heifetz, R. A. & Linsky, M. (2002, June). A survival guide for leaders. *Harvard Business Review, 80*(6), 65–74.

Heifetz, R., Grashow, A., & Linsky, M. (2009, July–August). Leadership in a (permanent) crisis. *Harvard Business Review, 87*(7/8), 62–69.

Henton, D., Melville, J., & Walesh, K. (2004, Spring). The rise of the new civic revolutionaries: Answering the call to stewardship in our times. *National Civic Review, 93*(1), 43–49.

Hesselbein, F. (1996). The 'how to be' leader. In F. Hesselbein, M. Goldsmith, & R. Beckard (Eds.), *The leader of the future* (pp. 121–124). New York: Jossey-Bass.

Hildebrand, K. (1955). *Achieving real happiness.* New York: Harper & Brothers.

Hoffer, E. (1951). *The true believer.* New York: Harper & Row.

———. (1973). *Reflections on the human condition.* New York: HarperCollins.

Hook, S. (1943). *The hero in history.* New York: The Humanities Press.

Huntford, R. (2010). *The race for the South Pole.* New York: Continuum.

Hursthouse. R. (2001). *On virtue ethics.* New York: Oxford University Press.

Ibarra, H. & Hansen, M. T. (2011, July–August). Are you a collaborative leader? *Harvard Business Review, 89*(7/8), 68–74.

Immelt, J. (2004, April). Things leaders do. *Fast Company.* http://www.fast company.com/48877/things-leaders-do.

Isaacson, W. (2011). *Steve jobs.* New York: Simon & Schuster.

Israel, A. (1998). *Amanda Berry Smith.* Lanham, MD: Scarecrow Press.

Jacques, E. (1985, June). Executive vision: A matter of time. *Small Business Report,* 8.

Jarvis, P. (1992). *Paradoxes of learning.* San Francisco, CA: Jossey-Bass.

Javetski, B. (2012, September). Leading in the 21st century: An interview with Michael Useem. *McKinsey Quarterly.* Retrieved on January 16, 2014 from http://www.mckinsey.com/insights/leading_in_the_21st_century/an_interview_with_michael_useem

Kahn, W. A. (1992). To be fully there: Psychological presence at work. *Human Relations, 45*(4), 321–349.

Kahneman, D., Slovic, P., & Tversky, A. (Eds.) (1982). *Judgment under uncertainty: Heuristics and biases.* New York: Cambridge University Press.

Kaiser, R. B., Hogan, R., & Craig, S. B. (2008). Leadership and the fate of organizations. *American Psychologist, 63*(2), 96–110.

Kanter, R. (1996). World class leaders. In F. Hesselbein, M. Goldsmith, & R. Beckard (Eds.), *The leader of the future* (pp. 89–98). New York: Jossey-Bass.

Kanter, R. B. (2008, January). Transforming giants. *Harvard Business Review, 86*(1), 43–52.

Karlgaard, R. (2004, November 19). Peter Drucker on leadership. *Forbes.* Retrieved from http://www.forbes.com/home/management/2004/11/19/cz_rk _1119drucker.html.

Kessler, S. (2012). Inside Starbuck's $35 million mission to make brand evangelists of its front-line workers. *Fast Company Magazine.* Retrieved from //www .fastcompany.com/ 3002023/ inside-starbuckss-35-million-mission-make-brand -evangelists-its-front-line-workers.

Kets de Vries, M. F. R. (1980). *Organizational paradoxes: Clinical approaches to management.* London: Tavistock.

Khurana, R. (2002). *Searching for a corporate savior: The irrational quest for charismatic CEO's.* Princeton, NJ: Princeton University Press.

Kidder, R. M. (2006). *Moral courage.* New York: Harper.

Kiechel, W., III. (1984, May). Sniping at strategic planning. *Planning Review, 12*(3), 8–11.

———. (2010). *The lords of strategy.* Boston, MA: Harvard Business School Press.

Kiefer, C. F. & Schlesinger, L. A. (2010). *Action trumps everything.* Duxbury, MA: Black Ink Press.

King, P. (Ed.). (1999). *Scott's last journey.* New York: HarperCollins.

Kirkland, R. (2012a, September). Leading in the 21st century: An interview with Ellen Kullman. *McKinsey Quarterly.* Retrieved on January 16, 2014 from http:// www.mckinsey.com/insights/leading_in_the_21st_century/an_interview _with_ellen_kullman

———. (2012b, September). Leading in the 21st century: An interview with Daniel Vasella. *McKinsey Quarterly.* Retrieved on January 16, 2014 from http://www.mckinsey.com/insights/health_systems_and_services/mckinsey _conversations_with_global_leaders_dan_vasella_of_novartis

Kobasa, S. C., Maddi, S. R., & Kahn, S. (1982). Hardiness and health: A prospective study. *Journal of Personality and Social Psychology, 42*(1), 168–177.

———. (1982). Hardiness and health: A prospective study. *Journal of Personality and Social Psychology, 42*(1), 168–177.

Kotter, J. K. (1990). *A force for change.* New York: Free Press.

———. (1997). *Matsushita leadership.* New York: Free Press.

Kouzes, J. M. & Posner, B.Z. (1993). *Credibility: How leaders gain and lose it and why people demand it.* San Francisco, CA: Jossey-Bass.

———. (1996). Seven lessons for leading the voyage to the future. In F. Hesselbein, M. Goldsmith, & R. Beckard (Eds.), *The leader of the future* (pp. 99–110). New York: Jossey-Bass..

Kuhn, T. S. (2012). *The structure of scientific revolutions: 50th anniversary edition.* Chicago, IL: University of Chicago Press.

LaBarre, P. (2003, May). The New Normal: Welcome to the first year of the rest of our lives. *Fast Company Magazine. 70.* Retrieved at www.fastcompany.com/46387/new-normal.

Labovitz, G. & Rosansky, V. (1997). *The power of aligning.* New York: John Wiley & Sons.

Lafley, A. J. & Martin, R. L. (2013). *Playing to win.* Boston, MA: Harvard Business Review Press.

Lamb, R. B. (1987). *Running American business: Top CEO's rethink their major decisions.* New York: Basic Books.

L'Amour, L. (1985). *The walking drum.* New York: Bantam Books.

Lau, D. C. & Liden, R. C. (2008). Antecedents of coworker trust. *Journal of Applied Psychology, 93*(5), 1130–1138.

Lewis, C. S. (2009). *The screwtape letters.* New York: HarperOne

Loehr, J. & Schwartz, T. (2001, January). The making of a corporate athlete. *Harvard Business Review, 79*(1), 120–128.

Lombardo, M. & Eichinger, R. W. (2009). *FYI: For your improvement – for learners, managers, mentors, and feedback givers.* Minneapolis, MN: Lominger International.

Lorenz, E. N. (1963). Deterministic nonperiodic flow. *Journal of the Atmospheric Sciences, 20,* 130–141.

Lubit, R. (2001). The long term impact of destructively narcissistic managers. *Academy of Management Executive, 16*(1), 127–138.

Lynn, A. B. (2007). *Quick emotional intelligence activities for busy managers: 50 team exercises that get results in just 15 minutes.* New York: AMACOM.

MacIntyre, A. (1984). *After virtue: A study in moral theology.* Notre Dame, IN: University of Notre Dame Press.

Maddi, S. R. (2002). The story of hardiness: Twenty years of theorizing, research, and practice. *Consulting Psychology Journal, 54,* 173–185.

———. (2005). On hardiness and other pathways to resilience. *American Psychologist, 60,* 261–262.

Maitland, I. (1997). Virtuous markets: The market as a school of virtue. *Business Ethics Quarterly, 7,* 17–31.

Mandela, N. (1994). *Long walk to freedom.* New York: Little, Brown and Company.

Mandelbrot, B. & Taleb, N. N. (2006, March 24). Mastering uncertainty. *The Financial Times.* 2–3.

McAdams, D. P. (1989). *Intimacy: The need to be close.* New York: Doubleday.

———. (1993). *The stories we live by: Personal myths and making of the self.* New York: Morrow.

———. (2001). The psychology of life stories. *Review of General Psychology, 5,* 100–122.

McAdams, D. P., Diamond, A., de St. Aubin, E., & Mansfield, E. D. (1997). Stories of commitment: The psychosocial construction of generative lives. *Journal of Personality and Social Psychology, 72,* 678–694.

McCraw, T. K. (2001). *American business, 1920–2000: How it worked.* Wheeling, IL: Harlan Davidson.

McCullough, D. (1979). *The path between the seas.* New York: Simon & Schuster.

McGregor, D. (1960). *The human side of the enterprise.* New York: McGraw-Hill.

McNamee, R. (2004). *The new normal.* New York: Penguin Group.

Metaxas, E. (2007). *Amazing grace.* New York: HarperOne.

Michelli, J. A. (2008). *The new gold standard.* New York: McGraw Hill.

Mintzberg, H. (1987, July–August). Crafting strategy. *Harvard Business Review,* 65(4), 66–75.

———. (1989). *Mintzberg on management.* New York: Free Press.

———. (1994a). *The fall and rise of strategic planning.* New York: Free Press.

———. (1994b, January–February). The fall and rise of strategic planning. *Harvard Business Review,* 72(1), 107–114.

Moffett, M. (2005, November 9). Barrio study links land ownership to a better life. *The Wall Street Journal,* A1.

Montgomery, C. A. (2012, July). How strategists lead. *McKinsey Quarterly.* http://www.mckinsey.com/insights/strategy/how_strategists_lead

Montefiore, A. & Vines, D. (1999). *Integrity in the public and private domains.* London: Routledge.

Morgenson, G. & Rosner, J. (2011). *Reckless endangerment: How outsized ambition, greed, and corruption led to economic armageddon.* New York: Times Books.

Morris, B. (2008). *1948: The first Arab-Israeli War.* New Haven, CT: Yale University Press.

Murray, A. (2010). *The Wall Street Journal essential guide to management.* New York: Harper Business.

Naim, M. (2013). *The end of power.* New York: Basic Books.

Nanus, B. (1992). *Visionary leadership.* San Francisco, CA: Jossey-Bass.

Neustadt, R. E. (1960). *Presidential power: The politics of leadership.* New York: John Wiley & Sons.

Nicholson, I. A. M. (1998). Gordon Allport, character, and the culture of personality: 1897–1937. *History of Psychology, 1,* 52–68.

Normann, R. (2002). *Service management.* West Sussex, England: John Wiley & Sons.

Nozick, R. (1989). *The examined life.* New York: Touchstone.

Organ, D. W. & Ryan, K. (1995). A Meta-analytic review of attitudinal and dispositional predictors of organizational citizenship behavior. *Personnel Psychology, 48,* 775–802.

Osborn, R. N., Hunt, J. G., & Jauch, L. R. (2002). Toward a contextual theory of leadership. *The Leadership Quarterly, 13,* 797–837.

Oudea, F. & Kirkland, R. (2013, November). Leading in the 21st century: An interview with Societe Generale's Frederic Ludea. *McKinsey Quarterly*. Retrieved on January 4, 2014 from http://www.mckinsey.com/insights/financial_services /leading_in_the_21st_century_an_interview_with_societe_generales _frederic_oudea

Owens, L. A. (2012). Confidence in Banks, Financial Institutions and Wall Street, 1971–2011. *Public Opinion Quarterly, 76*(1), 142–162.

Parker, M. (2009). *Panama fever.* New York: Anchor.

Parry, K. W. & Proctor-Thomson, S. B. (2002). Perceived integrity of transformational leaders in organisational settings. *Journal of Business Ethics, 35,* 75–96.

Pearson, C. M. & Clair, J. A. (1998). Reframing crisis management. *Academy of Management Review, 23*(1), 59–76.

Peters, T. (1988). *Thriving on chaos: Handbook for a management revolution.* New York: Harper Paperbacks.

Peterson, C. & Seligman, M. E. P. (2004). *Character strengths and virtues.* New York: Oxford University Press.

Pink, D. H. (2009). *Drive.* New York: Riverhead Books.

Pittinsky, T. L., Rosenthal, S. A., Welle, B., & Montoya, R. M. (2005). *National leadership index 2005: A national study of confidence in leadership.* Cambridge, MA: Center for Public Leadership, John F. Kennedy School Government.

Plato (1956). *Protagoras and memo.* New York: Penguin Books.

Plato (1968). *The Republic.* New York: Basic Books.

Podsakoff, P. M., MacKenzie, S. B., Paine, J. B., & Bachrach, D. G. (2000). Organizational citizenship behaviors: A critical review of the theoretical and empirical literature and suggestions for further research. *Journal of Management, 26,* 513–563.

Pollock, J. (1977). *Wilberforce.* London: Constable and Company.

Porter, M. E. (1998a). *Competitive advantage: Creating and sustaining superior performance.* New York: Free Press.

Porter, M. (1998b). *Competitive strategy: Techniques for analyzing industries and competitors.* New York: Free Press.

Prahalad, C. K. (2009, September 10). In volatile times, agility rules. *Business Week.* Retrieved on October 15, 2013 from http://www.businessweek.com/ stories/2009-09-09/in-volatile-times-agility-rules

Quinn, J. B. (1980). *Strategies for change.* Homewood, IL: Richard D. Irwin.

Rachman, G. (2011). *Zero sum game: American power in an age of anxiety.* New York: Simon & Schuster.

Rae, S. B. & Wong, K. L. (2004). *Beyond integrity.* Grand Rapids, MI: Zondervan.

Regine, B. & Lewin, R. (2000). Leading at the edge: How leaders influence complex systems. *Emergence, 2*(2), 5–23.

Richardson, G. (2002). The metatheory of resilience and resiliency. *Journal of Clinical Psychology, 58*(3), 307–321.

Rittel, H. W. J. & Webber, M. M. (1973). Dilemmas in a general theory of planning. *Policy Sciences, 4,* 155–169.

Rodman, P. W. (2009). *Presidential command.* New York: Alfred A. Knopf.

Rosenthal, S. A. (2012). *National leadership index 2012: A national study of confidence in leadership.* Cambridge, MA: Center for Public Leadership, Harvard Kennedy School.

Rousseau, D. M., Sitkin, S. B., Burt, R. S., & Camerer, C. (1998). Not so different after all: A cross discipline view of trust. *Academy of Management Review, 23,* 393–404.

Rumelt, R. P. (2011). *Good strategy bad strategy.* New York: Crown Business.

Ryan, R. M. & Deci, E. L (2000, January). Self-determination theory and the facilitation of intrinsic motivation, social development and well being. *American Psychologist,* 55, 68.

Sampson, A. (2000). *Mandela: The authorized biography.* New York: Vintage Books.

Scheier, M. F. & Carver, C. S. (1992). Effects of optimism on psychological and physical well-being: Theoretical overview and empirical update. *Cognitive Therapy and Research, 16,* 201–228.

Schein, E. J. (1992). *Organizational culture and leadership.* San Francisco, CA: Jossey-Bass.

Schultz, H. & Gordon, J. (2011). *Onward: How Starbucks fought for its life without losing its soul.* New York: Rodale Books.

Seligman, M. E. P., Park, N., & Peterson, C. (2005). Positive psychology progress: Empirical validation of interventions. *American Psychologist, 60*(5), 410–421.

Senge, P. M. (1990). The fifth discipline: The art and practice of the learning organization. New York: Doubleday.

Shamir, B., & Howell, J. M. (1999). Organizational and contextual influences on the emergence and effectiveness of charismatic leadership. *The Leadership Quarterly, 10*(2), 257–283.

Shamir, B., House, R. J., & Arthur, M. B. (1993). The motivational effects of charismatic leadership: A self-concept-based theory. *Organization Science, 4,* 577–594.

Sheldon, K. M. (2002). The self-concordance model of healthy goal striving: When personal goals correctly represent the person. In E. L. Deci & R. M. Ryan (Eds.), *Handbook of self-determination research* (pp. 65–86). Rochester, NY: University of Rochester Press.

Sheldon, K. M. & Kasser, T. (1998). Pursuing personal goals: Skills enable progress, but not all progress is beneficial. *Personality and Social Psychology Bulletin, 24,* 1319–1331.

Sinek, S. (2011). *Start with why.* New York: Penguin Group.

The Small Wars Council (2009). Retrieved on February 4, 2010 from http://coucil.smallwarsjournal.com/showthread.php?t=1198.

Smith, A. (1893). *An autobiography: The story of the Lord's dealings with Mrs. Amanda Smith, the colored evangelist.* Chicago, IL: Meyer & Brother Publishers.

Snyder, C. R. (1991). The will and the ways. *Journal of Personality and Social Psychology, 60*(4), 570–585.

Spencer, L. & Spencer, S. (1993). *Competence at work*. New York: John Wiley.

Sternberg, R. J. (Ed.). (1990). *Wisdom: Its nature, origins, and development*. New York: Cambridge University Press.

———. (Ed.) (2000). *Handbook of human intelligence*. New York: Cambridge University Press.

Taylor, D. (2001). *Tell me a story*. St. Paul, MN: Bog Walk Press.

Taylor, W. C. (2003). The leader of the future. *Fast Company Magazine*. Retrieved from http://www.fastcompany.com/online/25/heifetz.html.

Tec, N. (1986). *When light pierced the darkness: Christians rescue Jews in Nazi-occupied Poland*. New York: Oxford Press.

Toffler, A. (1984). *Future shock*. New York: Bantam.

Trevino, L. K., Hartman, L. P., & Brown, M. (2000). Moral person and moral manager: How executives develop a reputation for ethical leadership. *California Management Review, 42*(4), 128–142.

Tuchman, B. W. (1985). *The march of folly: From Troy to Viet Nam*. New York: Random House.

Walters, J. M. & Gardner, H. (1986). The theory of multiple intelligences: Some issues and answers. In R. J. Sternberg & R. K. Wagner (Eds.), *Practical intelligence* (pp. 163–182). New York: Cambridge University Press.

Weber, M. (1947). The theory of social and economic organizations. (trans. T. Parsons). New York: Free Press (Original work published in 1927).

Weick, K. E. (1979). *The social psychology of organizing*. Reading, MA: Addison Wesley.

Weiss, H. M. & Knight, P. A. (1980). The utility of humility: Self esteem, information search, and problem solving efficiency. *Organizational Behavior and Human Decision Processes, 25*, 216–223.

Wilberforce, W. (1982). *Real Christianity*. Portland, OR: Multnomah Press.

Yankelovich, D. (1981). *New rules: Searching for fulfillment in a world turned upside down*. New York: Random House.

Zyman, S. (2002). *The end of advertising as we know it*. Hoboken, NJ: John Wiley & Sons.

Index

CPSIA information can be obtained
at www.ICGtesting.com
Printed in the USA
BVHW042008261119
564880BV00011B/192/P